DOING ETHICS *in a* DIVERSE WORLD

DOING ETHICS
in a
DIVERSE WORLD

Robert Traer
Dominican University of California

and

Harlan Stelmach
Dominican University of California

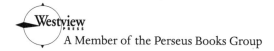
A Member of the Perseus Books Group

Copyright 2008 by Westview Press, a Member of the Perseus Books Group.

Published in the United States of America by Westview Press, A Member of the Perseus Books Group, 2465 Central Avenue, Boulder, Colorado 80301-2877.

Find us on the World Wide Web at www.westviewpress.com

Westview Press books are available at special discounts for bulk purchases in the United States by corporations, institutions, and other organizations. For more information, please contact the Special Markets Department at the Perseus Books Group, 2300 Chestnut Street, Philadelphia, PA 19103, or call (800) 255-1514, or email special.markets@perseusbooks.com.

Library of Congress Catalog-in-Publication data
Traer, Robert.
  Doing ethics in a diverse world / Robert Traer and Harlan Stelmach.
    p. cm.
  Includes bibliographical references and index.
  ISBN-13: 978-0-8133-4366-2 (pbk. : alk. paper)
  ISBN-10: 0-8133-4366-6 (pbk. : alk. paper) 1. Ethics, Modern—21st century. I.
Stelmach, Harlan Douglas Anthony, 1945– II. Title.
  BJ320.T73 2007
  170—dc22
                                                                         2007003744
The paper used in this publication meets the requirements of the American National Standard for Permanence of Paper for Printed Library Materials Z39.48–1984.

10   9   8   7   6   5   4   3   2   1

Contents

III. OVERCOMING AN ETHICAL PRESUMPTION

IV. APPLYING THE APPROACH

Preface

An introductory ethics book should help readers understand different theories and how to apply these to contemporary ethical issues. In *Doing Ethics in a Diverse World* we try to accomplish these goals by considering:

- Five kinds of ethical arguments to construct and test ethical presumptions.
- The rule of law as an analogy for doing ethics.
- The ethical presumptions of international human rights law.
- Religious as well as philosophical traditions of ethics.

First, instead of summarizing eight or more ethical theories as many introductory texts do, we describe **five kinds of ethical arguments** that use concepts familiar to everyone. Four of these ethical arguments affirm that some actions, or ways of being a good person, are inherently (or intrinsically) right, or good. These ethical arguments concern our duty, character, relationships, and rights. A fifth kind of ethical argument considers only the consequences of a proposed action to decide if the action is right.

We use these diverse arguments to **construct and test ethical presumptions.** By a "presumption" we mean our hypothesis as to how we should respond to an ethical issue. Different points of view give us greater perspective as to what our hypothesis should be. We then test our presumption with a thought experiment by considering what the consequences would likely be of acting on the presumption.

Taking this approach to doing ethics means we are not arguing for one ethical theory and against all other theories. Also, our approach offers an answer to the problem of ethical relativism, which arises with any description of various ethical theories without a way of using these theories to come to some decision. We use four kinds of ethical reasoning (about our duty, character, relationships, and rights) to decide what action we think we should take. Then we test our ethical presumption by a fifth way of ethical reasoning, which asserts that only consequences really matter.

To help readers understand this practical approach to doing ethics, we include a worksheet before chapter 9 and then use this worksheet to address the issue of HIV/AIDS in that chapter. Readers may find it helpful to refer to this worksheet and also to the diagram on page xii while reading chapters 10–15, which apply the approach to contemporary ethical problems.

Second, we use **the rule of law as an analogy for doing ethics.** Issues of public morality concern what the law should be, and the rule of law is a great ethical achievement. Moreover, everyone is familiar with legal presumptions such as the presumption of innocence. As these legal presumptions are also ethical presumptions, considering the rule of law gives us many helpful examples of how to address ethical issues. Our approach to doing ethics is like the way that laws are made, debated, and revised in a democratic society.

Third, laws protecting human rights are also ethical presumptions, and today these presumptions concerning our fundamental freedoms and the responsibilities of national governments are affirmed by **international human rights law.** Therefore, we include an explanation of international human rights law in the chapter on rights and use these ethical presumptions in considering how to respond to contemporary issues.

Fourth, in expressing the diversity of ethical thought in five kinds of arguments and constructing presumptions from these arguments, we con-

sider **religious as well as philosophical traditions of ethics.** The chapter
on duty includes Hindu teachings that were used by Mahatma Gandhi to
support his ethical affirmation of *satyagraha*, as well as a brief description
of Kant's philosophical approach. The chapter on character not only presents the thinking of Aristotle and Aquinas, but also the ethical teachings of
Lao Tzu and Confucius that rely on a Chinese understanding of *Tao*. The
chapter on relationships contains Buddhist teachings as well as feminist arguments about an ethics of care. The chapter on rights summarizes legal
and philosophical arguments, but also considers support for human rights
law within the major religious traditions of the world.

Doing Ethics in a Diverse World offers an inclusive and practical introduction to ethical reasoning. It builds on our commonsense understanding of
duty, character, relationships, rights, and consequences by considering diverse philosophical and religious arguments using these five ways of reasoning. It applies this approach by constructing and testing ethical
presumptions concerning issues such as abortion, capital punishment,
same-sex marriage, euthanasia, the war against terrorism, and our ecological crisis. Readers are invited to confirm their understanding of the text,
and to see how this approach may be helpful in addressing contemporary
ethical issues, by answering questions provided at the end of each chapter.

The authors hope that readers will enjoy studying this introductory text
as much as they did writing it.

Acknowledgments

A book like this reflects a lifetime of learning. Therefore, it is impossible to thank all those who have contributed. Both authors have had many fine teachers over the years, and we are grateful for them all. We have, however, been especially inspired by the teaching and writings of Robert Bellah, and so we dedicate this book to him. We are, of course, responsible for the text, but we are very grateful to Bob not only for his challenging work on ethics but also for his wise counsel over the years.

We also wish to acknowledge how much we have learned about ethics from our many colleagues. Moreover, we are grateful for the patience of our wives, children, and grandchildren, as we have often been slow learners of the many lessons they have taught us about ethics.

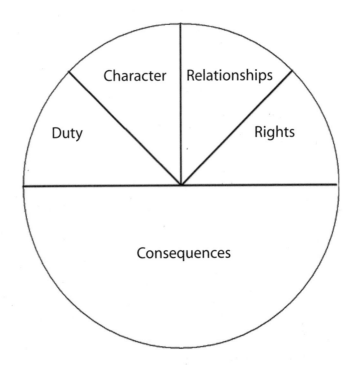

The diagram represents five kinds of ethical arguments. Four of these, which are depicted as sections of the circle above the horizontal line, involve assertions of what is inherently (or intrinsically) right or good. Claims about duty and rights define a right way of acting. Statements about character and relationships describe what being a good person involves.

In considering an ethical dilemma we use these four ways of reasoning to construct a presumption, which is our hypothesis as to the right action we should take and how we should conduct ourselves as we take this action. Then we consider the fifth kind of ethical argument, which claims any act resulting in consequences that are more beneficial than not is right. The consequences we predict may either confirm our presumption, as to how best to respond to an ethical issue, or may give us reason to reconsider.

PART I
Learning from Experience

We hope to clarify what is right, good, and fair by considering our experience, as people living in societies with diverse cultural and religious traditions.

We begin in chapter 1 by resisting claims to ethical certainty and rejecting arguments for cultural relativism. We accept that our knowledge is always incomplete, but nonetheless affirm that we may aspire to articulate moral presumptions that are, or may become, universal standards. For example, human rights and the rule of law are affirmed worldwide as moral presumptions, and we propose to rely on these presumptions in doing ethics.

Our approach to moral philosophy involves constructing presumptions that identify our duty and express our concern for building character, sustaining relationships, and protecting human rights. We recommend acting on these presumptions unless the predicted consequences are so negative that another choice seems more justifiable.

In chapter 2 we consider reasoning and the limitations of our knowledge. We distinguish deductive from inductive reasoning and suggest a largely inductive approach to doing ethics, which is analogous to the scientific quest for greater knowledge and understanding. As both religious and secular teachings reflect the human quest for greater understanding and meaning, our approach to doing ethics involves thinking critically about both.

We construct ethical hypotheses, "test" these presumptions by our reason and experience, and revise our presumptions as seems best by considering the likely consequences of acting on them. We acknowledge that we cannot predict all the consequences of our actions, because our knowledge and experience is limited. Therefore, how well we reason will depend on how and with whom we reason.

In chapter 3 we use the rule of law as a model for asserting ethical presumptions. When there is wrongdoing, we presume it is right to punish those who have done wrong, even by severely restricting their freedom. When no one has done anything wrong but a choice must be made as to how benefits or burdens are best to be allocated, we presume that the distribution should be fair.

The rule of law also clarifies a number of other moral presumptions. We must ensure procedural as well as substantive justice, and also apply the principle of proportionality in seeking a just result. In addition, we must clarify what evidence of adverse consequences is required in order to overcome a moral presumption and thus justify an alternative course of action.

1

Our Challenge

DOING ETHICS IN A PLURALISTIC SOCIETY

Doing what is right, being a good person, trying to achieve results that are fair—these are the main concerns of ethics. Making ethical decisions is not always easy, as you well know. Life is complicated. Yet, all of us have a great deal of experience in deciding what is right and wrong, in trying to be a good person, and in predicting how our choices may lead to the best possible consequences.

Therefore, we are asking for your assistance in considering some of the moral issues of our time. Our goal is to clarify our thinking so we might act more responsibly.

Making moral decisions can be difficult, but all of us have been training for this challenge since we were young. Doing ethics is built into us, as social beings, in our human development and in our language. We may well act unjustly and be selfish. Yet, we cannot live together without some sense of what is right and wrong, good and bad, fair and unfair. It is human nature to be ethical, to be concerned about acting morally, to want to be a good person, to resist wrongdoing, and to try to be fair in our relations with others.

Certainly, ethics is different than some of the other lessons we learned as children. It is not simply a skill that can be acquired like riding a bike, which involves repeating the attempt until our muscles and sense of balance enable us to ride without having to think about what we are doing. In doing ethics, we need to think carefully and clearly.

To improve our critical thinking, we will consider what a few leading moral philosophers have written about making ethical decisions. We will also reflect on the lives of those we most admire for being virtuous persons. Contemplating the thoughtful arguments of ethical writers as well as the exemplary character of outstanding individuals may help us see more clearly what ethical choices we should make.

Yet, there is more to ethics than learning from others, for we must also learn more fully who we are. Doing ethics involves a quest for greater self-knowledge. We not only study and draw on the moral wisdom of the past, but also discover and create new ways of taking the right actions and being good persons.

Embracing this challenge will involve asking questions, pondering alternatives, trying what seems best, admitting mistakes, seeing what works and what doesn't, evaluating our assumptions, and asking new questions. Moreover, it will mean doing this with others, who want as much as we do to act more responsibly.[1]

We assume that you come to this discussion with strong convictions, with experience in facing and making moral decisions, and with ways of explaining your judgments. You probably have some questions about ethical reasoning, as we do, and perhaps you share with us some misgivings about the relevance of moral philosophy for our daily lives.

The authors of this book have had moral conflicts with parents, children, and friends, and these conflicts have led us to question some of our moral presumptions and also our ways of reasoning. We assume this is true as well for many of you. We hope you have discovered as we have that these experiences may teach us important lessons and help us deepen our self-understanding.

We assume, moreover, that you are concerned about many of the significant moral issues that divide our society. Should public officials always tell the truth? Is our tax system fair? Do people suspected of terrorism have a moral right to due process of law? What is a fair wage or salary? Should same-sex marriage be permitted? Is capital punishment right or wrong?

Who should receive the benefits of welfare? Is abortion always wrong? Should federal funds be used for stem cell research? Who should have to pay for our public education system? And so forth.

It may seem that there is no way to reconcile those who disagree about the many issues of public morality, yet history reveals that divisive issues have at times been "resolved." A century ago, for example, women did not have the right to vote. For decades against stiff opposition, a few women argued for changing the law. Eventually, enough men who could vote were persuaded that it was morally wrong to withhold the right to vote from women, and the law was rewritten to reflect a new moral presumption for our society.

Much of our concern in this book will be with issues of public morality, such as the right to vote, and in chapter 10 we will look more explicitly at what public morality means for us and requires of us. Issues of morality concerning only our private lives are no less important for all of us. Yet, we will say less about private morality, as our public morality today leaves most of these issues to individuals and their families.

There is controversy, however, in deciding which moral questions should be public and which should be private. For example, sexual inter-course is a very private matter, but is also the subject of considerable public debate. Laws in many societies prohibit prostitution, incest, and polygamy, so these sexual issues are matters of public policy. With these exceptions, however, contemporary Western societies have generally repealed statutes that in the past restricted the private sexual activity of consenting adults.

Conflict over abortion also raises questions as to where we draw the line between private and public morality. On this as well as many other moral issues, even having a civil discussion may require a great deal of self-discipline. We have done our best to be clear and forthright, and we trust that you will enter into this discussion in the same spirit.

DIVERSITY, FREEDOM, AND RAPID CHANGE

Many believe that making ethical choices is more difficult now than in previous generations. Some say that the following words of William Butler

Yeats apply to our time, although he wrote them at the beginning of the
twentieth century:

> *Things fall apart; the center cannot hold;*
> *Mere anarchy is loosed upon the world,*
> *The blood-dimmed tide is loosed, and everywhere*
> *The ceremony of innocence is drowned;*
> *The best lack all conviction, while the worst*
> *Are full of passionate intensity.*[2]

How do you see the changes that make our time particularly difficult
for making ethical decisions? Here are some of our thoughts.

First, the vast migrations of people in the twentieth century, which continue to define the beginning of the twenty-first century, have created
more diverse societies all over the world. In the past there was greater consensus within communities about morals, especially when most people
lived in smaller cities and towns. In our multicultural cities, however,
people with various religious and ethnic traditions live side by side. If there
is to be a new and more compelling consensus about public morality in our
pluralistic society, we will have to work hard to achieve it.

Second, most of us enjoy a great deal of personal freedom. In traditional societies individual choice is more restricted by cultural and social
traditions. Today, some urge that our moral standards should be more fully
defined by the law, as in the past. Yet, in pluralistic societies the law continues to protect our individual autonomy. The debate over gay rights is only
one prominent example of the struggle today between those who want to
protect personal freedom and those who would impose greater restrictions
on personal conduct in order to uphold a particular moral standard.

Third, moral issues and disputes over personal freedom now divide our religious communities. Many Catholics use birth control measures prohibited
as illicit by church teachings. Protestant denominations are split over whether
or not gay persons or women should be ordained. Jews argue as to whether
their moral obligations to other Jews apply also to Gentiles. Some Muslims
disagree with Islamic teachings that explicitly justify social restrictions for

women. Hindus dispute whether India ought to have a secular government, as it now does, or a government that supports Hindu teachings and rituals.

Fourth, technological advances have created a large number of new ethical dilemmas. Breakthroughs in biology have led to fierce debates about genetically modified food, the cloning of animals, stem cell research, and many other choices that are now available to us. Computers bring pornographic pictures into our homes via the Internet, and millions of people download music and videos illegally. New technology offers more sophisticated medical treatments, but has also increased the cost of health care, raising difficult moral questions about the allocation of scarce resources.

Fifth, the role of women has changed dramatically. Women have been elected to head the governments of several nations and have attained positions of leadership in business, law, and medicine. Female scholars have studied and revealed the patriarchal bias that has shaped not only our social relations, but also the way we have understood both human culture and the natural world. This feminist insight has been much resisted, yet has powerfully altered many areas of study, including the disciplines of developmental psychology and moral philosophy.

Sixth, the sexual revolution that has accompanied the evolution of pluralistic society is unprecedented. The ability to prevent conception has enabled women to have sex without having children, and sexual relationships outside of marriage have become common at least in the West. People wear more revealing clothing in public, and nudity is legal in many societies on designated beaches or in private clubs. These "liberating" changes have not, however, freed women from the trade in sex, which today enslaves hundreds of thousands of young women, or from pornographic displays of the human body. Nor has freer sex necessarily led to healthier sex, as sexually transmitted diseases including HIV are rampant and AIDS is the cause of millions of deaths each year.

Seventh, economic globalization has made food and many commodities available to more consumers at lower prices, but has also meant a loss of livelihoods for millions of farmers and workers. Multinational corporations and institutions, such as the World Trade Organization, now exert greater control over trade than nation-states. Moreover, economic globalization has meant, in general, that the rich have become richer while the poor have (at least in relative terms) become poorer.

Eighth, terrorism has become a global reality, and the support of terrorist acts by some Muslims now affects international politics as well domestic policies in Western nations with respect to Muslim immigrants. After the terrorist attack on the World Trade Center in New York on September 11, 2001, there was an outpouring of sympathy and support for the United States. Subsequently, however, the war against terrorism waged by the United States in response to this attack has alienated much of the world.

Ninth, the threat of global warming now reveals that the human experiment on earth can no longer continue without taking into account the ecosystems of the earth on which all life depends. A more industrialized way of life and a growing world population make ethical choices about the use of our natural resources and the recycling of wastes absolutely essential, if human society is to avoid a catastrophic collapse.

We live in a diverse and rapidly changing world that allows us great personal freedom, but we do not always agree on how best to make use of our freedom. Moreover, we face ethical issues of enormous complexity and importance, and there is little agreement among us as to how to resolve these difficult problems.

> The ancient image of the Tower of Babel has been used by more than a few modern writers to describe the current state of discourse about ethics and values. There is no one "spirit of the times," but many—*too* many in fact—too many competing voices, philosophies, and religions, too many points of view on moral issues, too many interpretations of even our most sacred documents, our Bibles and Constitutions. Only the most unthinking persons can fail to be affected by this pluralism of points of view and not wonder, as a consequence, about the truth of their own beliefs.[3]

In *Doing Ethics*, we do not take the diversity of our time lightly. Therefore, we begin not by making strong assertions about what we take to be right, but by reminding ourselves of the limited capacity of human beings to understand our world.

OUR LIMITED KNOWLEDGE

Our present scientific knowledge clearly reveals that we cannot know all there is to know about our world and our place in it. As finite human beings, we know what we know through our own subjective observations, and so our knowledge is limited.

Advances in biology and neurology enable us to understand that we construct our perceptions of the world and of each other. Our eyes are not video cameras, and our ears are not tape recorders. We do not simply see and hear the world as it is. Instead, our minds compose from our sensory impressions the images and meanings that we take to be real.

Moreover, as we construct our knowledge of the world, every thought is associated with a feeling as it becomes a memory, and these memories are shaped by other memories that we have constructed from earlier experiences. In other words, what we know is always an interpretation of what there is to be known.

> Information from the eyes, ears and body is carried to primary sensory regions in the brain. From there, it is carried to so-called higher regions where interpretation occurs. . . . The surprise is the amount of traffic the other way, from top to bottom, called feedback. There are 10 times as many nerve fibers carrying information down as there are carrying it up. These extensive feedback circuits mean that consciousness, what people see, hear, feel, and believe, is based on what neuroscientists call "top down processing." What you see is not always what you get, because what you see depends on a frame-work built by experience that stands ready to interpret the raw information. . . . [4]

In constructing the world we rely on our language, our culture, the literature we read, and our personal experiences, as well as the data that comes from our senses. We do not perceive a world that is just there, external to us. Instead, we make our world.

This means that we are unable to see reality with complete objectivity. We cannot stand outside of our world and look at it, because in every moment we see our world through our construction of it. There is always a subjective aspect to our knowing. What we understand of the world is inevitably personal, because it is *our* understanding.

To attain greater objectivity, therefore, we must check our understanding with others. A conscientious scientist welcomes scrutiny of her research, so that her hypothesis may be verified or modified. The goal is always greater knowledge and a more accurate view of the world and our experience in it. Yet, we must not forget that a complete and final view of reality is impossible, because:

- Our knowledge is always limited to our particular time and place.
- The world is always changing, even as we are always changing.
- We cannot know how human beings will exercise their freedom.

What does this have to do with thinking about ethics? Our sense of responsibility is based on our knowledge of the world, and therefore involves a construction that we have made. How we understand what is right and wrong, or good and bad is shaped by our experience in life and by our discussion with others. In doing ethics, therefore, we must welcome critical discussion of our moral arguments, so we can improve our understanding of how best to address the ethical issues that we face.

The limitations of our knowledge are particularly evident when we try to decide what is best by predicting the foreseeable consequences of taking a particular action. The human experience of regret is strong evidence that we are not as capable of doing this as we would like to think we are. Reflecting on some of the past decisions we have made will quickly remind us of this fact. Moreover, we will recall that we are often unable to know how we will evaluate the consequences of an ethical decision until after we have made it and "lived with it" for awhile. We simply cannot predict all the consequences of exercising our freedom.

Would the future be completely predictable if we fully understood the laws of physics, chemistry, and biology that govern the universe? Is everything that happens, including the choices we make, merely the result of previous causes?

Prior to modern theories of relativity and quantum mechanics, some scientists and philosophers thought that human freedom was simply an illusion. Contemporary physicists, however, reject this deterministic view of reality, because at the quantum level there is irreducible uncertainty and only mathematical probability as to what will occur.

Within atoms, which make up all matter, energy transfers involve tiny packets, or quanta, and any measurement involving these energy transfers cannot determine precisely both speed and location. If we know the speed, we can only speak of the probable location, and if we know the location, we can only predict the probable speed. At the quantum level, therefore, reality is inherently indeterminate and uncertain.[5]

The social sciences are committed to predicting as well as explaining human behavior. Yet, the diverse theories of psychology, anthropology, sociology, and economics make predictions largely a matter of choosing between various approaches and methodologies. Forecasts about the future can never offer a guarantee.

Not surprisingly, the uncertainty of life is the main subject of literature, and the stories of every culture reveal its deepest moral struggles. Benton Lewis, an Apache Native American, says that stories change us. "Stories go to work on you like arrows. Stories make you live right. Stories make you replace yourself."[6]

The characters we love to read about in novels or watch in movies are as complex and unpredictable as we are. Like us, they cannot know fully the implications of the moral decisions they are making. By entering into their stories, however, we find clues to help us sort out our own dilemmas.

The stories that define a culture tell us a great deal about its ethics. Some of these are religious stories and are reflected in the symbols that continue to shape the self-understanding of a people. We are reminded of the story of the Buddha's renunciation as we look at a statue of him sitting quietly. Images of the crucified Jesus evoke other stories involving sacrifice and forgiveness. The many images in Hindu art express diverse feelings about the pervasive presence of divine power, whereas the lack of images in Islamic cultures reflects the teaching of the Qur'an that God is wholly transcendent and demands submission.

These ancient stories and images shape our understanding of life, perhaps primarily in unconscious ways. We live within them, and they shape our view of the world. Now that these and many other stories and images are informing our pluralistic societies, we should not be surprised that doing ethics has become more complicated.[7]

BEGINNING

Of course, acknowledging the limits of what we can know should not keep us from trying to know all that we can. We certainly can be more or less aware of how our thinking shapes our understanding of the world, and we may hope that considering different points of view will help us think more carefully and critically.

In *Doing Ethics* we take up this challenge in three parts. Part I begins with this chapter, which introduces the problem of doing ethics today and invites you to help in working out a credible approach. In chapter 2 we distinguish inductive from deductive reasoning and consider how to use each. We also explain why using moral presumptions is helpful, and we suggest that ethical discourse should include reflection on religious teachings as well as philosophical arguments.

Neither of these first two chapters presupposes any special knowledge of ethical theories. Each chapter appeals to the reader to join with the authors in considering our human experience, the circumstances of our contemporary pluralistic context, and the various ways that we think and reason together.

In chapter 3 we review the ideal of the rule of law. We expect the law to enforce the moral agreements of our society, and also to reflect our highest ideals. The law must be fair, and those responsible for the law must also be accountable to it.

Moral philosophy generally ignores the rule of law, but we argue that the moral presumptions of the rule of law are crucial for addressing issues of public morality in our pluralistic society. Moreover, we rely on the rule of law as a model for doing ethics by constructing presumptions and acting on these unless there is sufficient evidence that some other action is more justifiable.

In part II we consider moral theories under five main concerns: duty, character, relationships, rights, and consequences. Traditional ethical discourse, whether philosophical or religious, has generally emphasized duty and character. Today, those who propose that ethics should strengthen our human relationships are critical of moral philosophies that either rely on rules to enforce duties or emphasize character traits that usually reflect "masculine" virtues.

Asserting moral rights is a way of thinking about ethics that reflects political and social changes favoring democratic forms of government. International human rights law now supports group rights as well as individual rights, and includes economic, social, and cultural rights in addition to the more familiar civil and political rights. Human rights law is a contemporary way of doing ethics by asserting as law the social conditions necessary for protecting and promoting human dignity.

The chapter on consequences involves a shift in ethical thought of seismic proportions. Those who reason this way focus on the predicted outcomes of our actions, rather than on moral presumptions concerning our duty, our concern for character and virtue, our relationships, or our rights. In what is often called the utilitarian or consequentialist approach to ethics, we are to act on the basis of our prediction as to how the best results may be achieved.

Each of these approaches to ethics is reflected in various political and economic perspectives. Religious leaders and monarchs tend to promulgate duties, statesmen and philosophers are more likely to promote character and virtue, and revolutionaries and egalitarians strongly assert their rights. Feminists emphasize both rights and caring relationships, and people in business, politicians, and social scientists typically decide what is right by trying to predict the consequences of an action.

There is much to be learned from all these theories of moral philosophy. In *Doing Ethics* we use the first four approaches to create ethical presumptions. Then we consider whether or not the likely consequences of acting on these presumptions substantiate what we think is right or good or fair.

As in the rule of law, we should act on an ethical presumption unless those who question this presumption meet the burden of proof required to set it aside in favor of a different course of action. In chapter 9 we incorporate all five moral concerns into this way of doing ethics and illustrate this approach.

The concluding chapters in part IV test our ethical reasoning. Chapter 10 clarifies what we mean by public morality, and the following chapters consider health care issues, sexual ethics, the war against terrorism, economic justice, and our response to the current ecological crisis.

To illustrate what we hope to gain by working our way through the rest of *Doing Ethics*, we invite you to consider briefly the ethical problem of lying. Do you think lying is always wrong, or is it sometimes right? How would you explain your ethical convictions about this moral issue? The debate about lying has preoccupied moral philosophers and religious teachers for centuries. As there seems to be no consensus, should we simply conclude that whether or not lying is wrong depends on the situation?

We reject this relativistic conclusion. After reading what follows, we hope you will agree with us that everyone should presume lying is wrong. Each of us has a moral duty, as human beings, to tell the truth to others. Telling the truth also reflects a character trait we want to encourage, as candor is crucial for the integrity of a democratic society. Relationships depend on trust, and lying undermines trust. In addition, lying violates the rights of others, who must know the truth to make informed moral decisions.

For these reasons we argue that telling the truth should be our ethical presumption. As in the rule of law, we should act on a moral presumption until those who think otherwise meet the burden of proof required to set the presumption aside. Meeting this burden requires evidence that the consequences of telling the truth in a particular situation are sufficiently adverse to warrant making an exception to our ethical presumption against lying.

This is how we plan to move from ethical problems to decisions that we can explain and justify. We conclude each chapter with thought experiments that address questions and issues covered in the chapter. Our hope is that these inquiries will help us clarify our insights, as we pursue doing ethics in a diverse and rapidly changing world.

DOING ETHICS TOGETHER

I. Are human beings inherently ethical?

1.   At the beginning of this chapter we assert: "Doing ethics is built into us, as social beings, in our human development and in our language."[8] Can you think of examples that verify this claim? Raise one or more critical questions about this assertion.

2.   Think of a story or a television show that addresses a moral issue. Identify and explain the moral presumption of the narrative.

3.   Confucius, the ancient Chinese sage whose advice about doing ethics we will consider in chapter 5, said that knowledge involves knowing "both what one knows and what one does not know."[9] Suggest two presumptions about discussing ethical issues that you think take this understanding of knowledge into account. Each presumption that you assert might begin, "We should . . . "

II. What is really right and wrong?

We have argued that everyone should be open to other points of view, but also that we are able as moral and rational persons to come to some conclusions about what is right and good.

1. Give an example of how you have been open to other points of view. Did your openness change your mind? Explain your thinking.
2. State a moral presumption that you think is right or good and explain your reasoning.
3. Give an example of a moral presumption that asserts a right or a duty, which is affirmed by the rule of law, and make an ethical argument in support of this presumption.

III. Do consequences determine what is right?

A consequentialist approach to ethics asserts that we should decide what is best based on our prediction of the consequences of taking an action. The utilitarian version of this approach defends the proposition that we should do what will result in "the greatest good for the greatest number."

1. Raise a question about the limitations of this approach to ethics and give an example.
2. Suggest a consequentialist moral argument in support of the US war against terrorism. Raise a critical question about this argument.
3. Think of an ethical problem that interests you, and then identify an action you think would be best. Did you base your thinking on the likely consequences of taking this action? If so, what assumptions did you make in order to predict these consequences? If you didn't use a consequentialist approach to decide what action would be best, is your reasoning based on a sense of duty? Or, is it a character argument? Or, are you concerned with sustaining relationships? Or, would you be protecting a human right?

2

Reasoning Together

MAKING SENSE OF OUR EXPERIENCE

The story of blind men describing an elephant to one another is well known. One man feels the trunk and says the elephant is like a snake. Another touches the leg and describes the elephant as being like a pillar. A third puts both hands on the side of the elephant and concludes it is more like a wall.

Originally either a Hindu or a Buddhist tale, this teaching has been used by Jews, Christians, Muslims, and others to illustrate the wisdom of being humble about our assertions, because of the limitations of our knowledge. Our knowledge is limited and not comprehensive. We all "see" what "is" only in part.

The story, however, also reveals the possibility of knowing more by listening to others. In the traditional telling of the tale, each blind man simply argues for his own point of view. We quickly see their folly, but may not draw the important inference that dialogue is a way of clarifying our experience. By sharing their perceptions the blind men would have come much closer to knowing what an elephant actually is.

This chapter is about learning from one another by reasoning together. By *reasoning* we mean sharing our perceptions of the world and our understanding of these perceptions, often by telling stories or relating our experiences, and then thinking through what this means for how we are to live together. This is a *commonsense* understanding of reason.

We began with a story to remind us that reasoning is narrative as well as analytical or theoretical, and also to subvert the intellectual boxes, such as "philosophy" and "religion," that are used to categorize what we think we know. The story of the blind men and the elephant illustrates both the limitations of human reasoning and also the possibility that reasoning together, from different perspectives, will give us greater understanding.

Most books on philosophy argue that religious traditions offer no help in doing ethics, because each religious tradition claims a source of truth other than our reasoning. In his dialogue entitled *Euthyphro,* Plato (c. 429–347 BCE) sought to banish religious assertions from ethical discourse by having Socrates argue that the gods love what is good because it is good. Therefore, we should do what is good simply *because it is good*, and not because a god commands it.

How can we know what is good? Moral philosophers all agree that we must rely on reason, yet differ in their understanding of how we are to use our rational capacity to verify what is ethical. They also differ on how rational we are and the exact way in which we reason. In *Doing Ethics* we use a commonsense approach to reason and do not attempt to resolve what in philosophy is known as the "rational man" problem.

Some moral philosophers hold that ethics is primarily about duty or character. Others reason that nothing is right or wrong in itself intrinsically (or inherently), and that ethics involves weighing the likely good and bad consequences of any action.

We know that emotions play a big part in how we reason and that our "reasoning" is shaped by how we use metaphors and feelings to give meaning to information. Ethicists, however, differ about the role of intuition in moral reasoning, although most agree that ethics is not simply a matter of feeling that something is right or good.[1]

How then are we to work toward mutual understanding and perhaps even greater agreement? Should we ignore religious teaching and also broader views of human reasoning in order to limit our discussion to a more traditional understanding of rationality? We recommend, instead, that we try to learn about the "elephant" that philosophers call ethics from all the "blind men" who describe what "it" is.

In a society informed by diverse religious and philosophical traditions, it seems clear that no single perspective will give us a complete view. We affirm, however, that the diverse philosophical and religious teachings that shape our common life may not simply be an obstacle, as many moral philosophers suggest, but may be an asset for doing ethics together.

LEARNING FROM OUR DIVERSE WORLD

Suppose you are hiking and become lost. If you are with others who have hiking experience, you will probably feel more confident about finding your way. Taking into account the various points of view may be helpful in deciding which way to go.

The ethical teachings of philosophical and religious traditions offer a similar advantage, for these reflect long histories of thoughtful reflection. One can dispute absolute claims made by religious teachers, or first principles asserted by moral philosophers, and yet learn a great deal from the arguments and stories of both. Surely, every philosophical or religious tradition that has withstood the test of time can be helpful in discerning right from wrong, the moral good, and what is fair or unfair.

The religious and philosophical traditions are like streams that merge in the river of life, pushing against each other even as they flow downstream together. Our challenge today is to make our way safely across this swift river, as the waters from its many tributaries rush in and swirl around us.

To understand the currents of this river of life, which will help us make a safe crossing, we read philosophers, such as Aristotle, Immanuel Kant, and John Stuart Mill, as well as contemporary writers, who continue to revise the thinking of the Western philosophical tradition. We also study the writings of feminist scholars, who resist the patriarchal assumptions of traditional Western philosophy and argue for the importance of relationships in ethics. In addition, we suggest that Eastern traditions of thought, although frequently characterized as more religious than philosophical, offer some balance to the individualistic emphasis that tends to characterize Western philosophy.

Due to recent migrations as well as the greater availability of information, our contemporary diversity includes traditions of reasoning from many cultures. For instance, Confucius taught that ritual is essential for public ethics, a perspective almost entirely absent from moral discourse in the West. Also, African and Asian perspectives on human rights resist the individualistic emphasis of Western thought by defending a more consensual view of how the social conditions for human dignity may be achieved.

All religious traditions use reason as well as rely on claims of truth, and all philosophers not only reason but also assert premises that cannot be proven. Reasoning is limited by our knowledge, yet by reasoning we aspire to know more. We can and should learn from religious and nonreligious points of view. It is misleading to pose a choice between reason and religion, or between Western philosophy and other traditions of thought, if we hope to learn from the human experience reflected in the diverse cultures of our world. Our real choice, therefore, is how we reason and with whom.

MAKING SENSE OF EXPERIENCE

We suggest that reasoning is best understood in terms of how we make sense of our experience. We are reasoning when we see patterns or relationships, make inferences, require consistency and coherence, understand our empathy for persons in distress, consider likely causes, and predict possible consequences. We use this *commonsense* reasoning to explain our experience to ourselves and to others.

We are not always aware of our motives, yet reasoning with others may lead to greater self-awareness. Once we become aware of our motives, we may be able to distinguish rationalizations from reasons in order to achieve a more objective view of our differences with others. We take this sort of reasoning for granted, but our ability to think like this is quite extraordinary.

Using a contemporary image, we might say that reason is an essential part of the software of our minds. We can conceive of the mind as "running" on the neural structure of the brain like software runs on the hardware of a computer. The software of our minds, however, is not limited to using our experience to reprogram instinctual responses, although it does that. We also use our experience to speculate on the causes of what has happened and what has yet to happen.

In this sense reason is far more complex and creative than any software program we can imagine, because reasoning enables us to think about what we do not know and to project possible outcomes that may or may not happen.

For instance, on September 11, 2001, as we were horrified by televised images of airplanes flying into the World Trade Center, we immediately began to wonder why anyone would commit such a terrible act. Moreover, we soon were thinking about various ways we might try to prevent such a terrorist attack from happening in the future.

Reason takes us beyond our immediate experience and allows us to think about what might not have been, or what might be. This exploring, imaginative, speculating nature of reasoning transcends our material reality. Reason is not constrained, as we physically are, to a particular time and place. We can consider the vast cosmos and the tiny quark, not only now but also at the beginning and end of time. Our minds can "travel" faster than the speed of light, and can conceive of "things" that might never be.

This incredible ability to reason makes ethics possible. We reason not only to meet our needs for food and shelter, but also to discern what is right and wrong. We use reason not merely to continue to survive, but to consider and pursue the purpose of our lives. We reason together not simply to gain wealth and power, but also to seek peace and greater justice.

The fact that we are ethical at all, that we even bother reasoning about what is right and wrong, is astounding and should inspire us. Yet, we may be so aware of all the conflicts and violence in the world that we fail to appreciate the significance of our human nature. Our species is capable of being ethical and seems to be incapable of being unconcerned about ethics. Of course, individuals and groups may act in ways that are completely unethical, but we are all aware of this. Moreover, we are critical of such unethical conduct.

As reasoning creatures, we are free to make choices, but not free to ignore questions of right and wrong. As human beings, we can only live together more or less ethically, with more or less clarity about the moral decisions we make. We may act in unreasonable ways, but we are not free to stop reasoning about whether our actions are reasonable.

WAYS OF REASONING

The question, therefore, is not whether we will or should reason about ethics, but how best to do so. To answer this question, we will briefly consider how reason enables us to agree, to make distinctions, and to draw analogies.

First, reason allows us to come to agreement about some ethical choices, despite our differences. As reasoning beings, we are able to share our sense of right and wrong, despite all our cultural and religious differences. In addition, because we are able to reason together, we can agree on at least some moral issues, even if this means also agreeing to respect our right to disagree. For example, what is known as the golden or silver rule, as we shall see near the end of this chapter, verifies the possibility of moral agreement despite our different cultural and religious traditions.

Second, by reasoning we can make distinctions that help clarify our approach to doing ethics. We can distinguish reasoning about retributive justice, when a wrong has been done, from reasoning about distributive justice, which does not involve responding to a wrong that has been done but only concerns the fair allocation of a burden (such as taxes) or a benefit (such as social security). We can also see that reasons concerning moral duties and rights are different than reasons predicting likely consequences.

In addition, we can acknowledge that the reasons we give for our actions may be rationalizations for doing what we simply want to do. It would be unreasonable to resist the contemporary insight that all assertions concerning right and wrong reflect the interests of those making these assertions. Yet, the lesson to be learned here is not that all reasoning is fatally flawed. For critical reasoning—the kind of reasoning that questions and contrasts and is a bit suspicious of our motives—is how we have come to understand the danger of rationalizing our desires.

Third, we can reason by analogy to discover a similarity between unlike things. We began this chapter with a story of blind men describing an elephant. Reading this story as an analogy, we concluded that its meaning might be applied to our understanding of ethics. Similarly, we drew an analogy from the image of waters flowing from streams into a river.

Reasoning by analogy will be especially helpful in learning from religious teachings. Although we may reject the authoritarian claims that accompany a religious story or a dogmatic assertion, we may nonetheless reason by analogy to glean new insights into human experience and the difficulties of doing ethics in a diverse world. For example, we may reject the belief that the Bible was revealed by God, but we can discern that a Christian's faith in God is in some ways like a philosopher's faith in a fundamental presupposition.

In addition, we can and should reason with empathy. Our feelings are not necessarily contrary to our reason. Psychologists have taught us that reasoning, as though we have no feelings, means that we are repressing the feelings we have. Reasoning without feelings is not moral reasoning. We learned as children to be moral by relying on empathy for others as well as by formulating reasons for explaining what we feel to be right and wrong.

Michael Schulman and Eva Mekler, authors of *Bringing Up a Moral Child*, argue that: "Moral motivation is acquired through three psychological processes, which . . . [are] the three foundation stones of moral development. They are: 1) internalizing parental standards of right and wrong action; 2) developing empathic reactions to other people's feelings; and 3) constructing personal standards of kindness and justice."[2]

Of course, we must learn to explain our feelings, to give reasons for them, and to subject these reasons to critical examination. This kind of reasoning, however, should not replace our empathy, but instead should help us articulate our feelings. Ethics is not simply about rewarding those who are right and punishing those who are wrong, or calculating dispassionately how best to distribute scarce resources. Ethics involves acting with compassion and forgiveness as well as justice, and there are good reasons why this is so.

Inductive and Deductive Reasoning

Finally, we can and should rely on deductive and inductive reasoning—which we are using in a more general sense than in the philosophical discipline of logic. By deductive reasoning we mean applying a principle or a presupposition in different situations. For instance, if we affirm that hitting a child and causing bruising is wrong, then it is wrong for parents or teachers or older children or anyone else to hit and bruise a child. If child abuse is wrong, then every specific instance of child abuse is wrong. In formal logic this conclusion "necessarily" follows.[3]

Inductive reasoning is very different, because it begins with a question (or hypothesis) about what might be and then evaluates that question (or hypothesis) by testing it. In contrast to deductive reasoning, which moves from an assertion to what follows from the assertion, inductive reasoning moves from what might be, through experiments (or other forms of experience) to see if it really is or can be. In formal logic such an argument only supports a "probable" relationship.[4]

Deductive reasoning applies a principle to a problem, whereas inductive reasoning involves questioning, observing, and evaluating what we know about a problem as well as realizing what we don't know. For instance, we might use inductive reasoning to consider whether or not spanking constitutes child abuse, by interviewing experts in child development as well as parents and children in order to assess the effects of spanking on both children and parents.

Human beings necessarily use both kinds of reasoning, and no approach to ethics is merely deductive or inductive. In general, however, traditional forms of ethics have relied more on deductive reasoning, because people defending a religious, cultural, or philosophical tradition have claimed that certain principles or teachings were beyond questioning and were simply to be accepted and applied to particular situations. The traditional approach to ethics involves reasoning deductively from these principles, commandments, or authoritative teachings, to address various problems.

In our pluralistic context, however, there are at least two difficulties with this approach. First, not everyone agrees with the principles or teachings that are claimed to be the foundation for ethics. Yet, deductive reasoning requires agreement on principles and so, by itself, is not very helpful in a pluralistic society for resolving diverse views of public morality.

In our moral context there is no accepted universal teaching from which to derive ethical principles that everyone will accept. We cannot use deductive reasoning simply to apply the ethical teachings from the Christian Bible, or from the Torah, or from the Qur'an—as many Christians, Jews, and Muslims may do for themselves and for their religious communities. Also, there is no consensus about reasoning deductively from the ethical presuppositions of a renowned moral philosopher, such as Aristotle or Immanuel Kant or Confucius, in order to draw moral conclusions as to how we may achieve happiness or fulfill our moral duty.

Therefore, in our context of diverse and competing points of view, we conceive of scriptures and philosophers as offering hypotheses for doing ethics, and we describe these moral hypotheses as "presumptions." We evaluate our ethical presumptions by using thought experiments and other ways of reasoning inductively.

The second difficulty in relying largely on deductive reasoning is that moral principles are often broad statements that do not necessarily clarify how to respond to particular issues. If it is child abuse to hit a child and cause bruising, is it child abuse to deprive a child of food or to force a child into prostitution? If "child abuse" *is* "hitting a child and causing bruises," then the use of deductive reasoning alone will not enable us to come to the conclusion that seems obvious.

For most of us, child abuse includes a wide variety of ways that adults may mistreat children because of their size and dependence on adults. When we think of examples of abusing children, we are thinking inductively about what our rule concerning child abuse should include. Yet, no matter how broad the rule we devise, we may have to revise it as we confront new forms of abuse.

In doing ethics, we must use inductive as well as deductive reasoning. For example, when confronted by an ethical dilemma, such as whether it is right or wrong to spank a child, we begin by reasoning inductively about our duty to children, the character we hope to instill in them, strengthening our relationship with them, and protecting their human rights. From this reasoning process we construct a moral presumption concerning spanking. Then we use deductive reasoning to apply this presumption to a particular situation in which there is disagreement about whether or not spanking will constitute child abuse.

Before we act, if we have concluded by deductive reasoning that the likely consequences of acting on our presumption will not be best, we should use inductive reasoning to revise our moral presumption. After acting, we should reason inductively to evaluate the consequences of our action, and this may lead us to revise our moral presumption as to how to respond if we were ever to face a similar dilemma.

Of course, it isn't necessary to use words like *inductive* and *deductive* to describe how we reason. We do ethics by learning from others and from our experience. We clarify what we think is right, and then apply our conclusions to particular problems. As circumstances change, and after we have observed the results of our moral actions, we evaluate what we presumed to be right before we acted. Then we apply the insights we have gained from our experience and from the observations of others.

With reason, we pause before judging in order to try to see with greater objectivity. We may not always be aware of our motives, or of our self-interest, but we can think critically about the reasons that make sense to us, and so perhaps see if any of these reasons seem to be rationalizations. Discussing our reasoning with others is also a good way of achieving greater objectivity and perspective.

PRESUMPTIONS AND PROOF

Like the words *inductive* and *deductive*, the word *presumption* is not part of our everyday vocabulary. In *Doing Ethics* we refer to presumptions the way scientists speak of hypotheses to mean working statements of what we take to be right, at least until we have evidence that leads us to conclude otherwise. When we speak of ethical presumptions, we mean simply what we presume to be right based on the reasoning we have done so far.

For instance, we explained briefly in chapter 1 why we presume that telling the truth is right and lying is wrong. This presumption comes as the result of reasoning about our duty as human beings, our aspiration to model the kind of character we think is required in a moral society, our concern to build and maintain trusting relationships, and our commitment to respect the rights of others. Once we have constructed an ethical presumption, we assume it describes an action that is right.

Our moral presumptions are the rules or principles we follow, but we choose not to call them rules or principles because we want to emphasize that they are open to revision. We do not want to become defensive about an ethical presumption, once we have constructed it. We intend only to rely on it as being right or good or fair, until there is evidence that some other presumption would be better. Like the use of hypotheses in science, presumptions in ethics are provisional and subject to change, if there is sufficient evidence to call into question what we have presumed to be right.

For instance, if our presumption is that we should tell the truth, then the evidence for testing this assumption will include the likely consequences of telling the truth in a particular situation. Identifying these consequences will require careful observation, awareness of our tendency to rationalize, interpretation of causal relationships, and perhaps a lengthy study of the events that follow telling the truth. We may decide through this largely inductive reasoning process that our moral presumption, or hypothesis, should be revised or set aside, at least in certain circumstances.

Ethical presumptions that we have already suggested in the first two chapters include the following:

- All persons are equal before the law.
- We should tell the truth rather than lie.
- We should be compassionate as well as just.

The word *should* is often used in moral presumptions, but this verb is also used in commands as well as in other ways. "You should be quiet," may simply mean that someone wants you to be quiet, and not that you have a moral duty to be quiet.

In reading the first two chapters of this book, you may have noticed that the adjectives *moral* and *ethical* are being used interchangeably, as synonyms.

Some authors distinguish these two words, but for our purposes we use them without making any distinction between the two adjectives.

Finally, we should clarify what we mean by the word *proof*. We do not mean evidence that puts an end to all questions and all critical reasoning, for we do not believe human beings can attain such certainty. Instead, by proof we mean evidence and reasons that are persuasive.

Why would reasons be persuasive? Because these reasons seem inductively to make the diverse threads of our experience coherent, or deductively to be consistent with a moral presumption we hold. Because we conclude that the evidence and the arguments presented should persuade a person of goodwill and all those who are fair-minded. Because we know that those we respect and trust have found the evidence persuasive.

By "burden of proof" we mean the evidence we take to be required to overcome an ethical presumption. Once we construct a presumption, we presume it is right until evidence to the contrary based on likely consequences leads us, through inductive reasoning, to modify this presumption.

We are justified, therefore, in acting on an ethical presumption we have constructed. Those who oppose it bear the burden of proof of showing that the presumption is unwise. If they meet this burden of proof, then we should revise our presumption. Clearly, such a judgment requires some discussion with others, which is why we must consider now not only how we reason but with whom.

ETHICAL DEBATE

If we limit our ethical conversation to those who are like us, it will be hard to see what we take for granted as right or wrong, or as reasonable. In her book *Lying*, Sissela Bok argues that in all but private matters there should be public debate before lying is deemed justifiable. If public discussion is not feasible, then she urges debate that at least includes sufficient diversity to ensure critical reflection on different points of view.[5]

If we take her point seriously, then we will include in our ethical debate not only moral philosophers from the West, but also voices from other philosophical and religious traditions. Western philosophers differ in many respects, but share assumptions that are questioned in other cultures. There is no way, of course, to represent every perspective in our moral discourse, but if we err it should be on the side of inclusion rather than exclusion.

Our ethical discussion should also be open to religious advocates, who may believe that only their teachings are true. After overhearing a conversation about our ethical approach, a waiter in a Jewish restaurant urged the authors to study the revelation to Moses on Mount Sinai, which includes this statement, which our waiter recited from memory: "Hear, O Israel! The LORD is our God, the LORD alone. You shall love the LORD your God with all your heart and with all your soul and with all your might."[6] This passage follows a second rendering in the Torah of the Ten Commandments, which are read by many Christians as well as Jews as God's foundation for ethics.

Anyone who thinks this passage has relevance only for Jews or Christians should think again. Jewish scripture commands obedience to the one God, who prohibits murder, theft, adultery, and bearing false witness against others. Whether or not we believe these teachings are the revealed will of God, they have had an enormous impact on the history of ethics and law.

Moreover, monotheistic moral teaching in its Jewish, Christian, and Muslim expressions has the loyalty of about half of the world's peoples. Surely, there are lessons here for doing ethics.

Consider also a very different, but no less striking, point of view expressed as a narrative in the ancient heritage of India. The *Bhagavad Gita*, which is part of the epic Mahabharata, tells of a warrior named Arjuna, who concludes that war is futile and so decides not to fight in a battle. However, Krishna, one of the many gods of the Hindu tradition, persuades Arjuna that he has a duty to fight, because he is a soldier. Krishna also tells Arjuna that he cannot know whether the consequences of withdrawing from the battlefield will be better than what may come by doing his duty. We are, the story reminds us, mere mortals, and not gods.[7]

Gandhi relied on a symbolic understanding of this Hindu tale to argue that we should always strive to live the truth, and for him this meant fighting nonviolently for what is right. His experiments in applying this ethical presumption to resist the oppression of British colonial rule over India influenced Martin Luther King Jr. and the civil rights movement that struggled against segregation in the United States. Moreover, the examples of

Gandhi and King gave hope to Desmond Tutu and Nelson Mandela in South Africa, and helped to sustain a largely nonviolent movement in opposition to apartheid.

No one could have predicted that the telling, interpreting, and living of this ancient Indian story would have such consequences in the twentieth century.

Today, affirming our moral duty is less popular than asserting our human rights, but we would be foolish to ignore a tradition of ethical reasoning that has so powerfully shaped recent history. Moreover, we should consider carefully the claim illustrated in this ancient Hindu tale that we cannot know the consequences of our actions, and therefore should do our duty rather than simply act on our own calculation of what we think will yield the best results. In Western society, we trust too much in our ability to forecast the consequences of our actions, despite much historical evidence to the contrary.

We might also learn from the Qur'an, which begins with an Arabic affirmation that may be translated: "In the Name of Allah, the Beneficent, the Merciful."[8] Over a billion Muslims devoutly recite this phrase from the Qur'an, but nonetheless hold that Islamic morality involves strict rules and harsh punishments. Critics of Islam see these facts as contradictory. Yet, Muslims have no difficulty believing God is both harsh in judging those who persevere in wrongdoing, and merciful with those who repent of the wrong they have done.

One need not be a Muslim or even a religious person to think that we should repent of the wrong we have done or the good we have left undone. Doing ethics challenges us not only to decide what is just, and to act justly, but also to admit our wrongdoing and to forgive those who have wronged us.

Many other voices are worthy of being heard in our conversation about ethics, but for now we consider only one more. The Lotus Sutra relates that the Buddha told a story of a man who found his children playing in their house as it burned. In order to save them from being consumed by the fire, he called them to come out, but they were so entranced with their play that they ignored his warning. So, he promised them marvelous gifts, although he had none, and with this "false" promise enticed them from the burning building.[9]

This story may be used to justify lying to achieve a good result, at least in circumstances where the probable consequences seem dire and truthful speech unlikely to be effective. In the Buddhist tradition, however, the story is not told to undermine the moral presumption to tell the truth, for Buddhists precepts embrace being truthful. Reasoning by analogy, the story is told to illustrate how some people may need to receive a promise of rewards in order to act in their own best interest. It is a tale about the "truth" of human motivation.

Rather than suggest that the study of ethics is the only way we all will be saved from the dangers of our time, we promise instead that you will enjoy what lies ahead in *Doing Ethics*. This would be a false promise only if you proceed looking for an easy read. If, however, you hope to see more clearly how to make ethical decisions and how to explain your reasoning, then our promise of the delights to come may well be realized.

THE GOLDEN/SILVER RULE

Where does our sense of right and wrong come from? We cannot know, but surely it comes from who we are, as human beings, whether we understand our ethical nature as God-given or as the transcendent aspect of our humanity. We are able to act ethically, to learn from our mistakes, to aspire to be better persons, and to struggle for a more just society. History shows us this is so.

Yet, history also reveals that the human story is not simply a tale of moral improvement, for the past century was among the bloodiest ever. We should be humble and not simply conclude that we are more ethical than our ancestors were.

One ancient moral presumption that links us to the past is known by most of us as the golden rule. Many are able recite this ethical presumption from memory: "Do to others, as you would have them do to you."[10] In some cultures this moral presumption is stated in terms of what we should not do, and this formulation is often called the silver rule.

We should be encouraged to find in different cultural and religious traditions an ethical presumption of enormous significance that has not only been affirmed for millennia, but also is widely embraced today. Here is evidence that diverse peoples may nonetheless derive from their human experience a moral presumption that is close to universal.

- Buddhism: "Hurt not others in ways that you yourself would find hurtful." (Udana-Varga, 5:18)
- Christianity: "In everything do to others as you would have them do to you; for this is the law and the prophets." (New Testament of the Bible, Matthew 7:12)
- Confucianism: "Surely it is a maxim of loving kindness: Do not unto others that you would not have them do unto you." (Analects, 15:23)
- Hinduism: "This is the sum of duty: Do naught unto others which would cause you pain if done to you." (Mahabharata 5:1517)
- Islam: "No one of you is a believer until he desires for his brother that which he desires for himself." (Sunnah)
- Judaism: "What is hateful to you, do not do to your fellow men. This is the entire law: all the rest is commentary." (Talmud, Shabbat 31a)
- Taoism: "Regard your neighbor's gain as your own gain and your neighbor's loss as your own loss." (T'ai Shang Kan Ying P'ien)
- Zoroastrianism: "That nature alone is good which refrains from doing unto another whatsoever is not good for itself." (Dadistan-I-dinik, 94:5)[11]

The golden/silver rule calls us to see others as we see ourselves. It states the ethical presumption that we should treat other persons as an end—as having intrinsic worth, and not simply as a means to an end. We should intend that others enjoy what is good, even as we hope to enjoy what is good. As we will see in chapter 4, this is acting with what Immanuel Kant calls a "good will."

At our best, we want what is right for us and for others as well. To act ethically we need to have empathy for others, even for those who may seem to be our enemies. If we want our human dignity to be recognized and respected, and surely we do, then we must recognize and respect the human dignity of others. This is a duty that human beings owe to one another. Therefore, every person has a right to this respect from others.

We are able to reason together about what is right and wrong. Others have, and we can, too. In the next chapter we will see how referring to the rule of law, which is acknowledged today as a fundamental principle for justice, will help us address some of the most controversial moral issues of our time.

DOING ETHICS TOGETHER

I. Does ethics come from our human nature?

1. Use the three words—*motivation, reason,* and *feeling*—in a brief statement that sums up, for you, what ethics involves. What other words might you choose to describe what ethics means for you? Why are these words important to you?
2. Give two reasons why it might be reasonable to say that ethics "is a result of human nature."
3. State two ethical principles or moral rules that you agree with. Is either from a religious tradition? Identify two statements in this chapter that you especially agree with and explain why.

II. Are moral reasons simply personal preferences?

1. Pick a moral issue that interests you and construct an ethical presumption to address this issue. Give two reasons in support of this ethical presumption.
2. With respect to the issue you have chosen, how would you identify the evidence of adverse consequences that should be required to set your moral presumption aside?

3. It makes sense to say, "A good person does good deeds." It does not make sense to say, "Doing what is right makes one a right person." Think of other ways to illustrate how the words *good* and *right* are, and are not, interchangeable.[12]

III. *How may we distinguish rationalizing from reasoning?*

1. If someone were to assert that all forms of reason are simply rationalizations, how would you respond? Illustrate how we may distinguish reasoning from rationalizing.[13]
2. If you have an interest in the outcome of a moral choice, does this necessarily mean that your arguments for a particular decision are rationalizations? Explain your reasoning using an example.
3. Distinguish between a reason and an opinion. Give an example to help explain your thinking.

3
Rule of Law

THE ETHICS OF JUSTICE

The rule of law refers to the ethical ideal behind our contemporary view of law. Our conduct often falls far short of this ideal, but nonetheless our aspiration to uphold the rule of law remains as one of our highest ideals. By affirming the rule of law we embrace a whole host of moral presumptions about what is right, about what rights we all have, and about what must be done for justice to be served.

The rule of law is a way of reasoning about public morality. We expect that the law will not intrude into issues of private morality, but we demand that laws deal with at least some of our public controversies. The moral presumptions of the rule of law express the public ethical agreements of our society.

We are heirs today of a struggle for the rule of law that has lasted well over three thousand years. This struggle has been waged against rulers who have denied the claim that they should be governed by laws. The rule of law rests on two ethical presumptions: *no one is above the law*, and *everyone is entitled to equal protection under the law*. All other moral presumptions of the rule of law may be deduced from these *two pillars of faith* in our common humanity.

The Jewish, Christian, and Muslim scriptures teach that sovereigns are subject to the laws of God, and Greek and Roman assemblies made valiant efforts to impose the rule of law on their rulers. An important advance was achieved in 1215 when the Magna Carta restrained the power of English monarchs. Parliamentary governments soon followed, and slowly men (and later women) began to enjoy the freedoms of self-government. In the late eighteenth century the revolutions in America and in France led to new experiments in democratic government and to a clearer articulation of the rights of citizens under the rule of law.

In the nineteenth and twentieth centuries the rule of law has been extended to new nations around the globe, as resistance to colonialism and imperialism has led to more experiments in national self-government. With the formation of the United Nations after World War II the rule of law took a new global form, and contemporary international human rights law began in 1948 when the United Nations approved the Universal Declaration of Human Rights. This declaration and the many treaties ratified to enforce it have extended the rule of law, at least in principle, to all peoples on the earth.[1]

In chapter 7 we will examine the ethical presumptions of human rights law. Here we simply note that international human rights law applies to all people everywhere, whether or not their governments actually enforce the standards of international law. This means, we believe, that the moral presumptions of human rights law should now affect the way that ethics is done throughout the world.

The United States, however, has ratified only a few of the human rights treaties and has resisted the application of international norms to its citizens. Nonetheless, we suggest that international law has changed the moral presumptions of the rule of law, not only for all other peoples of the world, but also for Americans.

The rule of law not only affirms many moral presumptions of our public morality, it also offers a model for doing ethics. We are reasoning by analogy to the rule of law when we do ethics by constructing moral presumptions, which we take to be right and act on, unless the predicted consequences of taking such actions seem to offer convincing or compelling evidence that we should reconsider.

WRONGDOING

We begin our discussion of these ethical presumptions by reviewing a fundamental distinction in law concerning two kinds of justice. The first applies when someone has done something wrong, and we must decide what action taken in response to this wrongdoing would be right. The basic moral presumption that applies in this instance affirms that *no one is above the law.*

The second kind of ethical issue involves deciding what is right when there has been no wrongdoing, but a choice has to be made as to what action will be fair. The basic moral presumption that applies in this case is that *everyone should enjoy equal protection under the law.*

There is an important distinction between seeking justice after a wrong has been done, and seeking justice when there has been no wrongdoing. As we begin to consider an ethical issue, we should look to see if a wrong has been done. If so, we must analyze issues of retributive justice, which generally involve punishment. If there has not been any wrongdoing, then we need only address issues of distributive justice, which simply require that our choices are fair.

Consider a few examples. Someone who robs a bank breaks the law and thus commits a wrong. Drawing this conclusion does not tell us what our right action should be in response to the wrong that has been done. Should citizens form a posse, hunt the robber down, and string him up? Or, is this a matter for the police to handle? If the latter, we also need to clarify the rules that those charged with enforcing the law must follow in order for their response, to this wrong, to be right.

Probably all of us have seen enough crime shows on television to know some of what is required in criminal law for a right response to wrongdoing. The police have to inform suspects of their legal rights, our laws require a presumption of innocence for anyone accused of committing a crime, and juries are instructed that the burden of proof the prosecutor must meet for someone to be convicted of a crime is evidence of guilt beyond all reasonable doubt. These moral presumptions are essential for preserving the rule of law.

Now consider a second example of retributive justice. Suppose someone borrows money from you but doesn't pay it back, as the two of you have agreed. This is obviously wrong, but now what is right? Not so long ago debtors were put in prison, but we no longer think that is right. Today, the just remedy for not getting your money back is some form of compensation, which may well be less than what you lost, but gives you at least part of what you are owed. Terms like remedy, compensation, and restitution are used in civil law to discuss what is right when agreements and contracts go wrong.

As in criminal law, the civil wrongdoer has rights that must be protected, but in civil cases of wrongdoing there is no prosecution by the government. Instead, the person who is wronged may bring a lawsuit against the alleged wrongdoer. In a civil case the burden of proof is not guilt beyond all reasonable doubt, which in doing ethics we will identify as *compelling* evidence, but only a reasonable assessment that the evidence is persuasive, which in doing ethics we will call *convincing* evidence.

A third example of retributive justice would be responding to wrongdoing that doesn't involve breaking a law, such as telling hurtful lies. Doing something wrong as a way of getting revenge is one possible response, but we all were told as children that "two wrongs don't make a right."

If we are victims of such a wrong, reasoning by analogy from the rule of law may help us realize that we should respond in a way that respects the rights of the other person. We should presume that the person suspected of wrongdoing is innocent, until we have sufficient evidence that he actually committed the wrong. If we conclude that the person should be held responsible for wrongdoing, we should nonetheless act in a way that continues to respect his rights. For instance, we might confront the wrongdoer with the evidence and ask for an apology or some action on his part that will redress any injury caused by the wrong. We might even choose to forgive him, hoping he will be shamed into admitting that he was wrong, and then act more responsibly in the future.

All three of these examples pose issues of retributive justice. Much of the rule of law involves enforcing ethical presumptions against those who break the laws of our society, as well as ensuring that those who enforce the laws also abide by the ethical presumptions of the rule of law.

In what follows we will first take a closer look at retributive justice and then will consider distributive justice.

RETRIBUTIVE JUSTICE

Crime involves breaking the law, which is wrong, at least if the law is just. What if a law is morally wrong? Examples are easy to come by. Segregation was lawful in the southern states of the United States as late as the 1950s. Activists in the civil rights movement argued that segregation laws were morally wrong, and therefore urged disobedience to these laws.

How are we to decide if a law is right or wrong? If we are religious, we argue that to be morally right a law must comply with the law of God. If we are not religious, we may reason that acts violating the rights of others are wrong, because these acts either injure them or deny them their freedom.

Given the moral presumptions of international human rights law, we might affirm that our human dignity requires protecting the security of each person. Crimes are wrong because they violate the human rights that are necessary social conditions for human dignity. In the next chapter we will suggest that this requirement to protect each person's security creates a duty, as there is always a duty involved in upholding a right.

History reveals that the standards for retributive justice have changed. Religious and nonreligious arguments were used for centuries to try to justify slavery; and, after slavery was abolished, segregation in the United States was legal for another century. Now, however, slavery and segregation are repudiated everywhere as contrary to ethics and also international human rights law.

Thus, we may understand retributive justice not as a fixed set of rules or prohibitions, but as a way of reasoning from our moral experience about how to apply the moral presumptions of the rule of law in response to wrongdoing. Today, the International Covenant on Civil and Political Rights (ICCPR) asserts a number of moral presumptions concerning retributive justice:

- No one shall be subjected to torture or to cruel, inhuman or degrading treatment or punishment. (Article 7)
- No one shall be required to perform forced or compulsory labor. (Article 8)
- No one shall be subjected to arbitrary arrest or detention. Anyone who is arrested shall be informed, at the time of arrest, of the reasons for his arrest and shall be promptly informed of any charges against him. (Article 9)
- All persons deprived of their liberty shall be treated with humanity and with respect for the inherent dignity of the human person. (Article 10)
- No one shall be imprisoned merely on the grounds of inability to fulfill a contractual obligation. (Article 11)
- Everyone charged with a criminal offense shall have the right to be presumed innocent until proved guilty according to law. (Article 14)

In addition to these ethical presumptions concerning retributive justice, there is also a very important presumption that *punishment for wrongdoing should be proportional to the wrong done.* At one time murder and stealing a loaf of bread both were punished by execution, but putting someone to death for stealing bread is clearly disproportionate to the crime.

Legal presumptions about self-defense also reflect this moral presumption of proportionality. Life-threatening violence is only justifiable as an act of self-defense when there is a real and imminent threat to a person's life. Similarly, as we shall see in chapter 13 when we discuss the war against terrorism, the self-defense of a country does not justify going to war except as a last resort to protect its people.

DISTRIBUTIVE JUSTICE

As we have explained, distributive justice involves addressing an ethical issue when no wrong has been done, but there is nonetheless an issue of fairness that should be addressed. Can you think of an example? Suppose two persons are waiting for a heart transplant, but only one heart becomes available. Who should receive the heart? How should this question of distributing a scarce and precious resource be decided?

The moral presumption that governs distributive justice is having *equal opportunity under the law*. Actually doing this, by providing equity in resolving issues of distributive justice, is often very difficult.

The problems of distributive justice are widely debated in our society. How are we to decide who is eligible for what medical resources? How should money raised through taxes be spent fairly by our government to meet the many public needs of our society? The allocation of social costs also raises issues of distributive justice. What is fair taxation? If our system of health care is not serving those who are unable to afford health insurance, how might access to health care be made more equitable? If protecting national security means imposing greater costs and inconvenience on citizens, how is this burden to be fairly distributed?

Retributive justice involves imposing a penalty that is proportional to the wrong that has been done. Distributive justice involves allocating resources or responsibility in a fair way to avoid doing a wrong.

Equal Opportunity: Education

For example, if everyone has a right to an education, there are issues of distributive justice in securing this right. Deciding how we *could* provide such an education merely involves using our resources in the most efficient way. Asking how we *should* provide education for everyone implies that we think some choices are more ethical than others are.

Providing education for everyone involves distributing a resource as well as distributing the cost of providing this resource. Creating and sustaining a public education system that meets the requirements of distributive justice means guaranteeing equal opportunities for children to be educated and also a fair system of taxation to pay for this education.

The history of racial segregation in public education reminds us that a lack of equal opportunity may be the result of wrongdoing. Nonetheless, we need to distinguish the issues of retributive justice and distributive justice. Our response to racial discrimination in public education should be

punishment that is proportional to the harm done. Our response to unequal opportunity in public education should be changes in our schools
that seem to offer the greatest hope for ensuring equal opportunity for all.

Achieving this goal of distributive justice will require addressing difficult
ethical questions. How are we to define the "opportunity" that is to be offered through public education? Surely every child must have access to an
education without having to qualify by paying tuition, or by belonging to a
particular ethnic or religious group. Yet, must this opportunity be offered
to noncitizens as well as citizens? What about noncitizens who are illegally
in the country?

These questions are hard enough to answer, but hardly exhaust the ethical debate. We have yet to consider what "equal" adds to the "opportunity"
for education that is being offered. Equal in what respect? Equal in providing access for all those living within a certain geographical area? Equal in
the actual quality of the education offered? Equal in offering a diverse cultural experience that will help children learn how to get along in our pluralistic society? Equal in providing an educational program that is designed
to address the needs of each child?

In the United States, school districts historically relied on local property
taxes to pay the costs of education. This approach led to inequitable funding levels between schools in rich communities and schools in poor communities. Therefore, state governments began to provide significant
funding for public education, but relying on sales tax revenue means less
affluent families pay more proportionally for public education than those
with greater resources.

Referendums in some states have limited the ability of a state to collect
taxes for the support of education and other public services mandated by
law. Authorizing the sale of bonds to raise funds shifts the payback for today's educational costs to the next generation. Furthermore, although the
federal government provides funding for particular purposes and programs, it may mandate services that cost more than the funds granted to
the states to pay for these educational services.

All these issues are ethical as well as political and economic. The political argument involves individuals representing political parties and various

points of view in a debate about the appropriate responsibilities of effective government. The economic issues primarily concern methods of financing education and questions of efficiency.

The ethical debate arises from the presumption that public schools have a duty to provide each child with equal educational opportunities, and each child has a right to these opportunities. Morally, the funding of public education does not simply involve questions of cost-benefit analysis, but also requires supporting equal educational opportunities (however these opportunities may be understood) for all the diverse students attending public schools.

Equal Opportunity: International Law

There are also, of course, many ethical issues concerning equal opportunity in the administration of justice and in the protection of our civil rights and the rights of workers. The International Covenant on Civil and Political Rights (ICCPR) asserts some of these moral presuppositions:

- All persons shall be equal before the courts and tribunals. (Article 14)
- Everyone shall have the right to recognition everywhere as a person before the law. (Article 16)
- Everyone shall have the right to freedom of thought, conscience, and religion. (Article 18)
- Everyone shall have the right to hold opinions without interference. (Article 19)
- Everyone shall have the right to freedom of association with others, including the right to form and join trade unions for the protection of his interests. (Article 22)

Questions of distributive justice also arise in economic decision making. The allocation of annual profits among shareholders, employees, and officers of a corporation raises issues of distributive justice. Is it fair for corporate officers and executives to receive large bonuses, when employees are given merely cost of living increases and shareholders receive only modest returns on their investment? Should men and women receive equal pay for equal work and be given equal consideration for advancement in a company?

Article 7 of the International Covenant on Economic, Social, and Cultural Rights (ICESCR) asserts a number of presumptions that define distributive justice in the workplace. It states that everyone has a right to the enjoyment of remuneration that provides all workers, at a minimum, with:

- Fair wages and equal remuneration for work of equal value without distinctions of any kind, in particular women being guaranteed conditions of work not inferior to those enjoyed by men, with equal pay for equal work;
- A decent living for themselves and their families in accordance with the provisions of the present Covenant;
- Safe and healthy working conditions;
- Equal opportunity for everyone to be promoted in his employment to an appropriate higher level, subject to no considerations other than those of seniority and competence;
- Rest, leisure, and reasonable limitation of working hours and periodic holidays with pay, as well as remuneration for public holidays.

Issues of distributive justice are among the most difficult ethical problems we face. Resources are almost always scarce, and even when we have adequate resources the manner of their distribution among those who want and will likely benefit from these resources may be controversial.

Yet, we continue to affirm the second pillar of faith in the rule of law: that everyone is entitled to equal opportunity. We expect the government to tax and provide services in an equitable manner, and we expect corporations to compensate their stakeholders (officers, employees, and shareholders) in ways that are fair. We affirm that justice requires a fair distribution of benefits and burdens in both public and private decision making.

SUBSTANTIVE AND PROCEDURAL JUSTICE

Justice requires a just result as well as the use of just means to achieve this result. In other words, justice requires both substantive justice and procedural justice. This is true whether we are concerned with retributive justice or distributive justice.

The procedures required in retributive justice not only protect the rights of an accused person, but also protect our rights against being complicit in a wrongful conviction. If an innocent woman is found guilty of committing a crime, she is not the only person to suffer injustice. All of us, on whose behalf the government is enforcing the criminal law, suffer from the wrongdoing of public officials; to whom, at least implicitly, we have given our support.

In 2003 four men sentenced to death in Illinois courts for committing murder were pardoned by the governor, because a review of their cases using new techniques in DNA testing cast doubt on the justice of their convictions. Pardoning these men meant no one was punished for the crimes they had been accused of committing, so the government of Illinois failed to realize substantive justice for these murders. Yet, by freeing men who had been wrongly convicted, the government was able to provide the procedural justice denied these men during their trials.

Due process is also crucial in resolving issues of distributive justice. For example, before legislatures and school boards make decisions about public education, citizens should be able to make their views known. Resolving public issues of distributive justice requires both just results and the due process of law, if decisions made by elected officials are to be legitimate ethically as well as legally.

Does this same argument hold for doing ethics when there is no legal issue at stake? Suppose you are a member of a private club. Is there an ethical issue concerning how decisions are made about membership, privileges, and expenditures? In order to have moral credibility with its members, the club would need to ensure that at least its members have a voice in the decision-making process.

Anyone who has sat through long debates in a decision-making meeting of a private organization will appreciate the use of *Robert's Rules of Order* (or some other set of procedures) that provide clear and fair guidelines for making decisions. Procedures for group discussion and decision making are necessary simply to be efficient, but whether or not the procedures are fair is an ethical issue.

This example reminds us that not every moral issue is covered by a law. Moreover, even when there is a law addressing a moral issue, we may choose to affirm a higher moral standard than the law requires. For example, divorce laws seek to protect the rights of the spouses, as well as the best interest of the children, if the couple has any. Yet, we may affirm the moral presumption that it is best for all involved if couples getting divorced are cooperative and even forgiving.

BURDEN OF PROOF

When issues of distributive justice involving laws are adjudicated in civil courts, the burden of proof to be met by the party bringing the complaint is merely convincing evidence as viewed by a reasonable person. Retributive justice for a crime may deprive a person of his or her freedom, and so the burden of proof required before imposing such a punishment is compelling evidence beyond all reasonable doubt.

In cases concerning distributive justice the party initiating the complaint bears the burden of proof. In cases of retributive justice, the government brings the legal action not only on behalf of the immediate victim of a crime, but also on behalf of the whole society. Unlike contractual disputes, which involve conflicts between consenting parties, criminal acts are understood as directed against society itself. This is why the potential punishment includes incarceration for the protection of society, and not simply a monetary judgment to redress the suffering of the victim of the crime.

These distinctions in defining the burden of proof for civil and criminal cases reflect ethical concerns. We would consider it unethical, for instance, to take away the liberty of an accused person without evidence of guilt that is very compelling. Moreover, it has long been agreed that requiring an accused person to *prove* his innocence would also be unethical. In order to protect the moral presumption that a person is innocent until proven guilty, the burden of proof for finding someone guilty of breaking a law rests with the government.

Again, by analogy, might these distinctions in legal reasoning be useful in thinking through ethical issues that do not involve illegal conduct? In facing such an ethical problem, it may be helpful to identify who should bear the burden of proof, and also the evidence that should be required to meet this burden of proof.

Consider the question of whether or not it is wrong for an elected official to lie to the public. Asking who bears the burden of proof in answering this question means assessing whether or not there is an ethical presumption that officials should tell the truth. The first pillar of faith in the rule of law affirms that no one is above the law, so those who make and administer our laws must be held to its standards. Therefore, citizens have a right to expect that public officials will tell the truth.

Article 25 of the International Covenant on Civil and Political Rights states this moral presumption by affirming that every citizen has the right to "take part in the conduct of public affairs. . . ." Thus, every citizen has the right to hear the truth from government officials, and this is a human right that is necessary to ensure our human dignity.

The rule of law and international human rights standards put the burden for lying on a public official, who thinks a lie may in certain circumstances be justifiable. How substantial is the burden of proof that such an official must overcome to justify a lie? By analogy to the burden of proof required in criminal proceedings, we suggest the official must have *compelling* evidence to set aside the ethical presumption to tell the truth.

Deciding whether to lie to a child in order to protect the feelings of the child would seem to require meeting only a *convincing* burden of proof, which is considerably less than compelling. Yet, even in this instance we argue that our ethical presumption should be telling the truth. Adults should not simply assume they have the right to lie to children whenever they feel it would be best.

We suggest this kind of reasoning is helpful, in ethical reasoning as in criminal and civil law. So, after constructing an ethical presumption, we consider whether the evidence of adverse consequences, which is required to justify setting aside this presumption, should be compelling or merely convincing.

COMMON SENSE

We are using the rule of law as a model for doing ethics. We affirm democratic government and expect elected assemblies to resolve public moral conflicts, at least provisionally, by majority vote. Yet, we also expect our elected legislators to abide by the decisions of our courts that find legislation in violation of the rule of law.

In the United States, as in many other countries, the rule of law is protected by a constitution. For all countries, however, international law also promotes and protects the moral presumptions of the rule of law. The two pillars of the rule of law—that *no one is above the law*, and that *everyone is entitled to equal protection under the law*—are further elaborated in the many treaties that constitute contemporary international human rights law.

Thus, there is much that we can learn about doing ethics from international law, which is why we have referred to international human rights covenants to affirm many of the moral presumptions of the rule of law. Most of these presumptions are also upheld by the Constitution of the United States and by the constitutions of other countries as well.

In principle, these ethical presumptions appear to be common sense for many of us, because we learned about retributive justice and distributive justice as children. Remember when you hit your friend and your parents disciplined you? That was retributive justice. (You likely felt that your friend deserved his share of retribution as well.) When a parent told you to take turns on the swing with the other kids, this was distributive justice. When someone stayed on the swing too long, you knew that was unfair.

We learned about due process in school. When we had an argument with another student, a teacher who listened to both sides of the story before restricting one or both of us was being fair. We also learned in school about the moral presumption of proportionality. Detention for talking in class made sense, but being spanked or expelled was wrong. We know as well from our playground experience that fighting back in self-defense is different than beating up someone to get revenge.

Ethical presumptions are very familiar to us, although we have generally called them rules. We knew at home and at school that these presumptions were generally enforced without further justification. Perhaps we protested at times, but usually without success. So, we understand what it means to bear the burden of proof in overcoming a moral presumption, and how hard that can be.

Therefore, our life experience in dealing with moral issues has taught us many of the moral presumptions that are embodied in the rule of law. We know that constructing presumptions is a practical way of dealing with ethical problems, and we also realize that those who challenge an ethical presumption should have good reasons for doing so.

DOING ETHICS TOGETHER

I. Retributive justice.

Consider the following questions concerning the International Covenant on Civil and Political Rights (ICCPR), which most countries have ratified without qualification and the United States has ratified with reservations that limit the standards of the covenant to US law.

1. Article 14 of the ICCPR affirms the presumption of innocence. This places a costly burden on officials enforcing our criminal laws. How would you defend this moral presumption?

2. Article 9 of the ICCPR asserts that anyone arrested is to be informed promptly of the charges against him. Should this ethical and legal presumption be set aside for any reason? Give an example in your answer. Should compelling or only convincing proof be required, if this presumption is to be set aside?

3. Article 11 of the ICCPR affirms that debtors should not be imprisoned. Give two reasons for supporting this moral presumption. Does your reasoning include a consequence argument?

II. *Distributive justice.*

1. Article 16 of the ICCPR states that everyone has human rights everywhere. From the human rights protected by the ICCPR, which have been noted in this chapter, identify three human rights that the law should protect for undocumented immigrants.

2. Article 7 of the International Covenant on Economic, Social and Cultural Rights (ICESCR) affirms that men and women should receive "equal pay for equal work." Refer to one of the two pillars of faith in the rule of law to argue that this presumption is "morally right."

3. Article 14 of the ICCPR asserts that all persons shall be equal before the courts. What does this mean for deporting those who are illegally in a country? For those who are poor?

III. *Substantive and procedural justice, and the burden of proof.*

1. Give an example of providing due process to someone arrested on suspicion of committing a crime. Explain the importance of the moral presumption of due process in this instance.

2. What was the moral and legal presumption that prompted the governor of Illinois to pardon four men convicted of capital crimes? Did the governor's decision realize or set aside as less important the moral and legal presumption of substantive justice?

3. Would you require convincing or compelling evidence to justify: Lying to save a person's life? Pardoning someone convicted of murder? Explain your answers.

PART II
Creating an Ethical Presumption

Chapter 4 begins with Immanuel Kant's argument for doing our duty, by always acting with a good will to treat others as an end and never as a means to our own ends—out of respect for the dignity of human beings. This is one formulation of his famous categorical imperative. In another formulation, to ensure that we act on the basis of a good will, Kant affirmed that it is our duty to act as if our action would be applied universally. This categorical imperative, Kant argues, expresses a universal duty, because it is good for all people everywhere to accept it.

Gandhi's understanding of duty is similar, although shaped by Hindu notions of *dharma* and *karma*. He argues that everyone has a duty to seek the truth, and that this duty requires renouncing the fruits of our actions. Doing the truth requires resisting wrongdoing, but our resistance should always be nonviolent (*ahimsa*). We must affirm the human dignity of those who have wronged us, if we are to act without contradicting our duty to do what is right.

Chapter 5 describes the tradition of virtue ethics, which has its roots in the philosophy of ancient Greece and in the medieval natural law tradition. Unlike duty, which concerns what we should *do*, character involves who we should *be*. Aristotle suggests good habits make a good person, and Aquinas says those who know God's purpose will manifest it. The Chinese teachings of Lao Tzu and Confucius, which counsel living in harmony with Tao, offer ways of becoming the persons we are meant to be.

Our character often moves us to do more than our everyday notion of duty requires, and stories of great men and women stir us to try to realize our higher nature. This way of thinking about ethics involves aspiring to be a good person and to realize with others the common good.

In chapter 6 we consider the role of relationships in doing ethics. Empathy for others is not simply the second stage of moral development during childhood, but is also crucial for every ethical decision. A person who seeks only to do his duty may well neglect those closest to him. Aspiring to great virtue may blind us to the loving counsel of family and friends.

We agree with feminist writers who point out that praise for traditional understandings of duty and character have often masked unjust power relationships, and we join them in urging more inclusive decision making and less judgmental views of human development. We turn to Buddhist teaching to see how letting go of our desires may reveal what it means to be the sum of our relationships. We also suggest that this lesson may help us face the ecological crisis of our time.

In chapter 7 we argue that international human rights law is essential for doing ethics today. We suggest that civil and political rights, as well as economic, social, and cultural rights, affirm the moral presumptions that should guide our public decisions. Moreover, we hold that ethical presumptions asserting human rights require compelling reasons before being set aside. We also note that there is considerable support within religious traditions for the ethical presumptions of international human rights law.

4

Duty

DOING WHAT IS RIGHT

We know duty is important. We have a duty to our family, to friends, and to colleagues. We also have a duty to obey the laws of our society and, if we are religious, a duty to abide by the teachings of our tradition of faith.

Often this simply means living by the rules. Yet, we know that doing ethics requires reasoning as well. Not all rules are right, so we have to think critically about our duty to obey the rules. Moreover, because not all rules are right, it makes sense to change these rules to make them more just or fair.

To act morally we must clarify the reasons for doing our duty. For guidance in pursuing this challenge we turn to the writings of Immanuel Kant (1724–1804) and Mahatma Gandhi (1869–1948), who despite their differences understood ethics in much the same way as doing our duty for its own sake.

A GOOD WILL

There is a famous quip that "the road to hell is paved with good intentions." This old saw assumes that acting with good intentions simply means hoping that the results of our action will be good. When we do our duty, however, this is not what we mean by having good intentions. We mean intending to do what is right, because it is right. By good intentions we mean doing our duty, because it is our duty.

Immanuel Kant may help us see what it would mean to act with such good intentions (or right motives) apart from any calculation of the consequences. He described having the right intention as having a good will. This does not mean what we usually mean, when we say we have good intentions to bring about some worthy result. By a good will, Kant meant an intention (or motive) without self-interest.

We talk like this when we say a person is unselfish, or is acting without ulterior motives. For Kant, acting with a pure motive involves doing what is good because it is good. A good will means doing our duty because it is right, rather than acting in order to get something in return.

Consider a student who is registering people to vote. If she is doing this simply because she believes voter registration is morally the right thing to do, we will praise her for her selfless action. However, if she says she is registering voters so she can add this activity to her resume, or because she is being paid to register voters, then our assessment of her action will change. We may be glad she is registering voters, as there is general agreement that increased voter registration is important for the health of a democracy. We will not, however, see her participation in a voter registration campaign as being exemplary.

The consequences of the student's action seem to be the same regardless of her motive. People are being registered to vote, whether she is acting without any self-interest, or is seeking some benefit for herself. Morally, however, the two situations are different, at least according to Kant's understanding of ethics.

He argued that our reason enables us to act solely from duty, because our reason reflects the moral law within us. "Duty is the necessity of an action done out of respect for the [moral] law."[1] Respect for the moral law within us is not the same as obeying a law external to us, like the rules of a government or religious authority. Doing our duty means acting on the basis of conscience, which is our clue to the moral law within all people that gives us our dignity as human beings.

In summary, Kant believed that we should admire a person who acts with right intentions rather than with ulterior motives. By making this distinction, we reveal that human beings have the moral capacity to be concerned for others and not just for themselves. We know doing our duty means doing what is right—because it is right, and we are able to act in this way.

UNIVERSAL PRINCIPLES

Kant asserted that an action is ethical when it meets a rational test. If an action is done for the wrong reasons, or if an action will produce contradictory results, then it is morally wrong.

Suppose we lie to a friend when borrowing money by promising to repay the loan although we do not intend to. We may try to justify our lie by saying that the money was more important for us than the feelings of our friend. However, this would be rationalizing, rather than reasoning, as the argument we are making is self-defeating.

Our moral presumption would seem to be: "Lying to friends is right, because it helps us get what we want from them." Yet, lying to obtain money from friends will result in losing friends, and therefore also make it harder to borrow money. Because such an argument is self-defeating, we can see that it is an excuse rather than a reason.

A rational principle or presumption for moral action has to make sense in more than one instance, at least in similar circumstances. For instance, in criminal law it is rational to apply the presumption of innocence to everyone accused of breaking the law. It would be irrational to apply this presumption in cases where individuals are accused of robbery, but not in instances involving murder.

Where we find a lack of consistency in applying a moral presumption, we have good reason to suspect that the motive for our action is self-serving. In cases involving the law, this will likely mean that our distinctions are biased or discriminatory.

By using reason, Kant said, we can see why any moral principle that cannot be affirmed as a general presumption is wrong. The issue is not whether the consequences of acting on such a principle will be good or not. The *test* of a moral presumption is its universal application. In contrast, thinking hypothetically involves conditional statements, such as: "We would have taken an action, if we thought the action would have good

consequences." Kant held, to the contrary, that morality requires a categorical imperative—a principle we can defend as universal using reason.

The golden rule is such a categorical imperative. We can affirm as a universal principle: "Do to others as you would have them do to you." The
principle reminds us of our common humanity. We should not use others,
because no one should use others; we should respect other people, because
every person deserves respect.

By adhering to this rational principle, we may live a noncontradictory
life. We should embrace this duty because it is rational, not because some
religious authority says we should. Actions are moral, Kant taught, when
we do with a good will what reason reveals to be right.

Therefore, we should not obey laws in order to avoid the punishment for
breaking them. Instead, it is our *duty* to obey a law when reason confirms the
law is right, because its moral presumption applies to everyone and is therefore universal. We should always act with a good will (a right intention).

RESPECT FOR PERSONS

The categorical imperative can also be stated in a way that emphasizes respect for the dignity of each person. We diminish other persons, if we treat
them as less than an end in themselves by using them as a means for pursuing our own goals. The example of lying to a friend in order to obtain a
loan that we do not intend to repay illustrates using people as a means for
our own ends. It is unethical to use our friends as a way of attaining our
own happiness without any regard for their happiness.

Kant argued that each person has a will, and that this capacity to act as
a person is shared with all human beings. Our autonomy reflects our individuality, but the nature of our freedom is not unique to each person. Our
autonomy is an aspect of our rationality, and both the ability and the
necessity to reason are common to all people.

The extent to which human autonomy is recognized and respected may
vary from culture to culture and throughout history. Yet, each person,
Kant held, is a "self-legislating will." Because we are free, we each make
choices on our own. To be ethical these choices must be rational by con-

forming to the moral law within us. Thus, the categorical imperative affirmed by Kant is often stated in two forms:

1. Act only on that maxim (ethical presumption) through which you can at the same time will that it should become a universal law.
2. Act as to use humanity, both in your own person and in the person of every other, always at the same time as an end, never as a means.

As human beings, our moral presumption should be that we treat others as ends in themselves, not as means for our own benefit. Therefore, in addressing issues of public morality, we should ensure that our laws respect the human dignity of each person.

This means telling the truth, because respecting others requires honesty. Might the possible adverse consequences of telling the truth ever make lying justifiable? Kant thought not. He argued that violating our duty to tell the truth by lying to someone actually wrongs everyone, as it undermines the mutual respect for one another that is necessary for a just society.

Does it matter if others disagree with us about ethical principles? Kant clearly thought so, which is why he defended moral principles that he believed were convincing, because they could be shown rationally to be categorical imperatives. Even as lying shows a lack of respect for others, trying to find agreement through rational discussion is a way of supporting and strengthening mutual respect within our society.

FROM COMMANDMENTS TO CONSCIENCE

Kant thought that we only know the world through what we bring to it. He came close to saying that we create the world through our own perception of it, which is not too different from what many contemporary philosophers say today. According to Kant, we cannot know the world as a "thing in itself."

He believed there is a "real" world, but argued that this "world in itself" is outside space and time and thus unknowable as we know other things.

We are unable to observe the world in itself using our normal means of observation and reasoning, as we do in scientific inquiry.

Nonetheless, Kant asserted, we have a capacity for "pure reason" that enables us to know right and wrong, which is a structure of the world in itself. With pure reason we can transcend time and space, and in this freedom discern the moral presumptions that should guide our actions.

> Kant never claims that he discovered the categorical imperative. In fact he says . . . that it would be outright silly of anyone to claim that he had discovered the moral law as something really new, as if the world up to then had been ignorant of what constitutes moral duty or else had been quite wrong about such a duty. This supreme principle is, rather, ordinarily presumed in all moral judgments. . . .[2]

Kant developed his ethical arguments in a time when the scientific method was being used to challenge the very idea of autonomous persons making moral choices. If, as Newtonian physics held, every event were caused by a preceding event, then life would be entirely determined by past events. Were this actually the case, however, the ethical notion of *duty* would be nonsense.

This deterministic way of thinking allowed that God might be the first cause, but otherwise replaced traditional notions of divine law with the laws of nature as described by science. A comparative and historical study of the Christian Bible revealed that its teachings were recorded by an ancient culture, which took divine revelation for granted. Once the claims of divine authority and revelation were understood by social scientists as myths of a less rational age, the commandments of Christian scripture no longer had any special claim to define our moral duty.

Kant was a devout Christian, but he defended his views as a philosopher. Rather than argue for the authority of the Christian Bible, Kant found within each person the capacity for self-transcendence. He thought that the pure reason of our nature enables us to discern and act on the moral law.

Kant accepted the scientific conclusions of his time, but argued that our rational and moral freedom is proof of God, the source of the moral law.

Faith in God, Kant said, is not merely rational but also necessary for a moral society, because the desire for immortality motivates us to do our duty instead of simply seeking our own pleasure.

Conscience is the word commonly used to identify our awareness of the moral law within us, but today there is a danger in this identification because we may think of our conscience as simply our opinion. "Let your conscience be your guide" *should* mean following the moral law within each of us that may be known by pure reason. For many in contemporary Western culture, however, this statement merely means deciding as individuals what we think is best.

We are challenged, therefore, by Kant's moral reasoning to do our duty because it is right, not because it is the rule or needs to be done to avoid unpleasant consequences, or even because we individually think it is best. Letting conscience be our guide means using our reason to act on the basis of the moral law that is universal.

If we think about *duty*, as Kant says we should, we will affirm the following moral presumptions. We should:

- Give others the respect that all people deserve.
- Tell the truth and never lie.
- Treat others as autonomous, self-willing beings.
- Base our actions on a good will to be sure we are acting without self-interest.
- Do our duty because it is right, not because we seek to benefit.
- Always act in ways that affirm universal moral principles.

DOING OUR DHARMA

At the end of chapter 2 we mentioned the story from the *Bhagavad Gita* that inspired Gandhi's nonviolent campaign to free India from British colonial rule. In this story, Krishna says that Arjuna, as a human being, cannot know the consequences that will come from his actions. Therefore, Krishna argues that Arjuna should simply do his duty as a warrior and fight against his enemy.

In the ancient traditions of the Indian subcontinent, morality was understood primarily as doing one's duty (dharma). The society was divided into castes that reflected different activities: teachers and priests, soldiers, merchants, and laborers. To fulfill one's purpose in life, each person was to perform the duties prescribed by his or her caste. No one was encouraged to act autonomously. Instead, everyone was expected to do his or her duty.

The *Bhagavad Gita* affirms this tradition, but also teaches that we fulfill our dharma (and thus do our duty) by acting without any concern for the results of our actions. "Renounce attachment to the fruits," Krishna tells Arjuna.[3] The story asserts that moral action involves freely choosing to do our duty without any self-interest or concern for the consequences that may follow our actions.

Recalling this story may help us understand why Gandhi expressed concern about advocacy for human rights. He argued that moral action requires doing what is right for its own sake, not trying to attain a desired result. We should support human rights because they are right, Gandhi said, not because we stand to gain by doing so.

> If we all discharge our duties, rights will not be far to seek. If leaving duties unperformed, we run after rights, they will escape us like a will o' the wisp. The same teaching has been embodied by Krishna in the immortal words: "Action alone is thine. Leave thou the fruit severely alone." Action is duty, fruit is the right.[4]

In his nonviolent campaign for an independent India, Gandhi urged others simply to do what is right. In this way he embodied the ancient Hindu notion expressed in Sanskrit as *tat tvam asi*, which is usually translated as "that thou art." This phrase may be taken to mean that each of us is divine, that the human person is one with the transcendent, that there is ultimately no separation between you (and me) and reality.

Of course, this claim cannot be verified by empirical evidence, for there is no way to stand outside ourselves in order to see reality as it actually is. Yet, Gandhi and other Hindus have long affirmed that we can know, at least, that we are not only "other" than that which is true, moral, and universal.

Morality in the Hindu tradition is not a matter of doing our duty regardless of our motives, for to be "one with" our duty means having the right motive. A good intention, which involves giving ourselves to our duty, is required to be one with our actions. In becoming one with our moral actions, we also become one with the truth reflected in and through them.

FROM KARMA TO AHIMSA

Hindu teaching affirms that by doing our dharma we will eventually achieve release from the suffering of this world through karma, the chain of cause and effect that offers liberation from the cycle of death and rebirth. Karma reinforces the belief that all people should serve their community by performing their caste duties. This view of duty, however, is seen from a Western point of view as suppressing individual autonomy.

In the story from the *Bhagavad Gita*, Arjuna wants to exercise his freedom. He wants to act on his own conscience. Krishna speaks for the Hindu tradition by urging Arjuna to do his duty instead.

Kant turned from divine commandments to redefine the Western notion of duty as conscience, by which he means acting on our rational capacity to know and manifest the moral law within us. Gandhi transformed the Hindu notion of duty by embodying the moral presumptions to act with truth-power (satyagraha) and with nonviolence (ahimsa), which became the dharma of all Indians in their struggle for independence. One who practices satyagraha, Gandhi wrote, "will always try to overcome evil by good, anger by love, untruth by truth, himsa (violence) by ahimsa."[5]

The practice of satyagraha, Gandhi believed, requires embracing the religious disciplines of "self-purification and penance."[6] Gandhi taught that being self-giving, rather than assertive, is the way a person may realize true moral and spiritual freedom.

His commitment to living truthfully led Gandhi to read the story in the *Bhagavad Gita* in a figurative way. The violence that Krishna told Arjuna was his duty—because of his caste—became, for Gandhi, the nonviolence that is everyone's duty regardless of his or her caste. Truth, as Gandhi saw in the story, means acting without any desire to attain benefits from our actions.

This requires nonviolence, because violence always seeks to win a victory over an opponent. Only a nonviolent response to our enemies can bring them to embrace the truth, which must be shared to be true, and so cannot be realized by winning a battle or an argument.

For Gandhi, there was no distinction between morality and God, between doing our duty and being one with the divine. Doing our duty with good intentions means acting with faith in God. Renouncing the fruits of our actions in order to do our duty for its own sake involves living the truth. And truth, for Gandhi, is God: "To me, God is Truth and Love; God is ethics and morality; God is fearlessness. God is the source of Light and Life, and yet God is above and beyond all these. God is conscience."[7]

KANT AND GANDHI

By reviewing the moral presumptions that we derived from Kant's thought, we will see if we also find these in the teachings and nonviolent practice of Gandhi.

- Give others the respect that all people deserve.
- Treat others as autonomous, self-willing beings.

Certainly, Gandhi would say that we have a duty to respect others, for every human being deserves respect. Gandhi would be unlikely, however, to speak of others as autonomous, self-willing beings. Yet, he appeals to each person to embrace satyagraha and ahimsa, and only persons acting out of their own freedom could make such a momentous choice.

- Tell the truth and never lie.

Like Kant, Gandhi affirmed the moral presumption that we should always tell the truth. By telling the truth, we do our duty if we do so without any concern for the consequences of our action. By telling the truth to others we manifest our respect for them as persons who have a right to expect nothing less from us than the truth.

- Base our actions on a good will to be sure we are acting without self-interest.
- Do our duty because it is right, not because we seek to benefit.
- Act always in ways that affirm universal moral principles.

Gandhi would agree that we should not manipulate others for our own gain, and that we should carefully search our hearts to be sure we are not acting with ulterior motives. He also teaches that everyone should do their duty because it is right, not as a way of seeking rewards. Moreover, Gandhi's conviction that moral action, truth, and God are one is a Hindu way of affirming that we should always act in ways that manifest universal moral principles.

Kant and Gandhi assert similar moral presumptions, yet they were very different persons. Kant refrained from making theological affirmations, but doing ethics for Gandhi was an act of religious faith. Kant was reacting to the claims of empirical science, whereas Gandhi explained his teachings in language intended to appeal both to traditional Hindus and progressive Westerners. Kant was a rationalist. Gandhi might better be described as a religious humanist. Kant led a quiet life and wrote books. Gandhi led an independence movement, and wrote letters and essays arguing for political reform.

DOING ETHICS TOGETHER

I. The categorical imperative.

1. Describe the relationship between Kant's notion of good will and the categorical imperative. Give an example of a person with the motive or good will described in your statement.

2. State the categorical imperative using the language of means and ends, and give an example that illustrates how your statement should be understood.
3. What is the problem that Kant says we confront in trying to know the moral law? What solution to this problem did he offer?

II. *Gandhi's ethic.*

1. The *Bhagavad Gita* affirms that we are to renounce the fruit of our actions. Give an example of what you think this meant for Gandhi.
2. What is Gandhi's understanding of truth?
3. Why do you think Gandhi believed that nonviolence is the only way to overcome evil?

III. *Conscience.*

Both Kant and Gandhi affirmed that conscience should be our guide.

1. Does Gandhi seem to agree with Kant that our individual conscience expresses a moral law that is common to all people? Explain your thinking.
2. Do Kant and Gandhi each think of conscience as rational? Explain your answer.
3. How might we guard against an individualistic understanding of conscience? Express your thinking by modifying the moral presumption: "Let your conscience be your guide."

5

Character
BEING A GOOD PERSON

We believe that good people will do what is right. In this sense, ethics is all about character. Perhaps to make the world better we need only identify the character traits that define a good person, and then reinforce these traits by encouraging and rewarding those who embody them.

We take up this challenge by looking at two ancient traditions of thought, one from the West and one from the East. The natural law tradition begins with the ancient Greeks, although it was given this name only in the thirteenth century when Christian writers incorporated the thinking of Aristotle (384–322 BCE) into their reflections.

What we call the Tao tradition begins with writings attributed to Lao Tzu (c. 550 BCE) and Confucius (c. 450 BCE). By the Tao tradition we do not mean a combination of Taoism and Confucianism, but rather early Chinese teaching about living in harmony with the Tao, which later generations developed into two separate schools of thought.

In both the natural law and the Tao tradition, ethics involves clarifying what it means to be fully human. These two ancient and enduring traditions tell us who we ought to be by describing what human life actually is.

THE LAW "ABOVE" HUMAN LAW

We begin our reflections on the natural law tradition with a quote from *Antigone* by Sophocles (495–405 BCE), because the play dramatically illustrates why so many people believe in a moral law that is "higher" than any human law. Antigone defies the king's edict by burying the body of her brother, who was slain as a rebel. She justifies disobeying the law of the land by proclaiming her allegiance to an eternal law, which has greater authority than the decisions made by any human ruler:

> *Nor did I think your edict had such force*
> *that you, a mere mortal, could override the gods,*
> *the great unwritten, unshakable traditions.*
> *They are alive, not just today or yesterday:*
> *they live forever, from the first of time,*
> *and no one knows when they first saw the light.*[1]

If the king is "a mere mortal," so are we all. Nonetheless, Antigone affirms, we can know the eternal law, for the "unshakable traditions" are well known. In Sophocles' play, other people seem to recognize this higher law, but only Antigone has the courage to live by it even though doing so leads to her death.

We applaud individuals with the courage to live as they know they should, despite the terrible consequences they may suffer for doing so. We see in their courage a character trait we admire. The story of Antigone suggests that all human law must be measured against a higher moral standard, because:

- There is a natural law, and we can know it.
- We have natural capacities to reason and to be virtuous.
- Our character is good to the extent that we fulfill these capacities.

In the natural law tradition of character ethics, being good enables a person to do what is right. Being good fulfills our truest and highest nature. Furthermore, reasoning together about how we should live is what enables us to create and sustain a good society.

OUR PURPOSE

The ancient Greeks found a purpose in life that seemed to give order to and also transcend the ways of nature. Sophocles gave voice to this belief in *Antigone*, and—as we shall soon see—Aristotle found purpose in his observations of the world around him. Many centuries later Christian theologians, such as Thomas Aquinas (1225–1274 CE), would not only find purpose in life but argue that human and natural laws reflect the laws of God.

Seven centuries after Aquinas, Martin Luther King Jr. would write in his 1963 *Letter from a Birmingham Jail*:

> How does one determine when a law is just or unjust? A just law is a man-made code that squares with the moral law or the law of God. An unjust law is a code that is out of harmony with the moral law. To put it in the terms of Saint Thomas Aquinas, an unjust law is a human law that is not rooted in the eternal and natural law. Any law that uplifts human personality is just. Any law that degrades human personality is unjust.[2]

In our time many people do not believe that there is a divine dimension to the natural world and human life. Nonetheless, more than half the people on the planet express such a faith within various religious traditions and, for these people, as well as many others who are not religious, a "natural law" approach to ethics continues to make sense.

What might life mean, if we thought we were "created" and thus are alive for a purpose? How would this shape our character? If we believed that we were created by God, certainly we would also believe that our lives are not simply our own. Therefore, we would accept that we have a responsibility to act in certain ways. We might even affirm that we are called to do the will of God.

Because our knowledge as finite human beings is limited, we cannot prove or disprove the existence of an eternal and transcendent God. We can, however, consider how moral decision making may be affected by the belief that we are created in God's image (Jewish and Christian teaching); are called by God to submission by following the straight path (Islam); are able to be one with the divine (Hindu); or may awaken from our illusions (Buddhist teaching).

BEING HAPPY

Aristotle began his *Nichomachean Ethics* by inviting readers to consider what it would mean to be happy. He wanted the Athenians of his time to ponder this question, for he realized that their answers would affect not only their individual lives, but also the life of the city of Athens.

Aristotle's teacher, Plato (427–347 BCE), had grappled with this same question in the *Apology* in his famous account of Socrates' death. The ideas that "the unexamined life is not worth living," and that we should "be true to our principles" have been reaffirmed throughout the centuries, as the works of Plato have been read and discussed. We remember Socrates for his steadfast pursuit of the truth and for his moral character and virtue.

In contrast to Plato, however, Aristotle sought to answer these questions by closely observing nature. His studies led him to conclude that humans are "happiness-seeking" animals.[3] Aristotle saw the pursuit of happiness as good in and of itself, and he accepted this as a natural disposition for human beings. He also observed that human beings have the unique capacity to know their world and to make choices. Our capacity to reason and our freedom to choose are crucial for living in ways that we find fulfilling.

This means that we are creatures who seek happiness not only individually but also in our life together, as social beings. No one simply lives alone, for we all live with others in families, communities, and a society. Thus, Aristotle reasoned, human beings will only find happiness by working together for the common good.

Sixteen centuries later, the Christian theologian Thomas Aquinas also concluded that happiness is what we seek in order to fulfill our nature. Agreeing with Aristotle, he argued that to be happy we must do what is good, and avoid doing harm to ourselves and to others. Aristotle described this way of living in terms of making a contribution to the welfare of society. Aquinas also thought we would achieve the highest good as responsible members of our society, for he believed that God created society.[4]

Throughout this chapter we will suggest that in order to "do" what is good, we need to "be" good. In the natural law tradition, this understanding is rooted in our human nature and in our purpose to seek happiness. Aristotle and Aquinas thought that to attain happiness in life each person must develop civic virtues and act on these in order to contribute to society for the greater good of all.

To identify such happiness, Aristotle used the Greek word *eudaimonia*, which is usually translated as "flourishing." The natural law tradition teaches that every human being is intended, by nature or by God, to be a flourishing person within a flourishing society.

BEING REASONABLE

Both Aristotle and Aquinas believed that human beings are able to discern the purpose of life. Understanding our human nature through reason is the way we discover the natural law. This is how we realize that we have the capacity to live a purposeful life.

Aquinas argued that reasoning uses all of our capacities (he called them "inclinations") to discover our natural purpose. Contemporary readers of Aquinas understand this to mean that our knowledge of the natural law is never complete and grows throughout history. As our conscience develops, our understanding of what is truly natural also changes. This helps us explain the mistakes and wrong judgments of the past. It should also warn us that we are never so wise as to be immune from making serious errors of judgment.

If our judgments are always uncertain and may well be wrong, how can we rely on them to define our moral conduct? One way to face this problem is by reasoning together. Where will reason lead us? To greater knowledge, even though this knowledge will not be complete or final. As in science, our hypotheses can be more or less true, and we can test them. In science, we do laboratory experiments. In ethics, we perform living experiments. In the "laboratory" of life we learn about who we should be, and potentially who we are, by aspiring to lead more virtuous lives.

This means that we must control our appetites and desires, for we can only fulfill our unique nature by developing our reason. Only by cultivating our capacity to act rationally will we be able to maximize the other inclinations of our nature, which are also important for achieving happiness.

Perhaps this sounds like the message of many contemporary self-help books that are so popular in the West, but in ethics we seek above all the common good, rather than simply our own personal success. Aristotle and Aquinas were concerned with promoting public virtue, because they believed that individuals would only achieve happiness in life by creating a good society.

VIRTUES

We know that moral goodness is not simply inborn, but requires development. Achieving even the most mundane personal goods, such as hygiene, requires discipline and the development of good habits. A healthy or flourishing life takes many reminders, which is why Aristotle believed virtue could only be taught through a sound upbringing. (Give thanks for good parents and other role models!)

How we teach virtue is much debated, but there is general agreement that virtue is crucial for a healthy life, both for individuals and for our society. Nothing worth working for can be expected to happen without effort. An intention to be a good person is necessary, although it may not be sufficient. We cannot control many things that happen in our lives. Yet, we need to practice being good persons, if we are to become good persons.

Aristotle described the virtue of all virtues, moderation, as the golden mean. He saw that virtue requires practical wisdom. For instance, too much courage is foolhardy, and too much pride is vanity. Today we know that excessive loyalty can lead to blind patriotism and too much love can create unhealthy dependency.

Plato looked for the source of virtue in eternal forms, but Aristotle thought we must find our clues in the natural world and in human nature. Catholic teaching had long been comfortable with Plato's approach, for ideas about eternal forms were easily integrated with the belief in divine revelation. Aquinas, however, saw that Aristotle's reasoning was similar to the empirical investigations that were defining what would become modern science, and thus would have more credibility.

It is ironic that during the Dark Ages in Europe (400–1000 CE), Aristotle's philosophy was preserved in the Islamic schools of the ancient world. By the thirteenth century the cities of Paris and Naples, where Aquinas first studied, were alive with the works of Aristotle and his Muslim interpreters. As a Dominican monk, Aquinas embraced the task of reconciling issues of faith with the new "science."

Aquinas embraced Aristotle's method and reasoning, but not his idea that the natural world was independent of God. Aquinas believed that God is the author of natural law through what he identified as divine law. Aristotle wanted to know what makes us happy, and Aquinas wanted to reconcile faith in God with a scientific view of the world. Both wanted to know what it takes to live a fulfilled or "flourishing" life.

In reflecting on what virtue means in this tradition of moral philosophy, we need to acknowledge that the gender, class, and racial attitudes taken for granted in ancient Greece and medieval Europe were biased. Aristotle and Aquinas were clearly influenced by the mores of their eras, and both should be read critically. Their writings at times support aristocratic and patriarchal views, and in these ways they illustrate what we should avoid in doing ethics. Nonetheless, we can learn much from their writings, including being humble about our ability to transcend the moral "blindness" of our own time.

For Aquinas, as for many Christians, the highest virtues affording the greatest happiness are faith, hope, and charity. Within the natural law tradition that recognizes divine law, our purpose as human beings is to understand this law and live by it. Moral disciplines that foster good habits should also involve spiritual practice to nurture our faith as well as other virtues.

ETHICAL PRESUMPTIONS FROM NATURAL LAW

Although this tradition of thought uses the language of natural *law*, we have suggested that it is more about *character* than what we mean today by law. Ethical language concerning duty generally relies on principles, laws, and rules. In contrast, the natural law approach to ethics looks more to the examples of good persons, who are known for their virtuous character because they embody a moral standard that is "higher" than human law.

We agree with natural law thinkers that good habits help strengthen the virtues necessary for humans to flourish. From this tradition of moral reasoning, we conclude that we may derive at least the following presumptions. We should:

- Discern who we ought to be by examining the way things really are.
- Use reason to discover and fulfill the purpose of life.
- Resist human laws that contradict the higher law of our nature.
- Cultivate moderation, good habits, and responsibility.
- Strive for happiness through virtuous living that seeks the common good.

In this ethical tradition, doing what is good is most likely to happen when we become good people. In chapter 2 we wondered where our sense of right and wrong comes from. The natural law tradition answers that we know right from wrong by developing our moral capacity through reason and good habits. We learn to do what is right by becoming the good people that we are created (by nature or by God) to be.

TAO

The Chinese word *Tao* has taken on a life of its own in English. Usually translated as "way" or "the way," we are no longer surprised to see book titles such as the *Tao of Pooh*, *The Tao of Sobriety*, the *Tao of Quitting Smoking*, and the *Tao of Health, Sex, and Longevity*.

This pop culture use of the word *Tao* may seem vulgar, as the word has had profound and even sacred connotations for generations of Chinese. Nonetheless, the popular use of Tao today may reflect how the word was used in ancient Chinese culture. In this sense, Tao represents in the Chinese tradition what higher law, natural law, or divine law has meant in the West. Conforming to Tao means doing what is right and good because it is the order of nature or the natural order of society (or even the divine will). Although Taoist and Confucian understandings differ in significant ways, each tradition of thought follows this pattern.

The *Tao Te Ching* offers a poetic vision of the way of nature. Legend has it that Lao Tzu wrote this classic text as he was leaving China to retire and die in the wilderness. The *Tao Te Ching* has been read avidly in the West by those who hope to find in the way of nature the purpose and pattern of life that seems to be missing from Western culture. The Chinese, however, have also found that the *Tao Te Ching* has much to say about how society should be governed.

In the *Analects* of Confucius, Tao is not only the way of nature, but also the right way of life, the ideal way of human existence, and so the proper way of governing. The dominant image in the *Analects* is traveling on a path, a path that leads through cities and the countryside, among crowds and across canyons. It is the path through the world traveled by the wise man (the Great Man). Following this way is the source of wisdom, virtue, and also good government.

MERCY AND HUMILITY

The *Tao Te Ching* says, "The greatest Virtue is to follow Tao and Tao alone."[5] Virtue is not a character trait that a person can achieve through diligent practice. Instead, virtue is a way of being that a person may discover and then embrace, like finding a new trail on a hillside and following it. Virtue is not a benefit attained by persevering along a difficult way, but the delight that comes from finding and following that way.

This is why a "man of highest virtue will not display it as his own." In contrast, "Low virtue makes one miss no chance to show his virtue off." Virtue is a way of being, rather than an accomplishment. "High virtue is at rest; it knows no need to act. Low virtue is a busyness pretending to accomplishment."[6]

In this sense, the *Tao Te Ching* affirms, things are often not what they are said to be (or seem to be). Thus, in the Taoist tradition, all talk of virtue, morality, and compassion means that one has wandered off the path. "Truly, once the Way is lost, there comes then virtue; virtue lost, comes then compassion; after that morality; and when that's lost, there's etiquette."[7]

> Everyone under heaven says that my Tao
> Is great and beyond compare.
> Because it is great, it seems different.
> If it were not different,
> It would have vanished long ago.
> I have three treasures which I hold and keep.
> The first is mercy; the second is economy;
> The third is daring not to be ahead of others.
> From mercy comes courage;
> From economy comes generosity;
> From humility comes leadership.
> Nowadays men shun mercy, but try to be brave;
> They abandon economy, but try to be generous;
> They do not believe in humanity,
> But always try to be first.
> This is certain death.
> Mercy brings victory in battle
> And strength in defense.
> It is the means by which heaven saves and guards.[8]

Confucius agreed in the *Analects* that living according to Tao is how one may encourage virtue in others. Thus, it is foolish to seek a position of power in order to try to make others more virtuous. "Do not worry about holding high position," Confucius taught. "Worry rather about playing your proper role. Worry not that no one knows of you; seek to be worth knowing."[9] For Confucius, the virtuous person "concentrates on the task and forgets about rewards."[10]

Can such virtue be learned? Both the *Tao Te Ching* and the *Analects* agree that virtue can be learned, but Confucius also thought that virtue could be taught. This is why Confucius lectured on "literature, conduct, loyalty, and reliability."[11] He spent his life traveling and teaching others how to live a virtuous life, so the entire society might be uplifted by the good example of a few individuals.

Confucius saw that virtue could be understood and explained in terms of the various roles we have. A person of virtue would respect those with greater power, be gracious to dependents, be just with subordinates, and always act with humility. "Kung-sum Ch'iao possessed four virtues characteristic of Great Man: humility, respect for superiors, graciousness toward dependents, and a sense of justice toward subordinates."[12]

In the *Analects,* Confucius also explains that "balance" is essential for virtue. "When substance overbalances refinement, crudeness results. When refinement overbalances substance, there is superficiality. When refinement and substance are balanced, one has Great Man."[13] This is not the same as Aristotle's principle of moderation, for Confucius is concerned with balance between what is done (substance) and the way it is done (refinement). The virtuous individual (Great Man) not only does what is right, but also does it in the right way.

In this respect the *Tao Te Ching* and the *Analects* diverge in their understanding of how to follow Tao. The *Tao Te Ching* relies almost entirely on conforming to images from nature, whereas Confucius teaches the importance of ceremonies, music, and public rituals.

CIVILITY

The virtues that Confucius emphasized are social. In the book *Confucius: The Secular as Sacred,* Herbert Fingarette points out that: "*shu* (mutuality in human relations), *chung* (loyalty) and *hsin* (good trust toward others)—all inherently involve a dynamic relation to other persons."[14] Confucius did not see virtue as an inner state, but as a public involvement with others that reflects Tao. Therefore, the most powerful expression of virtue is in ritual.

For Confucius, virtue is not simply being humble, compassionate, brave, and upright. This is the substance of virtue, but refinement is also necessary. Ritual actions embody this refinement, literally, through the physical motions and expressions that are involved. In addition, words are given unique meaning through the symbolic actions in ceremonies.

"The ceremonial act is the primary, irreducible event," Fingarette argues. "Language cannot be understood in isolation from the conventional practice in which it is rooted; conventional practice cannot be understood in isolation from the language that defines and is part of it."[15]

This argument is hard for us to grasp, because we are so quick to think of ceremonies and rituals as external forms that easily may become conventional (by which we usually mean superficial). We will not understand Confucius, however, unless we realize why he taught that symbolic behavior expressed in ceremony and ritual is crucial for public virtue. "Rite brings out forcefully not only the harmony and beauty of social forms, [and] the inherent and ultimate dignity of human intercourse; it brings out also the moral perfection implicit in achieving one's ends by dealing with others as beings of equal dignity. . . . "[16]

Properly done, public ceremonies inspire us to be more virtuous. Confucius argued that virtue not only concerns character traits, but also orders our social life according to Tao. Fingarette quotes the *Analects*: "The Master said, govern the people by regulations, keep order among them by punishments, and they will evade shamelessly. Govern them by moral force (*te*), keep order among them by ritual (*li*), and there will be not only shame but correctness."[17]

Confucius taught: "Not to follow the rites in being humble is annoyance. Not to follow them in exercising care is timidity. Not to follow them in acts of bravery is confusion. Not to follow them in uprightness is rudeness."[18]

Imagine trying to teach civility. How are we to develop mutual respect? A good beginning, perhaps, would involve reinforcing good manners, saying please and thank you, and learning how to disagree with someone without starting an argument. For those who successfully complete our civility class, we might even have a graduation ceremony!

How quickly we turn to ceremonies and rituals to celebrate what we have learned. Perhaps this is not merely a "nice thing to do," but reflects our human nature. In our legislatures, parliaments, and courtrooms, we have various ritual forms that express respect for the law and those with responsibility for enforcing it. These ritual acts are not merely archaic rites from a previous age; they are the means by which we remain civil.

Even more simply, we all understand that using good manners and showing respect in the way we greet one another is important for encouraging civility, and these behaviors involve not only words but also nonverbal actions. Shaking hands is our standard greeting in the West and, because of globalization, has been adopted in much of the world. Nonetheless, any American who has shaken hands with an older Japanese man has probably been aware that it felt awkward. This is because bowing has long been the Japanese ritual way of showing respect for other people.

Civility requires that we present ourselves to strangers in a way that indicates we mean them no harm. Because we are strangers, we should not expect our words to be sufficient. Through ritualized, conventional gestures, whatever they may be, we seek to allay the fears of others.

Confucius teaches that moral education involves studying literature, music, and the civilizing arts. This means learning good manners as well as how to fulfill the ceremonial roles required of all those with public responsibilities. For students who lack discipline, Confucius says the response of a good teacher will not be judgment but encouragement. Eliciting shame, rather than guilt, will more likely inspire greater effort by those who have yet to understand the importance of developing the good habits that constitute civility.

TAO AND NATURAL LAW

The *Tao Te Ching* and the *Analects* of Confucius point to Tao as the pattern for human life. Each text comes from a cultural context that is very different from our own, and also unlike the European cultures in which Western philosophers and theologians developed the theory of natural law. Yet,

these writings have endured and offer us insights that we might apply to
our contemporary world.

Our challenge, therefore, is to construct moral presumptions from our
sense of Tao, as expressed in the *Analects* and the *Tao Te Ching*. Drawing on
this tradition of moral reasoning, we suggest that we may derive at least
the following principles.

We should:

- Discern who we ought to be by examining the Way
  things really are.
- Use *ritual to embody* and fulfill the purpose of life.
- *Seek to shame unjust leaders by acting with civility.*
- Cultivate *balance*, good habits, *mercy*, and *humility*.
- Strive for *harmony* through virtuous living that seeks the
  common good.

We have stated these moral presumptions in a way that parallels those
we derived from the tradition of natural law, but we have noted the differences. The first statement is identical, except Tao is usually represented in
English as "Way," so we have kept the initial capital letter in our statement.

The second statement differs considerably, as our moral presumption
derived from the natural law tradition uses the phrase "reason to discern"
rather than "ritual to embody." Confucius used reason to develop his
teachings, but his emphasis was not on our rational capacity. Instead, he
pointed to our ceremonial or ritual nature. For Confucius, the most important lesson to be learned is that we learn by doing. According to Tao, therefore, ethics involves doing what is right in the right way, and this requires
public rites.

The third statement differs the most. From the natural law tradition, we
derived the moral presumption to "resist human laws that contradict the
'higher law' of our nature." Within the natural law tradition, the importance of government reflecting what is right is framed in legal language,
using the phrase "higher law," "divine law," or "moral law" to represent
that which has greater authority than human law. In Chinese thought,

however, the language is very different. Confucius teaches that we should respond to unjust leaders by being civil and virtuous, which will shame them and in that way prompt them to be more civil and virtuous.

In the fourth statement from the natural law tradition, we derived the moral presumption to cultivate "moderation, good habits, and responsibility." From the Tao tradition, we constructed the moral presumption to cultivate "balance, good habits, mercy, and humility." Moderation and balance are not the same, as balance concerns maintaining both substance and refinement, rather than simply finding the mean between having too little or too much of a virtuous trait.

We also suggest that the assertive and individualistic connotations of "personal responsibility" in Western thought are absent from Eastern ethical teaching, which characterizes civility in terms of acting with mercy and humility within the community. Humility was not a virtue for Aristotle, as he thought it involved too little self-regard, but later Aquinas affirmed humility as a Christian virtue. Today in the West, however, we seem to have returned to the Aristotelian view, as being assertive is praised far more than being humble.

Finally, the fifth statement from the two traditions differs only in one word. The principle drawn from natural law speaks of striving for "happiness," whereas the parallel statement derived from our reflections on the tradition of Tao points to striving for "harmony." Presumably, if there is harmony, there will be happiness, and vice versa. Yet, we should acknowledge that the differences between the two traditions of thought are as important as the similarities.

Drawing on both of these ethical traditions, how might we state most simply our ethical presumption concerning character? We should strive to realize the common good by virtuous living.

DOING ETHICS TOGETHER

I. Character.

Suppose you were giving a lecture on character ethics.

1. What three moral presumptions would you use to sum-
    marize the natural law position?
2. What three moral presumptions would you use to sum-
    marize character ethics as taught by both the *Tao Te
    Ching* and by Confucius in the *Analects*?
3. Do you think seeking happiness and seeking harmony
    are the same? Explain by comparing the views of Aristo-
    tle and Aquinas with the views of Lao Tzu and Confucius,
    as explained in this chapter.

II. *Moral virtues.*

1. Explain what Aristotle meant by "the golden mean" and
    give an example.
2. State as a moral presumption what both Antigone and
    Martin Luther King Jr. affirmed about knowing right and
    wrong.
3. Think of someone you admire as a moral person, and
    identify the virtues that make his or her character so ad-
    mirable. Give an example of how this person has mani-
    fested one of these virtues. Do you think that this virtue
    reflects more of an Eastern or Western way of thinking
    about character? Explain your answer.

III. *Good government.*

1. Do you agree with Aquinas that a just law reflects the
    moral law, which reflects divine law? If so, how are we to
    know the divine law? If not, what makes a law just?
2. How is Aristotle's concern for cultivating virtues and
    forming good habits related to good government? What
    does Aristotle mean by moderation? Give an example of
    a moral presumption that seems to be shared by Aristo-
    tle and Confucius.

3. What does Confucius mean by balance? Why does Confucius argue that rituals are important for good government? Give an example to illustrate his thinking.

6

Relationships

CARING AND LETTING GO

We are who we are, in large part, because of our families, friends, colleagues, and community. None of us is simply an individual. Each of us represents and reflects our relationships.

In one sense, this is an obvious fact. When considering our duty to respect others, we have assumed that there is some relationship to these people. Otherwise, why would we have any duty to respect them? Yet, in our discussion of duty as a way of doing ethics we have emphasized living by universal moral principles. This more abstract and impersonal way of thinking about ethics ignores, or at least makes it harder to see, our relationships and their significance.

When assessing the importance of character for doing ethics, we have been concerned with how aspiring to live with greater purpose and sensitivity might encourage others to be more virtuous. The pursuit of happiness, we have suggested, requires striving for the common good. In considering what being good people might mean, we have certainly assumed some kind of relationship with others. For without such a relationship, why would our character and virtuous conduct have any meaning for other people?

Now, however, we look at what has been largely implicit so far, and in looking at how relationships affect our understanding of ethics we will see that a shift in language is involved. In drawing on ethical thought that is ex-

plicitly concerned with relationships and care for others, we will find ourselves saying almost nothing about duty, and very little about character as an
individual trait. Instead, we will use language that is more personal and social.

Although a concern for moral relationships is present in the writings of
ancient Greece and in Jewish and Christian ethics as well, its prominence today in moral philosophy is the result of a feminist critique of the traditional
language of duty and character, which primarily concerns individual acts.
We begin, therefore, with this recent critical view of moral philosophy, before considering Buddhist teachings about the interrelated nature of all life.

THE FEMINIST CHALLENGE

In 1982, Carol Gilligan, a professor at the Harvard School of Education,
published the book *In a Different Voice: Psychological Theory and Women's Development*. Her study directly challenges the use of abstract principles and
rules in contemporary moral philosophy in the West, and has been crucial
for the feminist construction of an alternative ethical approach.

Gilligan argues that women think differently than men about moral issues, because women are more motivated by feelings of empathy. In addition, Gilligan asserts that this more caring approach to ethics is not "less
developed" as an ethical approach, in comparison with the way that men
have tended to think about ethics in terms of rules and principles.

Gilligan writes critically of developmental theories of ethics, such as
Lawrence Kohlberg's six stages of moral development, which identify empathy as a lower moral stage. In Kohlberg's theory the responsibility derived from a person's relationships is the third stage of moral development.
Reaching stage four involves subordinating relationships to the rules of the
social group. At stage five ethical decisions are based on principles of justice, and at stage six a person acts on abstract moral principles that all humanity should follow.

For Kohlberg, the last three stages of moral development involve subordinating empathy and caring for others to rules and principles. Gilligan's
argument is that this approach reflects the bias of male moral philosophers
and male developmental psychologists.

To illustrate this point, Gilligan reflects on an example in Kohlberg's work known as the Heinz dilemma. A man named Heinz is trying to save his dying wife. Her only hope seems to be a drug discovered by a pharmacist, which the pharmacist is selling for two thousand dollars, although it only costs him two hundred dollars to make the drug. Heinz offers one thousand dollars for the drug, but the pharmacist won't accept less than two thousand dollars, even though Heinz says that he will pay the balance later. Desperate, Heinz considers stealing the drug. Would this be wrong?

In Kohlberg's study, Jake, an eleven-year-old boy, responded quickly to this moral dilemma by concluding that Heinz should steal the drug. What is Jake's reasoning? "For one thing," Jake explains, "a human life is worth more than money, and if the druggist only makes $1,000, he is still going to live, but if Heinz doesn't steal the drug, his wife is going to die."

When asked why life is worth more than money, Jake answers: "Because the druggist can get a thousand dollars later from rich people with cancer, but Heinz can't get his wife again." When asked to explain this statement, Jake adds: "Because people are all different and so you couldn't get Heinz's wife again."[1]

Amy, who is also eleven years old, responds very differently. When asked if Heinz should steal the drug, she replies: "Well, I don't think so. I think there might be other ways besides stealing it, like if he could borrow the money or make a loan or something, but he really shouldn't steal the drug—but his wife shouldn't die either."

When asked to explain her thinking, Amy answers: "If he stole the drug, he might save his wife then, but if he did, he might have to go to jail, and then his wife might get sicker again, and he couldn't get more of the drug, and it might not be good. So, they should really just talk it out and find some other way to make the money."[2]

When the interviewer suggests that Amy should make a choice, because if Heinz does not steal the drug his wife will die, Amy continues to resist the terms of the hypothetical problem. She maintains that Heinz and the druggist ought to resolve the dilemma by finding an alternative or coming to a compromise.

From Kohlberg's point of view, Amy's moral development is stuck at stage three, because she sees moral issues in terms of maintaining relationships and working things out. Jake, on the other hand, has advanced to stage four or five, because he decides what is right on the basis of an impersonal principle. ("A human life is worth more than money.")

Gilligan argues that it is perfectly reasonable for Amy to resist the win-lose choice posed by the hypothetical, and for her to maintain that relying on an impersonal principle is inadequate. Amy wants a win-win solution that allows all the parties to get at least some of what they want. Her hope that this is possible may reflect her faith in the power of empathy, as she seems to think the pharmacist will moderate his demand if Heinz continues to talk with him about the situation and possible alternatives.

Gilligan maintains that Amy's way of doing ethics should not be understood as a lower stage of development in comparison with using impersonal rules or principles to resolve moral dilemmas. Gilligan agrees with Kohlberg that there are stages of moral development, but argues that empathy and caring are as important for moral decision making as the more abstract capacities that develop later.

If we accept that ethics involves integrating our feelings with our ability to think in terms of abstract moral principles, Gilligan's argument certainly seems convincing.

Other feminist scholars also argue that an *ethics of care* offers an important corrective to traditional moral philosophies that emphasize impersonal reasons. Virginia Held has written: "Caring, empathy, feeling with others, being sensitive to each other's feelings, all may be better guides to what morality requires in actual contexts than may abstract rules of reason, or rational calculation. . . . "[3]

PERSONAL ETHICS

One way of trying to settle this dispute involves emphasizing relationships when dealing with ethical issues that are primarily personal, and relying on impersonal rules and principles to address public moral controversies. Yet, we should avoid too sharp a distinction.

It seems likely that parents facing moral issues at home will rely more on an ethics of care than will legislators debating a law. As any parent knows, however, it is important in raising children to have rules, and enforcing these consistently and fairly is an important part of caring for children.

Taking turns is one such rule, as is keeping your hands to yourself. We could think of many others. With these rules there is also, in a caring home, a sense of being loved and accepted, even if a child breaks a rule and is punished for doing so. The rules only work well because of the loving relationships that sustain the life of a family.

We accept the feminist critique that using rules and principles may reinforce an impersonal approach to ethics that lacks compassion. We agree with all theories of justice that wrongdoing should be punished. Yet, in raising children we know that forgiveness and offering a second chance are as important as enforcing the rules. In a caring family, justice is administered fairly, but with a loving motive. It is a mistake to ignore relationships in the name of being fair.

In this sense, an ethics of care is personal not only because it concerns intimate or family issues, but also because it requires acting in a way that is more compassionate. This quality of acting is what we mean by care or empathy. Certainly, we can be caring even when we are acting on principles or enforcing rules. We can refuse to see ethical issues in an impersonal way, even when these issues involve social and public concerns.

For instance, elected officials have a duty to enforce the law fairly in carrying out their responsibilities, and they do not have a duty to care about each individual in their constituency. Yet, officials who do care about the people they represent bring a different moral quality to their decision making. We expect our officials to do their duty, but we also want them to be personally concerned about the people in their constituency.

For similar reasons we generally have high regard for citizens who volunteer in our community. There is no duty that requires them to perform this service, but we respect those who care enough to give freely of their time in order to help others.

As caring is a virtue, being concerned with relationships has much in common with our discussion in chapter 5 about doing ethics with an emphasis on character. An ethics of care may be understood as a revised way of emphasizing the kind of persons we are. Character ethics historically has praised the virtues identified with statesmanship, a public role that until very recently was available only to men. In contrast, an ethics of care gives priority to relationships and to compassion and empathy, virtues identified with women and with resolving family concerns.

The story of Antigone reveals that an ethics of care has ancient roots. In chapter 5 we considered her protest to illustrate the moral presumption that human laws should be subordinate to a "higher law," and we praised her for her courage and compassion. Here we note that she exemplifies what many feminists mean by acting with care.

Antigone buries her brother and by doing so violates the rule of the king. She describes her action not as the duty of a sister, but as an expression of her love for her brother. She embodies empathy for those slain in battle, even if they are judged to be guilty of breaking the law and so deserve the punishment they receive.

We want someone to intercede with the king in order to prevent Antigone from being put to death for disobeying his rule. Similarly, we empathize with Amy, who wants someone to intervene in order to negotiate a compromise between the pharmacist and Heinz, so Heinz's wife may receive the medicine she needs. When enforcing a moral rule or principle seems to require an either/or decision with a harsh result, we want to find an alternative with the character of a both/and result that we believe will be more compassionate.

We want not only just principles and fair rules, but also relationships marked by respect and concern for others. Tempering justice with compassion is what we mean by an ethics of care. Doing ethics, we believe, involves considering our relationships, as well as acting with concern for our duty and character.

THE CURRENT DEBATE

Critics of an ethics of care raise at least three objections. First, the focus on personal relationships seems to limit an ethics of care to those we know personally, as it seems unreasonable to expect that we should care in the same way for those we do not know. For these critics an ethics of care seems to be applicable only to family situations, or perhaps to groups of friends or colleagues. Certainly, most moral philosophers believe that social issues and questions of retributive and distributive justice require a more impersonal approach to ethics.

Second, because an ethics of care is concerned largely with feelings or intuition, rather than abstract reasoning, this approach to ethics seems to offer no way to formulate consistent guidelines for making decisions. How can those who feel differently about a moral concern hope to resolve their differences? Most moral philosophers argue that subjective feelings must be put aside so we can reason together with greater objectivity as we consider ethical issues.

Third, although those advocating an ethics of care are critical of rules and principles, it seems that their position might be expressed by a few principles. For instance, "maintaining or strengthening relationships" looks like a principle, as does the emphasis in health care on "doing no harm." Whether or not these are called principles, they seem to function in an ethics of care like principles. So, critics say, the issue is simply deciding which principles we should use.

Those who defend an ethics of care respond to the first concern by pointing out that the empathy we develop in childhood enables us to identify with the suffering of strangers as well as the feelings of those closest to us. Moral development, therefore, may be conceived as a way of strengthening our sense of empathy. Even as we develop our reasoning capabilities, we should also develop our capacity to care for others.

This is not a strange idea; it reflects common sense. Thousands of people respond to news of a disaster somewhere in the world by giving donations to help those who are homeless or injured. Empathy, which involves considering what it would feel like to be in another person's position, is the starting point of all moral action.

Religious traditions have long taught that we can care for strangers, if we realize that we are united by our common humanity. Moral teachings based on the story of creation in the scriptures shared by Jews and Christians emphasize that each person, regardless of race or religion, is a child of God. Buddhists teach that everyone is a potential Buddha, and that women and men from different castes or cultures all have the capacity to awaken and respond to conflicts in life with compassion.

In response to the second criticism of an ethics of care—that having more concern for feelings means rejecting reason—we have argued that doing ethics requires attending to both of these aspects of our humanity. Developing our capacity for empathy is as important as learning to reason abstractly, if we are to be moral persons. Feeling for others may help us understand their predicament. In addition, empathy may help us see that abstract reasons, which are always said to offer an objective solution to an ethical problem, may instead be rationalizations for a self-serving point of view.

Seeing that an ethics of care has much in common with character ethics may clarify this point. Caring virtues, such as compassion and generosity, express our feelings, and most of us would agree from our experience that encouraging these virtues in young people requires more than teaching the skills of abstract reasoning. In fact, those we admire most for being exemplary, ethical persons are both convincing in the reasons they give and caring in the way they express their convictions.

The third criticism of an ethics of care, which argues that it does have principles despite assertions by feminists to the contrary, is perhaps theoretically correct, but seems to miss the practical point. Relying on principles or rules, as Jake does in responding to the Heinz dilemma, is far different than looking at a moral problem with a concern for strengthening (or at least not harming) the relationships of those involved.

Theoretically, a concern for empathy or a commitment to do no harm may seem like a principle, but responding with empathy leaves open the possibility of compromise. For instance, Amy's hope for resolving the Heinz dilemma is that those involved in the dispute will keep talking until they find a better alternative than initially seems to be available in the hypothetical.

We might also distinguish the use of ethical principles from an ethics of care by recalling the difference between deductive and inductive reasoning, which we discussed in chapter 2. Moral philosophies that assert abstract principles of justice use deductive reasoning to apply these principles to a particular situation. Jake uses the principle that "a human life is worth more than money" to reason deductively that, in the situation faced by Heinz, this justifies a theft by Heinz.

Amy's approach is very different. She looks for clues in the situation that would support an alternative hypothesis, as to what the best action might be. Her "thought experiment" is a way of reasoning inductively in order to formulate a new moral presumption.

Inductive reasoning enables us to see the complexity of a moral issue as crucial for constructing a new presumption (hypothesis) as to how best to proceed. Rather than applying an abstract principle, which ignores the complexity of the problem, clues may be found amidst the conflicting arguments (and relationships) as to what sort of moral action in a particular situation might make the most sense.

CARING

Our hypothesis is that empathy and caring as well as rules and principles are important for constructing ethical presumptions. This means that we must consider not only our duty and the principles and rules that express our duty, as well as our character expectations and goals, but also how responding to an ethical dilemma reflects empathy for all those involved and a commitment to care for these relationships.

We may illustrate the significance of adding an ethics of care to our approach by considering a person who is contemplating whether or not to enlist in the armed forces. From the perspective of duty each citizen has a responsibility to respect the laws of his or her country, and to help protect the rule of law. Certainly, enlisting in the army might be an ethical duty, and in many societies military service is a legal obligation as well.

There are also good reasons why a person might consider service in the army to be morally virtuous and self-giving, and not simply patriotic. Courage and perseverance are among the virtues that likely will be required of any enlistee, and enlistees give up a good deal of personal freedom in order to serve their country.

What would a concern for relationships (or an ethical approach emphasizing care) add to this assessment? When thinking of duty and character, we tend to think of ourselves as individuals. A concern for relationships will challenge us to consider those who will be affected by the decisions we make.

If a person thinking about joining the army is married, certainly this decision should involve his or her spouse. Even if a person who is contemplating enlistment in the army is single, he or she will have significant relationships that will be deeply affected by this decision. Parents, siblings, other close relatives, colleagues at work—all those who will be directly affected by this decision should be invited to talk about it and, in that way, to have a role in making the decision.

Considering relationships adds to our ethical approach a concern for those who should be involved in making a moral decision. This is not the same as calculating *how* others will be affected by our decision, which is a way of speculating about the consequences of our decision. Empathy and care require us to *involve in our decision making* those who are close to us and who care for us.

Thinking about ethics this way might be compared with tuning an orchestra. The individual musicians must each tune their instruments, but for the orchestra to play in tune the musicians must tune together. That is, they tune to one another, and not separately. As they perform a piece, every member of the orchestra is involved in keeping the orchestra in tune. The musicians are related by their roles in the orchestra, and each musician is responsible to all the others (and not merely to the conductor). The harmony they produce, by tuning and remaining in tune as they play a piece, is the sum of their relationships.

This metaphor seems to emphasize only our personal relationships, but it may be expanded. The technicians who record the orchestra must also do their part to keep the music in tune. Disc jockeys who play the recording on the radio have to exercise care in order to maintain this same quality. Those who manufacture the radios and stereos that play the music are also involved in quality control, and everyone who listens to the music may allow its harmony to "tune" them as well.

There is always a larger context for every moral decision, which includes not only those directly involved, but also those who may become involved in the ramifications of the decision.

Consider once again a person wondering whether or not to enlist in the army. The larger moral context of this decision includes not only the citizens that soldiers hope to protect by serving in their country's armed forces, but also the people who might be injured or killed by someone who becomes a soldier. Perhaps our sense of duty encourages enlistment and armed service, but empathy for the victims of armed conflict should caution us against dismissing as collateral damage the suffering that soldiers inflict on the civilians of other countries.

If we take into account our natural environment, then using modern weapons even in a just cause, such as national defense, is not obviously the best moral choice. The devastating consequences of modern warfare both for communities and the environment should make us pause and reflect carefully before concluding that any war is morally justified.

Caring means that doing our duty and encouraging virtuous conduct are not sufficient for making a moral decision. We also need to assess what our relationships mean for acting ethically. Although those supporting an ethics of care caution against impersonal principles and rules, we suggest that the following moral presumptions point to what caring may mean. As hypotheses, not as rules, our concern for relationships implies that in facing moral issues we should:

- Ensure that decisions are made in an open and conclusive manner.
- Discern how to act with empathy for those related to us.
- Do no harm even if we are not certain we can do any good.
- Live in a way that expresses care for others and for the natural world.

LEARNING FROM THE BUDDHA

Two and a half millennia ago a man taught that our individuality is actually an illusion. Gautama Siddhartha, who would be known to history as the Buddha, taught a path to overcome suffering. The Buddhist way involves letting go of our attachment to our false sense of ourselves in order to discover who we really are.

The life of the Buddha is a parable of what life might offer. The Buddha renounced both his privileges as a wealthy upper-caste Hindu and also a harsh life of asceticism that he first thought offered the only spiritual and ethical alternative. Instead, he "awoke" and embraced a life of simplicity and gratitude. After his enlightenment, he chose to teach what he knew and to live with others in community. He avoided disputes about philosophical questions that cannot be answered, and devoted himself to living in a way that reveals what we can know and do.

We might say that he let go of the desires that today we often think of as defining our goals in life. The Buddha taught that everything is transient, that nothing is permanent. Therefore, striving for one thing or another is illusory, as it will cease to be what it was after we attain it. The Buddha saw that by renouncing these attachments, instead of clinging to them, we might find ourselves as we really are, in relation to all that is and will be.

The Buddha taught a way of life, not a moral philosophy. Yet, the Buddhist way of life is rich in its ethical implications. There are many differences among Buddhists, who for centuries have followed this path, but all agree this way involves "taking refuge in" (entrusting ourselves to) the Buddha, the dharma (his teachings) and the *sangha* (the community of Buddhists).

The dharma expresses the Buddha's realization of interdependence. Our lives are linked with all that is, which is why it is illusory to think we are individuals. The dharma offers a way of becoming who we might be, by letting go of our desire to separate ourselves from other people and from nature as well.

The sangha, or the Buddhist community, is the means by which we may discover who we are through our relationships with others and with the Buddha and the dharma. In community, we may discern that we are not individual egos, but are part of the wondrous rhythm of life.

Living in a sangha is certainly different than living in a family, but such a life is ordinary in many ways. In the book *Unsui: A Diary of Zen Monastic Life* we find Buddhist monks not only meditating, studying, chanting, and begging, but also gardening, cleaning, cooking, bathing, helping one another, and receiving guests.[4] There is a reason why the disciplined life of the sangha is full of the tasks of ordinary life. The Buddha discovered that enlightenment involves discerning the true meaning of life in everyday activities and relationships. Life is only special if we appreciate how special it is simply to be alive.

The disciplines of the sangha are not a substitute for the ordinary tasks of living, or a way to rise above menial work in order to be more spiritual. If monks were to hire servants to do the dirty work of the monastery, the monks would become attached to their leisure. By doing menial tasks the monks may come to know that enlightened living means letting go of the desire to escape the ordinary tasks of life.

What does this mean for doing ethics? The language of duty is not apt for Buddhists, as this way of thinking separates our ends and means, and also our motivations from our actions. For Buddhists, ends, means, motivations, and actions are all linked in making us who we are.

Character ethics would come closer conceptually to the Buddhist point of view, except for the traditional emphasis on individuals who are exemplary in their virtue. Buddhists would not choose to think of themselves as worthy of praise, even if others might have this opinion. Buddhists emphasize their shared life with others, not what distinguishes them from others.

A concern for relationships is at the heart of Buddhist moral thought. Buddhists urge that we consider all the interrelationships of our lives in thinking about what is right. Every human action is like the creation of a new universe with implications and consequences that extend far beyond our understanding. What we do involves our relationships with all other human beings, and not only the person or persons we think will be affected.

NONVIOLENCE

Human life and animal life are part of the interdependence of our world, and Buddhists seek to do no harm at least to those animals that appear to suffer as we do. For Buddhists, right conduct requires nonviolence, and killing other sentient beings is seen as an act of violence.

Specifically, by sentient beings Buddhists mean all animals that appear to try to avoid pain rather than simply behaving according to reflex actions. We may debate which animals feel pain as human beings feel pain, but anyone who has seen an injured mammal will have no doubt about its suffering. Moreover, many other animals also learn to try to avoid pain.

Buddhist monks, who traditionally obtained their food by begging, ate whatever was given to them including scraps of meat. Their vow was not to kill, but this did not mean they were necessarily vegetarians. Later in the Buddhist tradition, the vow was broadened by some orders to mean not eating meat as well as not killing sentient beings. Contemporary Buddhists vary in what they eat, as some are strict vegetarians and others consume meat.

Buddhists follow what is called the Eightfold Path to overcome suffering. In addition to right views, right thought, right speech, right action, right effort, right mindfulness, and right concentration, the Buddhist way of life also requires right livelihood. For lay Buddhists this means earning a living only in ways that avoid inflicting harm or killing. A Buddhist would not work in a slaughterhouse, nor would a Buddhist work with animal hides in factories making leather. Most lay Buddhists also would not work in industries that make weapons and would be opposed to investing in these industries.

In addition, most Buddhists would not seek to derive income from the making alcoholic drinks, or other drugs that can stimulate our desires. These activities are all seen as contributing to human suffering, and human suffering also contributes to the suffering of all sentient beings. For Buddhists, right livelihood means making a living from work that shows care for all sentient beings and the natural world that sustains life.

Although pursuing the Eightfold Path may seem like obeying a list of rules, this would be a misunderstanding. These practices and other Buddhists precepts are guides to follow rather than laws to be obeyed. Proceeding along this path is a way of "tuning" to all that lives and to its passing. The orchestra of life is always playing, and the music is always changing. Everything is impermanent, unpredictable, and interrelated.

Buddhist thought differs from what we have described as an ethics of care. Buddhists extend the idea of caring relationships beyond the people we generally feel related to, even beyond all human beings, to include caring for everything that lives.

Buddhist teaching can be seen as paradoxical, because care and empathy involve relationships, whereas overcoming suffering requires letting go of these relationships. For Buddhists, however, this paradox is really an illusion. Accepting the transitory nature of all life and every relationship enables us to care about others and also to let go of the desire to cling to our relationships.

This sense of interrelatedness might foster an ecological ethic. If we understood ourselves as related to and dependent on the flow of life, as well as the ecosystems that sustain every habitat, we might live with greater care for all beings on earth.

LETTING GO

Buddhist teachings and practice offer us a striking challenge. We are invited to let go of our attachment to individual concerns in order to find ourselves anew in relationship with all that is, which makes us who we are. If we try to apply Buddhist insights in our ethical approach, we might construct at least the following moral presumptions. We should:

- Have empathy for all sentient beings as we make ethical decisions.
- Realize that the consequences of our actions are both unpredictable and unending.
- Care for our natural world by living more simply and more ecologically.

Although there are differences between an ethics of care and Buddhist thought, these two approaches to moral living share a concern for acting with empathy for others and with a greater awareness of the relationships that shape every moment of life.

DOING ETHICS TOGETHER

I. *The Heinz dilemma.*

1. What seems to be the rule or principle that Jake uses to justify stealing? Explain his reasoning and why you find it persuasive or unpersuasive.

2. Construct a moral presumption that you believe represents Amy's thinking. How does this presumption differ from a rule or a principle?
3. Using the concept of duty, formulate a moral presumption that you think offers a good response to the Heinz dilemma. Now do the same using character language. Do these two moral presumptions differ in meaning, or only in the words you have used?

II. Who should be involved in making a moral decision?

Consider a moral problem that you have faced. Then reflect on the following questions.

1. If you involved others in helping you decide what to do, describe how that made a difference. If you didn't involve others, do you now have second thoughts about having made this decision on your own? Explain your thinking.
2. As a parent, would you help your child learn how to make decisions the same way your parents taught you? Or, would you use another approach? Explain your thinking.
3. Do you think there are some moral decisions that are exclusively an individual matter? If so, give an example and explain your thinking. If not, explain why not.

III. An ethics of nonviolence.

1. Do you agree with the moral presumption that human beings should not use violence against sentient animals without a good reason? If so, explain what you would consider a good reason for doing violence to an animal. If you do not agree, explain your thinking.
2. Do you think the ego is a problem for acting ethically? Or, does it take a strong ego to do what is right when others disagree? Explain your reasoning.

3. Does it matter for doing ethics whether or not we are aware that everything is impermanent (always changing)? Explain how a Buddhist would likely answer. What do you think?

7

Human Rights

AUTONOMY AND HUMAN DIGNITY

Protecting human rights is of great concern today, for human rights are necessary social conditions for human dignity. Therefore, we now consider how international human rights law affirms many of our most important moral presumptions.

The emphasis in our time on rights marks a movement away from traditional societies, which are dominated by a concern for religious commandments and duties defined by social and family status. In the late eighteenth century, political movements supporting natural rights sowed the seeds of personal freedom that in the second half of the twentieth century have born fruit as international human rights law.

The International Bill of Human Rights consists of the Universal Declaration of Human Rights, which was approved by the United Nations General Assembly in 1948 without a dissenting vote, and the International Covenant on Civil and Political Rights (ICCPR) and the International Covenant on Economic, Social and Cultural Rights (ICESCR), which are the two main treaties that give effect to the 1948 declaration. These two major treaties were ratified by a sufficient number of countries to come into force under international law in 1976.

Many international treaties addressing specific issues have been ratified, and these also define current international human rights law. Among these, with the date each treaty came into force under international law, are the following:

- The Convention on the Prevention and Punishment of the Crime of Genocide (1951)
- The International Convention on the Elimination of All Forms of Racial Discrimination (1969)
- The Convention on the Elimination of All Forms of Discrimination against Women (1981)
- The Convention against Torture and Other Cruel, Inhuman or Degrading Treatment or Punishment (1987)
- The Convention on the Rights of the Child (1990)
- The International Convention on the Protection of the Rights of All Migrant Workers and Members of Their Families (2003)

There are regional human rights treaties as well. These include the following, with the date each treaty came into force under international law:

- The European Convention on Human Rights (1953)
- The American Convention on Human Rights (1978)
- The African Charter on Human and Peoples' Rights (1986)

These treaties now define the moral presumptions concerning our fundamental rights as human beings. Moreover, in addition to the civil and political rights of individuals, these rights include the economic, social, and cultural rights of both individuals and groups, as well as peoples' rights to self-determination.

WHERE DO RIGHTS COME FROM?

There continues to be controversy among moral philosophers as to how rights may be justified. Movements in the eighteenth century for democracy and representative government attributed fundamental rights to God or to human nature. The American Declaration of Independence in 1775 made the following affirmation famous: "We hold these truths to be self-evident, that all men are created equal, that they are endowed by their Creator with certain inalienable Rights, that among these are Life, Liberty and the pursuit of Happiness."

This declaration asserts God-given rights that cannot be relinquished, which is what "inalienable" means. Before the end of the eighteenth century, the French revolution proclaimed that "the rights of man" were natural rights, which are inherent in the humanity of each person. In the nineteenth century, as Western societies became more diverse and more secular, the claim that rights are God-given gave way to the notion that civil and political rights are rooted in our human nature as reasoning and autonomous persons.

At the start of the twentieth century, legal rights were understood as the liberties guaranteed to citizens by their national governments. This theory of positive law prevailed until after World War II, when the victorious Allies had to face the horrifying fact that Nazi Germany had acted legally, according to German law, in committing what were characterized after the war as genocide and other crimes against humanity.

The United Nations and a new era of international law were conceived to embody the ethical presumption that some moral rights transcend the laws of nations. As these universal rights are understood to be necessary for our human dignity, both the UN Charter and the Universal Declaration of Human Rights affirm that protecting international human rights is the moral duty of every nation and all people.

Moral philosophers continue to argue about rights claims, as these have not been (and cannot be) derived by deductive reasoning from a single premise. Human rights owe more to history than to philosophy, for they have arisen from inductive reasoning about the state of the world in the middle of the twentieth century. Most philosophers continue to argue that human rights can only be individual rights, as groups by their very nature suppress individual autonomy. Yet, the instruments of international human rights law assert group rights and people's rights in addition to individual rights.

The International Covenant on Civil and Political Rights (ICCPR) and the International Covenant on Economic, Social and Cultural Rights (ICESCR) begin by affirming the right of self-determination, which is stated as the right of all peoples "to freely determine their political status and freely pursue their economic, social and cultural development." (Article 1.1 in each covenant) Both covenants also assert the right to nondiscrimination, which is affirmed in the UN Charter and the Universal Declaration of Human Rights. In Article 2.2 of the ICESCR, this moral presumption reads as follows:

> The States Parties to the present Covenant undertake to guarantee that the rights enunciated in the present Covenant will be exercised without discrimination of any kind as to race, color, sex, language, religion, political or other opinion, national or social origin, property, birth or other status.

The ICCPR makes the same affirmation in Article 2.1. Under international human rights law, men and women have equal rights and are to enjoy equal protection of the law.

These two covenants also affirm that some rights, such as the right to enjoy one's culture as a minority community or to participate in a trade union, require protecting group rights and not only individual rights. Because international human rights law includes group rights as well as individual rights, international law provides a check on the individualistic emphasis in both philosophical and legal arguments in the West in support of human rights.

We are affirming the ethical presumptions of human rights law not because these rights provide an unchallenged philosophical foundation for moral decision making. Nor do we claim that there is a legal consensus on human rights. Philosophers and legal scholars continue to argue about the nature of human rights and the difficulties of enforcing these moral presumptions. Despite these unresolved issues, we rely on human rights in doing ethics because international human rights law asserts these ethical standards as the necessary social conditions for human dignity. Moreover, the moral presumptions of international human rights law now are affirmed around the globe.

In our time, at least, we must consider human rights if we are to do ethics in a way that makes sense to us and to our contemporaries. Therefore, having assessed the moral duty that facing an ethical problem seems to require, and our hopes concerning public virtue and our caring relationships, we now consider how moral action should support the protection and realization of our human rights.

INTERNATIONAL HUMAN RIGHTS LAW

The Universal Declaration of Human Rights begins by affirming that "recognition of the inherent dignity and of the equal and inalienable rights of all members of the human family is the foundation of freedom, justice and peace in the world." It claims that "disregard and contempt for human rights have resulted in barbarous acts which have outraged the conscience of mankind," and asserts that "a world in which human beings shall enjoy freedom of speech and belief and freedom from fear and want has been proclaimed as the highest aspiration of the common people."

US President Franklin D. Roosevelt articulated these "four freedoms," which are affirmed in the Universal Declaration of Human Rights. After his death, his widow, Eleanor Roosevelt, chaired the commission that drafted the 1948 Declaration.

The Universal Declaration also proclaims: "the peoples of the United Nations have in the Charter reaffirmed their faith in fundamental human rights, in the dignity and worth of the human person and in the equal rights of men and women and have determined to promote social progress and better standards of life in larger freedom."

Most of the specific rights in the Universal Declaration are familiar, as they reflect the constitutional and legal rights asserted by the United States and the other Western countries that won World War II. These rights are set forth in detail in the ICCPR and include the following moral presumptions:

- Everyone has the right to liberty and security of person. (Article 9.1)
- No one shall be subjected to arbitrary arrest or detention. (Article 9.2)

- All persons deprived of their liberty shall be treated with humanity. . . . (Article 10.1)
- All persons shall be equal before the courts and tribunals. (Article 14.1)
- Everyone charged with a criminal offense shall have the right to be presumed innocent until proved guilty according to law. (Article 14.2)
- Everyone shall have the right to freedom of expression. . . . (Article 19.2)
- The right of peaceful assembly shall be recognized. (Article 21)
- All persons are equal before the law and are entitled without any discrimination to the equal protection of the law. (Article 26)

Less well accepted by many US citizens, as human rights, are the social and economic rights affirmed by the Universal Declaration, which Franklin D. Roosevelt characterized as our "freedom from want." These human rights are delineated in the ICESCR.

In addition to rights, the Universal Declaration affirms that: "Everyone has duties to the community in which alone the free and full development of his personality is possible. . . . " (Article 29) This ethical presumption reminds us that our freedom must be exercised within a community of law, which will need to restrict our freedom in some ways in order to protect it.

A free society also requires that we perform our duties to the community voluntarily, and not simply because we may otherwise be punished. This is why Article 29 of the Universal Declaration states that the only limitations on these human rights are those "determined by law solely for the purpose of securing due recognition and respect for the rights and freedoms of others and of meeting the just requirements of morality, public order and the general welfare in a democratic society."

The standards in the International Bill of Human Rights and other human rights treaties represent not merely current international law, but also ethical presumptions that are widely accepted. Therefore, in our approach to doing ethics we consider these norms as we construct presumptions to address specific moral issues.

We acknowledge that these human rights cannot be verified as absolute, universal presumptions, even though they are asserted in a Universal Declaration, are implemented as international law through many treaties, and have received much support around the world. Civil and political rights arose within the cultural traditions of the West, and economic, social, and cultural rights continue to be disputed, particularly by Western philosophers and US lawyers and politicians. In addition, nations everywhere violate these human rights.

Yet, global support for the moral presumptions of international law is strong evidence that today these human rights assert what many people in the world believe are the necessary social conditions for the realization and protection of their human dignity. Thus, using inductive reasoning, we see these facts as evidence for doing ethics. The moral presumptions of international law not only reflect the consideration of the world's governments, but also have won the allegiance of people from diverse cultural and religious backgrounds.

Today international human rights law defines many of the presumptions that express our global public morality, despite the refusal of the United States to ratify most of these treaties. The US government has ratified the ICCPR, but with reservations that limit these rights to the standards in US law. The US government has not ratified the ICESCR, and there is no indication that it will soon do so.[1]

By ratifying the International Covenant on Economic, Social and Cultural Rights, governments assume obligations to recognize many individual and group rights, including:

- The right to work. . . . (Article 6)
- The right of everyone to the enjoyment of just and favorable conditions of work. . . . (Article 7)
- The right of everyone to social security. . . . (Article 9)
- The right of everyone to an adequate standard of living for himself and his family, including adequate food, clothing, and housing. . . . (Article 11)

- The right of everyone to the enjoyment of the highest attainable standard of physical and mental health. (Article 12)
- The right of everyone to education. (Article 13)

The ICESCR states that each government has a duty to make progress, according to its economic development, in securing the social and economic standards necessary for human dignity. This standard of "progressive realization" contrasts with a government's duty to enforce civil and political rights immediately. The reason for these different standards is that ensuring civil and political rights does not depend on economic development, whereas realizing economic, social, and cultural rights does.

In the United Sates, social and economic *needs* are addressed by legislation that provides assistance for the poor who qualify. These "entitlements" are distinguished from human rights. Nonetheless, it is reasonable to argue that the standards of international law, which define the social conditions that most national governments have agreed are necessary for human dignity, also establish ethical rights and duties for Americans.

HOUSING, HEALTH CARE, AND CAPITAL PUNISHMENT

We propose to do ethics by constructing ethical presumptions based on an assessment of our duty, character (public virtue), relationships, and *rights*. We will also define the burden of proof required to overcome an ethical presumption in order to justify pursuing an alternative course of action.

For example, consider the issue of providing shelter for the homeless. Religious leaders from many traditions argue that an affluent society has a moral duty to assist people who cannot afford the cost of shelter. We might derive this same moral duty with deductive reasoning from the golden rule.

The International Covenant on Economic, Social and Cultural Rights asserts that housing is a human right. The Committee responsible for implementing the ICESCR has argued that this right should not be understood as "merely having a roof over one's head," but as the right to "live in security, peace and dignity."[2]

The United States has not ratified the ICESCR, and so has not assumed this legal obligation. Yet, it voted for the Universal Declaration of Human Rights, which proclaims that: "Everyone has the right to a standard of living adequate for the health and well-being of himself and of his family, including food, clothing, housing and medical care and necessary social services, and the right to security in the event of unemployment, sickness, disability, widowhood, old age or other lack of livelihood in circumstances beyond his control." (Article 25.1)

Therefore, it is reasonable to conclude that the US government has a duty to house those without shelter, as it did in the fall of 2005 when hurricanes left thousands living along the Gulf of Mexico without homes. International human rights law and also the golden rule support the ethical presumption that everyone has a right to housing. Those who disagree bear the burden of proving that their position represents a more ethical choice than enforcing the standards of international human rights law.

Might considering human rights change our moral presumption about capital punishment? The International Bill of Rights does not prohibit the death penalty, but restricts its use. Most nations now presume that capital punishment is morally wrong and no longer permit it.

In the United States, however, the Supreme Court has ruled that the Eighth Amendment of the Constitution, which prohibits "cruel and unusual punishment," does not abolish the death penalty. Therefore, whether or not capital punishment is permitted is left to each of the fifty states. As the ruling of the US Supreme Court asserts the moral presumption for the country, citizens who oppose the death penalty bear the burden of proof required to set this presumption aside.

In the ethical debate about universal health care, who has the burden of proof? A major medical ethics text, which was written for US universities, declares that: "There is not in our society a legally recognized claim-right to health care." The author notes that hospitals receiving federal funds "have a legal duty to treat people faced with life-threatening emergencies until they are stabilized." Yet, in the United States, he says: "I have no legal right to health care, and, if someone refuses to provide it, I cannot seek a legal remedy."[3]

A legal right to health care exists, however, wherever nations have ratified the International Covenant on Economic, Social and Cultural Rights, and more than three-quarters of the world's nations have done so. The care may be minimal, if a country is poor and largely undeveloped economically, but the right is protected for everyone, whether a citizen or an undocumented immigrant.

Along with the right to housing, the right to health care is affirmed in Article 25 of the Universal Declaration of Human Rights, and in 1948 the United States voted to approve this declaration. Therefore, we affirm that everyone in the United States should have a right to health care, and that those who oppose recognizing a right to health care should bear the burden of proof necessary to overcome this presumption.

HIGH MORAL STANDARDS

We have argued that the uncertainties of human knowledge prevent us from knowing that our moral presumptions are absolute. Yet, international law prohibits governments from "derogating" (setting aside) obligations to protect certain human rights, which makes them absolute for all practical purposes. Article 4.1 of the ICCPR states that when facing a national emergency, governments must nonetheless continue to enforce the following moral and legal presumptions:

- No one shall be arbitrarily deprived of his life. (Article 6.1)
- Anyone sentenced to death shall have the right to seek [a] pardon. . . . (Article 6.4)
- Sentence of death shall not be imposed for crimes committed by persons below eighteen years of age and shall not be carried out on pregnant women. (Article 6.5)
- No one shall be subjected to torture or to cruel, inhuman or degrading treatment. . . . (Article 7)
- No one shall be held in slavery . . . and the slave trade . . . shall be prohibited. (Article 8.1)

- No one shall be held in servitude. (Article 8.2)
- No one shall be imprisoned . . . [for] inability to fulfill a contractual obligation. (Article 11)
- No one shall be held guilty of any criminal offence . . . which did not constitute a criminal offence . . . at the time it was committed. (Article 15.1)
- Everyone shall have the right to recognition everywhere as a person before the law. (Article 16)
- Everyone shall have the right to freedom of thought, conscience and religion. (Article 18.1)

Other human rights, such as the right to privacy (Article 17) and the right to join trade unions (Article 22), do not have the same moral status. Yet, a strong argument has been made that the right to food is an absolute right, at least in its formulation in the ICESCR as the "right of everyone to be free from hunger." (Article 11) In the International Bill of Human Rights, this is the only right described as "fundamental" because it asserts a minimum condition for human dignity.

Human rights affirm presumptions with high moral standards. Thus, *compelling* evidence should be required before these presumptions are set aside by those who hope in a particular situation to realize a greater good by not enforcing these rights.

RELIGIOUS SUPPORT

Traditional religious teachings have emphasized duties, but many contemporary religious leaders have actively supported the development of international human rights law. In 1945, O. Frederick Nolde, who represented the Protestant denominations forming the World Council of Churches, persuaded a reluctant US secretary of state to include human rights in the UN Charter. Nolde also led the lobbying effort by Protestant leaders in support of the Universal Declaration of Human Rights. A representative of the American Jewish Committee, Judge Joseph M. Proskauer, collaborated with Nolde in this effort.

In 1948 the Roman Catholic Church was wary of supporting any declaration that did not attribute all rights to God, but Monsignor Angelo Giuseppe Roncalli privately reviewed the draft and later, after he became Pope John XXIII, made international human rights law the cornerstone of Catholic social ethics.[4]

Debate continues among religious leaders over human rights law, but advocates for human rights may be found in every religious tradition. Protestant Christians remain divided over whether rights advocacy is too political, yet the World Council of Churches, which includes Orthodox churches as well as Protestant denominations, actively supports human rights around the world.

The Catholic Church since Vatican II (1962–1965) has included the moral presumptions of human rights law in its training of clerical and lay leaders. Archbishop Oscar Romero, who was murdered in 1980 in El Salvador, is but one notable example of the many Catholic advocates who have been martyred in the struggle for human rights in countries where these rights are commonly violated.

The phrase *dignitas humana* first appeared in Catholic ethics in the nineteenth century, but it was not until the encyclical *Pacem in Terris* by Pope John XXIII that "human dignity" became the foundation for Catholic social teaching. *Pacem in Terris* begins with a ringing declaration of human dignity and inalienable human rights:

> Any human society, if it is to be well ordered and productive, must lay down as a foundation this principle, namely, that every human being is a person, that is, his nature is endowed with intelligence and free will. Indeed, precisely because he is a person he has rights and obligations flowing directly and simultaneously from his very nature. And as these rights are universal and inviolable so they cannot in any way be surrendered.[5]

The Pastoral Constitution on the Church in the Modern World, *Gaudium et Spes*, affirms that human rights are necessary social conditions for human dignity:

> [T]here is a growing awareness of the exalted dignity proper
> to the human person. . . . Therefore, there must be made
> available to all men everything necessary for leading a life
> truly human, such as food, clothing, and shelter; the right to
> choose a state of life freely and to found a family, the right to
> education, to employment, to a good reputation, to respect,
> to appropriate information, to activity in accord with the up-
> right norm of one's own conscience, to protection of pri-
> vacy and to rightful freedom in matters religious too.[6]

Contemporary Catholic social teaching clearly asserts economic and group rights as well as individual civil and political rights.

Jews support the human right of self-determination, which is affirmed in the International Bill of Human Rights. Many Jews, however, also believe God's gift of land to their ancient ancestors, as recorded in the Torah, gives the Jewish people a divine right that outweighs the moral and legal claims raised by Palestinians in defense of their land and their human rights.

Other Jews support equal human rights for Palestinians as well as for Israelis. In 1989, Rabbis for Human Rights, an organization founded by Israeli rabbis from the Orthodox, Conservative, and Reform streams of Judaism, began to defend the human rights of Palestinians. These rabbis assert that the ethical teachings of Judaism command respect for all peoples, which today involves defending their human rights.

Rabbi David Rosen, an Orthodox founder of Rabbis for Human Rights who now represents the American Jewish Committee internationally, argues that Jews must defend human rights. "When I speak of our ethical values, I mean first and foremost that every human being is created in the image of God. Moreover, I would go further and say that, if we don't behave in accordance with this value, we are not truly Jewish."[7] The Jews active in Rabbis for Human Rights agree with Rabbi Rosen that, "human rights apply to all people regardless of religion or race or nationality."[8]

The facts of history, however, verify that many of the Zionist leaders during the war in 1948 favored expelling Arabs from Palestine, and terror

was justified by some to implement this policy.[9] Many Jewish Israelis condemn such "ethnic cleansing," yet also agree with Rabbi Ehud Bandel, the
first executive director of Rabbis for Human Rights, who asserts that:
"Zionism is the national liberation movement of the Jewish people.
. . . Those who have fought each other for self-determination can only be
reconciled, if there is mutual respect for the right of self-determination."[10]

Muslims, like Jews, are also divided over human rights. Some believe the
Qur'an commands them to resist and fight non-Muslims in a time of war,
when Islam is threatened, which is how they see the danger posed today by
secular Western culture. Other Muslims see the United Nations as creating
a time of relative peace, which allows Muslims to struggle to protect Islam
without going to war. These Muslims endorse many of the ethical presumptions affirmed in international human rights law.

Muslim support for human rights, however, is conditional. Muslims believe that human rights come from Allah (God), so wherever Muslims who
support human rights find a conflict between international law and their
understanding of the Qur'an, they reject international law and support the
Qur'an.[11]

The rights of women are an especially contentious issue among Muslims. Riffat Hassan writes: "Having spent seven years in study of the
Qur'anic passages relating to women, I am convinced that the Qur'an is
not biased against women and does not discriminate against them." She acknowledges, however, that "under the pressure of mounting fanaticism
and traditionalism in many areas of the Muslim world" human rights are
disappearing:

> I am particularly concerned about serious violations of hu-
> man rights pertaining to the rights of women, the rights of
> minorities, the right of the accused to due process of law,
> and the right of the Muslim masses to be free of dictator-
> ships. In the end we have what seems to be an irreconcilable
> gulf between Qur'anic ideals and the realities of Muslim
> life.[12]

In contrast to Hassan's reading of the Qur'an, many Muslims believe it imposes on women a more restricted role in society, which a husband may enforce on his wife by punishing her, if she does not submit to his authority.[13]

Hindus embraced human rights when India became an independent nation. The new constitution of India established a secular government and guaranteed international human rights including the right to religious freedom for the many religious minorities of India. The constitution also outlawed caste discrimination among Hindus.

Traditional Hindu teaching emphasizes duty. When Gandhi was asked about the Universal Declaration of Human Rights, he replied as a good Hindu:

> I learnt from my illiterate but wise mother that all rights to be deserved and preserved came from duty well done. Thus, the very right to live accrues to us only when we do the duty of citizenship of the world. From this one fundamental statement, perhaps it is easy enough to define the duties of Man and of Woman and correlate every right to some corresponding duty to be first performed.[14]

Gandhi linked this view of human rights to the ancient Hindu teaching of renouncing the fruit of our action: "If we all discharge our duties, rights will not be far to seek. . . . The same teaching has been embodied by Krishna in the immortal words: 'Action alone is thine. Leave thou the fruit severely alone.' Action is duty, fruit is the right."[15]

There is now, however, a strong political movement among Hindus to make their tradition the official religion of India. Opponents in India of this political agenda fear it may result in the loss of civil rights, by making caste discrimination legal once again and by favoring Hindus over other religious groups. Thus far, however, democratic elections in India have not only confirmed the country's secular government, but have continued to facilitate the peaceful transfer of power in a society with more than a billion people who speak more than eight hundred languages.

Soon after Indian independence, four million Hindus of the Untouchable caste chose to convert to Buddhism as a way of affirming their human rights. They followed B. R. Ambedkar, who was born an "Untouchable" but became a prominent lawyer and leader of the movement for Indian independence. Ambedkar urged conversion by members of his caste to Buddhism, because Buddhists practice a "universal morality which protects the weak from the strong, which provides common models, standards, and rules, and which safeguards the growth of the individual. It is what makes liberty and equality effective. . . . "[16]

Most Buddhists, however, have been reluctant to identify the dharma with human rights, and Buddhist scholar Masao Abe has written that "the exact equivalent of the phrase 'human rights' in the Western sense cannot be found anywhere in Buddhist literature."[17]

Yet, Dr. Tilokasundari Kariyawasam, past president of the World Fellowship of Buddhist Women and deputy director general of education in Sri Lanka, writes: "Buddhism is an all pervading philosophy and a religion, strongly motivated by human rights or rights of everything that exists, man, woman, animal and the environment they live in." She claims that the rights "the Buddhist woman has enjoyed for centuries are revolutionary and daring," and suggests that concern "for human rights is seen in the efforts of women to ensure great equality of access to and participation in Buddhism."[18]

Buddhists in Southeast Asia have asserted their human rights against tyrannical rule, and the government of Sri Lanka (a largely Buddhist country) is trying to negotiate a peaceful settlement with Tamil insurgents (who are Hindu). Most countries with large Buddhist populations have ratified human rights covenants, although these countries have failed in many ways to enforce the moral presumptions of international law. Sadly, countries with large Buddhist populations share this shortcoming with other countries where the population is largely Christian, or Hindu, or Jewish, or Muslim.

In traditional Chinese society acting in harmony with Tao was never understood in terms of asserting personal rights. In the twentieth century, however, war and revolutionary struggle have led to a Chinese-controlled government on Taiwan, which proclaims civil and political rights, and to the People's Republic of China on the mainland, which emphasizes economic, social, and cultural rights.

Since the 1970s more than one reformer in China has argued that human rights may be derived from the duties of the Confucian ethical code. Wei Jingsheng asserts that: "We must reject the dregs of Confucianism, that is, the fantasy that tyrants can ever be persuaded to practice benevolent government. But the *essence* of Confucianism, which we do want to keep, is the concept that people are born with equal rights."[19]

Many today argue that human rights are a Western idea, both historically and culturally. Yet, Chinese scholar Wm. Theodore de Bary suggests that human rights are being adapted into Chinese thought in the same way that Buddhist concepts coming from India were assimilated by the Chinese in the early Middle Ages.

> In my own view nothing is to be gained by arguing for the distinctively Western character of human rights. If you win the argument, you lose the battle. That is, if you claim some special distinction for the West in this respect, or assert some inherent lack on the part of Asians, you are probably defining human rights in such narrow terms as to render them unrecognizable or inoperable for others. If, however, you view "human rights" as an evolving conception, expressing imperfectly the aspirations of many peoples, East and West, it may be that, learning from the experience of others, one can arrive at a deeper understanding of human rights problems in different cultural settings.[20]

AN AUDACIOUS FAITH

The UN Charter begins: "We the peoples of the United Nations determined ... to reaffirm faith in fundamental human rights. . . . ," and the Universal Declaration of Human Rights opens with similar words. In these affirmations, "faith" means trusting the moral capacity of humankind to protect, through the rule of law, the necessary social conditions for human dignity.

The moral presumptions of this faith include the human rights that we have identified in this book.

The International Covenant on Economic Social and Cultural Rights (ICESCR)

- The right to work.
- The right to the enjoyment of just and favorable conditions of work.
- The right to social security.
- The right to food, clothing and housing.
- The right to be free from hunger.
- The right to the highest attainable standard of physical and mental health.
- The right to education.

The International Covenant on Civil and Political Rights (ICCPR)

- No one shall be arbitrarily deprived of life.
- Anyone sentenced to death shall have the right to seek a pardon.
- Persons under 18 who commit a capital offense shall not be put to death.
- The death penalty shall not be carried out on pregnant women.
- No one shall be subjected to torture or to cruel, inhuman or degrading treatment.
- No one shall be held in slavery and the slave trade shall be prohibited.
- No one shall be held in servitude.
- Everyone has the right to liberty and security of person.
- No one shall be subjected to arbitrary arrest or detention.
- All persons deprived of their liberty shall be treated with humanity.
- No one shall be imprisoned for debt.
- All persons shall be equal before the courts and tribunals.

- Everyone has the right to be presumed innocent until proved guilty.
- No one shall be punished for an offence that was not a crime when committed.
- Everyone has the right to recognition everywhere as a person before the law.
- No one shall be subjected to arbitrary or unlawful interference with his privacy.
- Everyone has the right to freedom of thought, conscience and religion.
- Everyone shall have the right to freedom of expression.
- The right of peaceful assembly shall be recognized.
- Everyone has the right to join trade unions.
- Every citizen has the right to take part in the conduct of public affairs.
- All persons are entitled to equal protection of the law.

The ICESCR and The ICCPR

- All peoples have the right of self-determination.
- All men and women have the right to equal treatment under the law.

These moral presumptions express the faith of both religious and secular people in the rule of law and in the possibility of doing ethics together.

Dr. Martin Luther King Jr., in accepting the Nobel Peace Prize, proclaimed an "audacious faith" that "peoples everywhere can have three meals a day for their bodies, education and culture for their minds, and dignity, equality and freedom for their spirits."[21] These moral presumptions, which are embodied in international human rights law, assert the necessary social conditions for human dignity. Therefore, in doing ethics we will not set them aside unless there is *compelling* evidence that an alternative course of action would be better.

Whether we are religious or secular, embracing this faith in human rights and the rule of law will help us face the difficult ethical decisions that must be made in our time.

DOING ETHICS TOGETHER

I. Enforcing human rights.

1. Give a reason why the human rights in the International Bill of Rights are "morally right." Does the fact that governments frequently violate these rights undermine your argument?

2. Governments that have ratified human rights treaties are required to submit reports on their enforcement procedures and progress. Characterize the moral assumption behind this approach to enforcing human rights law. Is there evidence that this approach works?

3. The United States ratified the ICCPR with reservations that limit the standards of the treaty to the norms of US law. How might this affect the debate in the United States about subjecting suspected terrorists after they are captured to sleep deprivation and other aggressive means of interrogation?

II. A right to health care?

About a third of the American people do not have health insurance. Most of the adults without health insurance have jobs, but cannot afford the health insurance plan offered by their employer.

1. Use international human rights law to argue that Americans have a right to health care. What other arguments might you use to support this moral presumption?

2. Give an example of a government program in the United States that provides citizens who qualify an "entitlement" for health care. How does an entitlement program differ from enforcing international human rights law?

3. If the US government were to ratify the ICESCR, what standard would be used to measure whether the government was meeting its obligation to provide health care? How does this standard differ from the standard used for enforcing civil and political rights?

III. Other moral presumptions of the ICCPR.

1. Article 2 prohibits discrimination based on sex and also discrimination against religion. In countries where leaders of the dominant religious community claim that men have greater rights than women, how can the equal rights of women be realized?[22]
2. Article 11 asserts that no one should be imprisoned for a debt. Give a reason for supporting this moral presumption. Explain what sort of retributive justice would be fair for debtors.
3. Article 18, which asserts as a moral presumption "the right to freedom of thought, conscience and religion," has been interpreted to protect the right of religious groups to try to convert others. Give an argument supporting this interpretation, and an argument opposing it.[23]

PART III
Overcoming an Ethical Presumption

Once we construct an ethical presumption we are not finished, for we need to test the presumption against our prediction of the likely consequences of acting on it.

Chapter 8 explains why the dominant contemporary approach to ethics emphasizes predicting consequences rather than fulfilling duties and protecting rights, or considering character and virtues or relationships and caring. Social scientists tend to support this approach to ethics, which asserts that moral decision making simply involves calculating the likely results of our actions.

In an era when democracy is praised if often not practiced, John Stuart Mill's utilitarian principle of "the greatest good for the greatest number" seems very convincing. Moreover, when the whole of life is increasingly viewed as a vast, global marketplace, arguments emphasizing a cost-benefit analysis to determine what is right appear self-evident to many.

Yet, because human beings are free, we cannot know the consequences of our actions, but can only attempt to predict how others will react. In doing ethics, therefore, we suggest that the possible consequences of our actions should not be decisive unless these predictions are sufficiently adverse to overcome the ethical presumption we have constructed by considering our duty, character, relationships, and the human rights that are at stake.

In summary, our approach to doing ethics requires that we:

Construct an ethical presumption by identifying what must be intended and done to:

- Fulfill our ethical duty.
- Strengthen our moral character.
- Sustain caring relationships.
- Enforce and realize human rights.

Consider the likely consequences of acting on this ethical presumption to see if these consequences:

- Support our presumption, or
- Are sufficiently adverse to call this presumption into question.

Make our decision:

- If the predicted consequences confirm our presumption, we should act on it.
- If the consequence arguments meet the burden of proof to overcome our presumption, we should revise our ethical presumption, and act on this revised presumption.

We see this approach to doing ethics as both supporting the rule of law and offering a practical way to address issues of social justice. In chapter 9 we test this approach by using the worksheet preceding the chapter to consider four ethical issues raised by the HIV/AIDS crisis.

8

Possible Consequences

UTILITARIAN AND COST-BENEFIT ARGUMENTS

Consequences matter. This may seem obvious but so far, in constructing moral presumptions, we have given little attention to consequences. We have been concerned with acting in the right way, or being a good person, almost as though the consequences do not matter.

Yet, they do. Remember the Buddhist story about the man who lied to his children when they were absorbed in their play within a burning house? Because he was unable to convince them to leave the house, he promised them treats he didn't have so the children would come to him and be saved from the fire. Consequences clearly matter, but we never know before we act what all the consequences of our actions will be. Trying to entice children from a burning house with a promise of treats may not work. To save the children we might need to run into the house and, against their will, remove them from the danger.

A prediction of good consequences, however, might well be the reason given to justify employing morally questionable means. Often characterized as "the ends justify the means," this is clearly a dangerous approach, because it may be used to excuse actions that violate human rights. In chapter 13 we will examine this issue by reviewing arguments supporting the use of torture to extract information from suspected terrorists and also the reasons given by the US government for initiating wars in Afghanistan and Iraq.

Despite the danger of using unethical means to pursue what are thought to be good and probable outcomes, many moral philosophers argue that there is no better way to decide what choice is best than by evaluating the likely consequences. They admit that we are unable to know with certainty what the results of an action will be. Yet, they assert that making a decision on the basis of the predicted consequences will generally result in the best outcome.

We think like this all the time. Whenever we weigh the pros and cons of making an ethical decision, and then decide what to do based on our calculation of the possible outcomes, we are engaged in what moral philosophers generally describe as a consequentialist approach to ethics.

UTILITARIANISM

This way of doing ethics became popular in the latter part of the eighteenth century. David Hume (1711–1776) first proposed a theory of utilitarianism, but Jeremy Bentham (1748–1832) and John Stuart Mill (1806–1873) became its most prominent advocates.

Bentham was committed to reforming the laws and public institutions of England. In response to those claiming the divine right of kings, Bentham argued that evaluating right and wrong by assessing the consequences of our actions justified political and social change. For Bentham, ethics involved simply a factual assessment of our foreseeable future. "Nature has placed mankind under the governance of two sovereign masters, pain and pleasure. It is for them alone to point out what we ought to do, as well as to determine what we shall do."[1]

In his book *Utilitarianism*, John Stuart Mill provided the most convincing presentation of this approach to ethics. Rather than relying on moral duties claimed to be based on divine revelation or the will of the sovereign, Mill proposed that we should act to achieve the greatest good for the greatest number of people.

> According to the Greatest Happiness Principle . . . the ultimate end, with reference to and for the sake of which all other things are desirable (whether we are considering our own

good or that of other people), is an existence exempt as free as possible from pain, and as rich as possible in enjoyments.[2]

It is hard today to appreciate how revolutionary this argument was in its own time, but it meant nothing less than abandoning the accepted moral rules of traditional religion and culture.

This new moral theory was used to justify revolution as well as a war to end slavery. In the face of intractable injustice, which had long been defended as the will of God or the sovereign who ruled for God, arguing instead for the greatest happiness of all people was a radical challenge.

Utilitarianism simply means doing what will have the greatest utility or usefulness, where utility or usefulness is measured as happiness or pleasure. Instead of relying on religious revelation or on the moral duties or virtues derived by reason from philosophical theories, those assessing consequences to make ethical decisions assert that we should use our own power of practical reasoning to understand what is best for us and for our society.

There is disagreement, however, as to how happiness or pleasure is best measured. Bentham proposed a quantitative calculation, whereas Mill argued that assessing possible consequences should also involve qualitative considerations. Neither position adequately explains how pleasure and pain are to be measured, or how the pleasure of some is to be weighed against the pleasure or pain of others.

For example, providing emergency shelter for those who are homeless would increase their happiness, but taxing homeowners to pay for a shelter program would probably make some homeowners unhappy. A quantitative measurement would compare the number of happy people against the number of unhappy people. A qualitative measurement might give added weight to the grateful happiness of those receiving shelter, in contrast to the begrudging unhappiness of those paying higher taxes.

How would we weigh these different kinds of happiness or unhappiness? The utilitarian approach does not provide a clear answer to this question.

In addition, officials have to consider whether shelters are the best way to address the issue of homelessness. Alternatively, they might construct public housing, which would house fewer people than shelters, but provide subsidized housing for lower income families over a longer period of time. Or, the funds could be spent on training programs for students, so they might be more successful in securing jobs and earning enough money to pay for their housing.

It is unclear how these possible benefits involving subsidized housing or public education could be measured and weighed against the short-term benefits of a shelter program for the homeless.

Similarly, those responsible for expending taxes on public services face a wide range of demands and must decide how best to allocate the limited funds they have. A city trying to cope with homelessness might also be urged to build more parks or to fund the construction of a football stadium. Advocates for parks would argue that the happiness of children and joggers is important, whereas football fans would claim that the revenue generated in the community by the stadium and the pleasure of those able to attend the games would maximize benefits.

Those who make decisions about spending public revenues hear such appeals all the time, and often use a consequentialist approach in disbursing funds. It seems unlikely, however, that their calculation of consequences actually measures the happiness or unhappiness of all those affected by their decisions.

A second difficulty with the utilitarian approach involves ignoring moral duties or rights. The Tuskegee Study of Untreated Syphilis, which was sponsored by the United States Public Health Service from 1932–1972, offers but one infamous example. Syphilis-infected black men living in Alabama were given placebos (sugar pills) instead of treatment that might have provided them some benefit, so researchers could study the course of syphilis among black Americans to measure their natural resistance to the disease.

The US Public Health Service failed in its duty to provide care for those who were ill, because it calculated that the knowledge to be gained by studying untreated syphilis in black Americans was more important (would yield the greatest good for the greatest number of people). Obtaining information about a disease was the end, and the means of achieving this end involved denying the rights of the subjects in the study. The end was claimed to justify the means.

Today, some argue that suspected terrorists should be held indefinitely in order to prevent them from engaging in terrorist acts, although this involves violating their human rights as asserted under international law and also the laws of most nations. This argument is consequentialist for it claims that the likely danger of releasing these men, or of trying them for a crime and not securing a conviction, which would result in their freedom, outweighs the commitment of our government to uphold the moral presumptions of human rights law.

A third problem with the utilitarian approach is that we cannot be sure about the consequences that will result from our actions. Until we act, consequences are only possibilities, or at best probabilities. Even a quick glance at history will reveal that people often act with a mistaken view of the consequences of their actions. For instance, supporters of the war in Iraq predicted that success would come quickly, and yet the war in Iraq has lasted longer than U.S. involvement in World War II.

Economist F. H. Knight suggests that in considering consequences it is helpful to distinguish levels of uncertainty. When we know the probabilities of the possible outcomes of an action, as when we throw dice or calculate from considerable statistical evidence the likelihood of a chain smoker dying from lung cancer, we have an uncertainty that Knight identifies as a "risk." In contrast, when we know the possible outcomes but lack sufficient data to assign accurate probabilities to these outcomes, we are confronted by what Knight identifies as "uncertainty." When we do not even know the possible outcomes of an action, Knight says we should admit to "pure uncertainty" or "ignorance."[3]

With greater experience and knowledge, our predictions may come closer to what actually happens. The more data we have, the more accurately our inductive reasoning can at least calculate the probabilities of the possible outcomes. Using Knight's language, we no longer face uncertainty but can calculate the risks of our actions. Therefore, we can plan for such risks with insurance programs that assign costs to the various probable outcomes.

This is not the case, however, when we do not even know the range of possible outcomes of an action. A consequential approach to ethics dominates the debate about environmental policy, yet economists Herman E. Daly and Joshua Farley argue that this approach cannot be used to address all of the issues we face.

> Estimating stocks of natural resources or reproductive rates for cultivated species is basically a question of risk. Estimating reproductive rates for wild species is a question of uncertainty, since we cannot accurately predict the multitude of factors that affect these reproduction rates, but we do know the range over which reproduction is possible. Estimating ecological thresholds, conditions beyond which ecosystems may flip into alternative states, is a question of pure uncertainty, since we have limited knowledge of ecosystems and cannot predict the external conditions that affect them. Predicting the alternative state into which an ecosystem might flip when it passes an ecological threshold, and how humans will adapt, are cases of absolute ignorance involving evolutionary and technological change.[4]

As useful and necessary as consequential thinking is, we need to be reminded that many situations are so complex or new that we cannot know all the possible outcomes much less assign them probabilities. This is true, for instance, of predicting the weather, because of its complexity, and of calculating the effects of genetically modified (GM) food, because GM food is so new that there is little data on which to base a prediction concerning its long-term consequences.

RULES AND PREFERENCES

One other difficulty with the utilitarian approach to ethics is that, at least in principle, it requires considering all the possible consequences before taking an action, which is clearly impossible. To solve this problem, many utilitarian thinkers have modified their approach and support what is called Rule Utilitarianism, as contrasted with the classical theory now known as Act Utilitarianism.

Those who promote Rule Utilitarianism accept the argument that the results of every action cannot be accurately foreseen and are difficult to measure, and they also acknowledge that taking the time to project the outcomes of every act before acting is impractical. Therefore, they recommend making rules based on an analysis of the *past* consequences of many similar actions. They reason inductively from the data of past experience to formulate a rule.

We might use this reasoning, for example, to justify a rule against lying. In a particular instance, lying could yield the greatest good for the greatest number of people. Yet, after considering many situations, we might well conclude that the general good of society is better served by telling the truth. The happiness of the majority seems to require that people keep the promises they make to one another, that elected officials do not deceive the public, that doctors tell the truth to their patients, and so forth. Thus, according to Rule Utilitarianism, rather than assessing the consequences of each act, we should simply follow the rule and refrain from lying.

Many of our social rules have been derived with this kind of thinking. Traffic rules reflect an estimate of the general harm that will occur without such rules. From the point of view of Act Utilitarianism, a driver might be justified in ignoring a stop sign if no traffic was approaching, as the only happiness at stake would be the driver's. According to Rule Utilitarianism, however, all drivers should stop even when there is no immediate danger, because the rule must be upheld in order to achieve the greatest good for all.

A variation on Rule Utilitarianism is known as Preference Utilitarianism. This approach makes generalizations about what action is best by asking people before any action is taken what outcomes they would prefer. Considering preferences offers another way of trying to resolve the difficulty of measuring happiness.

Those who pursue this approach use surveys, polls, and focus groups to assess what actions, if taken, will be more or less acceptable to people. Whether these actions are reduced to formal rules, or merely summarized as guidelines or objectives, this approach to ethics allows a prediction of consequences based on how the people to be affected by a particular action think they will feel about it, if it happens.

This form of utilitarianism is often used by social scientists as it increases their ability to predict the consequences of implementing new social policies. We know, however, that many people do not know how they will feel about consequences until after these consequences have actually occurred. Moreover, no prediction of consequences can be completely accurate, which means that even relying on our preferences does not guarantee that most people will be happy after an action is taken.

We recognize that Rule and Preference Utilitarianism offer alternative ways of constructing ethical presumptions. Rule Utilitarianism involves reasoning inductively from an analysis of past consequences to formulate a rule that we should follow. Preference Utilitarianism uses stated preferences, which are predictions of what the consequences will be if a certain action is taken, to derive an ethical presumption as to how we should act.

In doing ethics, however, we do not rely on either Rule Utilitarianism or Preference Utilitarianism, because neither consequential approach allows us to consider ethical arguments and insights concerning duty, character, relationships, and rights. In previous chapters we have examined some of these ways of thinking about taking responsibility or being more responsible, and we want to continue to draw on these traditions in considering how to respond to ethical issues.

The sole concern of utilitarianism, however, is assessing consequences. There are no duties to uphold or rights to protect, and there is no reason to act with virtue or to strengthen relationships—unless past consequences verify that these ways of taking moral action and being good persons will result in the greatest good for the greatest number of people.

That is, all forms of consequentialist ethics ignore arguments for inherently or intrinsically right actions (our duty and human rights) or ways of being good (virtues and caring for others). The calculation of what should be done, which in Rule Utilitarianism and Preference Utilitarianism means what the moral presumption should be, involves only weighing the benefits and detriments of predicted consequences.

In doing ethics we take a more inclusive approach to moral reasoning. We first consider ethical arguments about what we should do or who we should be, based not on assessing the likely consequences, but instead on reasoning that has to do with the inherent or intrinsic worthiness of an act or a way of being. Next, we use these considerations to construct a moral presumption. Then we assess the likely consequences of acting on this presumption, to see if our predictions either support our presumption or call it into question.

COST-BENEFIT ANALYSIS

Perhaps because of the many unknowns in predicting consequences and also the widespread use of social science in our time, it is now common to use cost-benefit analysis as a way of weighing the likely benefits of taking an action against the foreseeable consequences that will be detrimental.

Home, car, and health insurance companies make such analyses seem easy. Mathematical tables based on the probability of accidents, how long the average person will live, costs of replacing homes, cars and body parts, and the inflation rate, are used to project probable costs. Top this off with a profit margin, then divide by the number of people in the insurance pool, and you can calculate the cost per person for the benefit of having insurance coverage.

Where the possible consequences of an action are sufficiently well known, so that we can calculate the probabilities of the various possible outcomes, a cost-benefit analysis may be very useful—if the consequences are easily quantifiable. This is often true in medicine, where we take it for granted that the costs of medications, professional staff, and equipment must be taken into account. If there are alternative therapies with a similar probability of success, we will readily agree that the most cost-effective approach should be chosen in order to stretch the health care funds available so that more people can be treated.

When we do not know the possible outcomes of a decision, however, there is no way to use a cost-benefit approach to determine the best course of action. Consider again the ethical question of housing the homeless.

Suppose it costs the same per year to provide a shelter for one hundred people or to house twenty people in subsidized housing. Obviously, the shelter is more cost effective per person. Yet, unforeseeable consequences are likely. There might well be protests in the community against the shelter, requiring public hearings and a greater investment of time by officials and their staff. If crime increases in the area around the shelter, there would be increased costs for security. In other words, a cost-benefit analysis comparing a shelter with subsidized housing will consider only the most obvious short-term consequences, ignoring the possible costs and savings over a longer period of time.

Certainly, our ability to predict consequences diminishes as we extend the period of time to be considered; yet these future consequences may well outweigh the short-term outcomes. For this reason we must resist the pressure in contemporary society to think *only* about short-term results, because these seem to be more predictable and measurable. In reality, we all know that many of the social and economic decisions being made today based on cost-benefit analyses have very long-term consequences.

Even when we know the possibilities and can calculate probabilities, it may nonetheless be "wrong" to assign numerical values to these anticipated outcomes. For example, there is ample evidence to predict various dangers in the workplace and the costs of requiring safety measures. Yet, the human right to a safe work environment cannot be reduced to a financial calculation, which is why human rights law resists a consequentialist approach to deciding issues of human dignity.

Similarly, we can see in the way that courts use cost-benefit analyses to settle legal disputes how such an approach is helpful in addressing some ethical issues, but not suitable for resolving all conflicts that involve duty and rights. When courts assess damages for a breach of contract, the ethical issues concerning a broken promise and the resulting unhappiness will be translated into a dollar amount. Where the loss suffered by a party is not simply financial, but involves physical or mental suffering, a court will likely accept a figure in dollars as reasonable compensation. Civil courts use such cost-benefit analyses all the time to seek fair resolutions of legal conflicts.

Courts are not, however, simply applying utilitarian reasoning to resolve ethical issues. Courts measure consequences in dollars, but also require that parties to a contract abide by their agreement. Courts enforce the duty to keep promises, whether or not the result of their decision yields the greatest happiness for the greatest number of people.

Promises under the law create presumptions of duty and rights, and these moral presumptions are what the courts enforce. Courts use cost-benefit analyses not to determine who is liable for the breach of contract, but to calculate the losses that should be compensated by the party who has broken his or her promise.

A HUMANE SOCIETY

Many advocates of a consequentialist approach to ethics argue that our society is more humane, because of this way of thinking. After all, striving for the greatest good for the greatest number is very much what we aspire to do under democratic government.

Taking into account the happiness of all people, and not only the duties or character traits that may primarily benefit the powerful, certainly does seem to be a moral step forward. This approach fits the way we make political decisions and market consumer products, because it reflects what most people want.

Moreover, those advocating a utilitarian approach to ethics were also among the first to express concern about the pain and suffering of animals, and were active in establishing Humane Societies for stray and injured animals. Writing in England, Jeremy Bentham argued that:

> The day *may* come when the rest of the animal creation may acquire those rights which never could have been witholden from them but by the hand of tyranny. The French have already discovered that the blackness of the skin is no reason why a human being should be abandoned without redress to the caprice of a tormentor. . . . What else is it that should trace the insuperable line? Is it the faculty of reason, or perhaps the faculty of disclosure? But a full-grown horse or dog is beyond comparison more rational, as well as a more conversable animal, than an infant of a day, a week, or even a

> month old. But suppose it were otherwise, what would it
> avail? The question is not, Can they *reason?* nor Can they
> *talk?* but, *Can they suffer?*[5]

Before such advocacy by utilitarian thinkers, moral philosophy was concerned only with the suffering of human beings.

Christian teaching holds that animals do not have souls and that God has given human beings dominion over all the plants and animals of the earth. (In fact, however, in the Genesis story of the Torah and the Christian Bible, God does not give animals to human beings for food until Noah and his ark of animals survive the flood.)

Jews and Christians read this creation story as scripture, and Muslims also accept that Allah (God), as Creator, has subordinated animals to human life. Therefore, teachings in these three religious traditions have generally been unconcerned about the suffering of animals, although Jews and Muslims slaughter animals for sacrifice and food according to the rules that are laid down in their scriptures.

In Hindu and Buddhist cultures some animals have been treated with great respect, and in many indigenous traditions animal life has been understood as related to human life. Yet, it is clear that all over the world animals are seen primarily as a human resource.

We eat animals, use their skins for clothing, and put them in zoos for our amusement. We exterminate animals that we find inconvenient or believe pose a danger to us. We confine (and may love) animals as pets, and use them in experiments to test drugs, cosmetics, and whatever else we think may be dangerous for us. We use animals, for our own good, as "guinea pigs."

If we agree that the suffering of animals is an ethical issue, then we must consider the likely consequences of the way animals are used in research, kept in zoos, and raised for our food.

Among contemporary ethicists, Peter Singer has been a leading advocate for including animals in utilitarian calculations of pleasure and pain. He has opposed the indiscriminate use of animals in research by arguing that their suffering often outweighs any benefits that may be derived for human beings.

Moreover, Singer has promoted vegetarianism because of the suffering that is involved in the way animals are now raised for food.

> The case for vegetarianism is strongest when we see it as a moral protest against our use of animals as mere things to be exploited for our convenience in whatever way makes them most cheaply available to us. . . . Even when animals are roaming freely over large areas, as sheep and cattle do in Australia, operations like hot-iron branding, castration, and dehorning are carried out without any regard for the animals' capacity to suffer. The same is true of handling and transport prior to slaughter. In light of these facts, the issue to focus on is not whether there are some circumstances in which it could be right to eat meat, but on what we can do to avoid contributing to this immense amount of animal suffering.[6]

Singer also relies on a utilitarian approach to argue that our present ways of raising animals for food is not only unnecessarily harmful to animals, but also does great harm to the environment that both we and animals require for life.

> Intensive animal production is a heavy use of fossil fuels and a major source of pollution. It releases large quantities of methane and other greenhouse gases into the atmosphere. We are risking unpredictable changes to the climate of our planet—which means, ultimately, the lives of billions of people, not to mention the extinction of untold thousands of species of plants and animals unable to cope with changing conditions—for the sake of more hamburgers.[7]

ENVIRONMENTAL ETHICS

We take up issues of ecology in chapter 15, but note here that policies to protect the environment are largely based on a consequentialist approach to ethics.

The concern for global warming is verified by pointing to the consequences of carbon dioxide emissions from our gasoline-burning cars and our coal-burning power plants. Those who lobby on behalf of preserving the diversity of plant and animal species resist corporate actions and government initiatives that seem to ignore the fact that the unintended consequences of economic development and growth are destroying life in the forests and oceans.

In these debates about global warming and the extinction of species, we hear that dire consequences create a duty to change our wasteful way of life. Certainly, we agree with this call for greater stewardship of the earth's resources. In this instance employing Rule Utilitarianism makes good sense.

Nonetheless, we argue that we also have a duty to respect the ecosystems of nature even apart from their utility for human life—simply because these natural systems are the source of all life and thus are intrinsically worthy of our respect and care. In addition, we suggest that a concern for character and virtues may enable us to live a flourishing life not only in civil society, but also as people who come from and belong to nature.

We do not agree that those who speak of human relationships with the earth, and its plant and animal life, are necessarily being sentimental. Nor do we think it wise simply to consider the consequences of our choices and how our actions may result in the greatest good for human beings and their natural environment. A duty to care for the environment may arise from recognizing its inherent worth.

Perhaps a consequentialist approach will prove to be best in addressing ethical issues about our environment, if it takes into account the effects of our decisions on ecosystems as well as human beings. This is the position of environmental ethicist Robin Attfield, who explicitly criticizes all moral theories other than consequentialism.

> One strong ground for accepting this view is as follows. If reasons for action are ultimately grounded in intrinsic value and disvalue, and it is states of the world that have such value and disvalue, then the reasons that make actions, policies, and practices right and/or obligatory must

be grounded in foreseeable differences that can be made to the value and disvalue of states of the world. Hence it must be right or obligatory, as consequentialists maintain.[8]

Attfield agrees with Singer that only the balance of good over bad outcomes, which are foreseeable, should determine the right course of action. He argues that the intrinsic values presumed by notions of duty, character, relationships, and rights only make sense if understood as actual realities, or what he calls "states of the world." These facts are, he says, nothing other than the consequences of our actions. For Attfield, therefore, the bottom line in ethics is not acting on moral presumptions, but achieving the consequences we hope for when we assert these presumptions.

In response to this argument, we suggest that limiting ethics to the assessing of predicted consequences in order to achieve a desirable outcome ignores too much of our ethical language and experience. Consequentialists shun considerations of duty, character, relationships, and rights, believing that the foreseeable outcomes of our actions are facts that trump every assertion of intrinsic or inherent worthiness. Yet, are predicted consequences actually facts? We suggest that many predicted consequences are not even probabilities, but merely possibilities. Moreover, we know from history that our actions always produce unintended consequences, and that some of these may be extremely undesirable.

Therefore, we recommend calculating the likely consequences *only* after constructing an ethical presumption by considering our duty, our character aspirations, our relationships, and the rights at stake in the action we are contemplating. We believe this approach to doing ethics will enable us to consider important concerns in making an ethical decision that would be neglected, if we were to act only on the basis of our assessment of the foreseeable consequences.

BURDEN OF PROOF

Certainly, we should not do ethics today without taking into account the possible consequences of the decisions we make. We live in a world of our own making, and not simply in the "state of nature." We know that what we do has consequences, and that these matter. We do not experience life as a string of random events, but as largely shaped by causality. In doing ethics, therefore, we must be concerned about what good (or bad) will come from the good that we intend to do.

We think it best, however, to make predicting consequences the *last* step in our moral analysis. We first construct an ethical presumption by considering our duty, character, relationships, and rights. After we assess what we expect to follow from taking an action based on this presumption, *then* we weigh the possible consequences of acting on this presumption. The outcomes we foresee will often reinforce our ethical presumption. At times, however, the possible consequences of acting on a moral presumption may seem sufficiently adverse that we should consider pursuing an alternative course of action. Reasoning inductively from these predicted consequences might lead us to revise our moral presumption.

To return to our housing example, suppose officials who have formed a moral presumption to provide a shelter for those who are homeless learn that a neighboring community is planning to close its shelter, as soon as the new shelter opens. If a consequence of opening a new shelter would be the closing of an existing shelter, this unfortunate result ought to cause those supporting the new facility to review their options.

Or, consider a health care example. A physician has a duty to tell the truth to her patients, so they can give informed consent for their treatment. However, what should a doctor do, if one of her patients asks her not to tell him the truth, because he thinks he will respond better to treatment if he doesn't know how severe his condition is? A physician not only has a duty to inform her patient—who has a right to be informed so he can give consent to his treatment—but also to provide the best possible care. Weighing the consequences of telling the truth, therefore, might lead the doctor to set aside her duty to inform the patient fully, in order to abide by his request.

A harder case would be the argument made in 2003 by the US government that a preemptive war against Iraq was justified, because Iraq (we were told) had weapons of mass destruction. A government has a duty to provide security for its people and a right to self-defense when the nation is threatened. Yet, international law clearly affirms the moral presumption that war should be a last resort.

Were the predicted but uncertain consequences of invading Iraq sufficiently foreseeable as well as dire enough to justify a preemptive war? After no weapons of mass destruction were found in Iraq, were the possible consequences of ending a dictatorship and creating a constitutional government sufficiently good and likely to justify the continuing loss of life and the devastation of the land?

In doing environmental ethics, we argue that a concern for moral presumptions based on our sense of duty, character, relationships, and human rights will prove essential in choosing the course of action that will both preserve our ethical heritage and our ecosystem. We should respond with critical reasoning to any claim that "foreseeable consequences" are simply facts that trump all ethical presumptions concerning what we should do and who we should be.

Hindsight warns us to be wary of predicting the future. What we think we foresee may be illusory, and what we fail to foresee may become very real.

DOING ETHICS TOGETHER

I. Should doctors abide by the requests of their patients?

"A study published in the March 2002 issue of the *Journal of the American Geriatric Society* found that 60 percent of the 1,185 Medicare patients surveyed at five teaching hospitals told their doctors to focus on making them comfortable rather than on extending their lives. Yet evidence indicated that more than one-third of the people expressing this wish had it ignored. They were treated more and lived longer than the two-thirds whose wishes were respected. Either their doctors forgot about their preferences, or they deliberately ignored them."[9]

1. Relying on these facts, what ethical "rule" or presumption might you make about the treatment of Medicare patients at these hospitals?

2. Does this account offer evidence in support of using Preference Utilitarianism to decide ethical issues? Were the patients, who did not receive comfort care despite their request for it, treated ethically? Explain your answers.

3. If doctors deliberately ignored the preferences of their patients, might you argue that in doing so they acted ethically? If so, make the argument. If you think not, give your reasoning.

II. Is happiness all that matters?

1. Suppose one person lies about another person. Does this only become wrong when the first person learns about the lie and feels wronged? Or, is this lie wrong even if the first person never learns about it? Explain your thinking.

2. Would you say that having friends is good because it makes you happy? Or, that having friends is good even when it doesn't make you happy? Does this distinction matter for how we think about ethics? Give an example as part of your explanation.

3. Suppose you are away from home on business and have a chance to have sex with someone you meet in the hotel. Would this be right, if it would make you both happy and no one else would know about it? Explain your answer.

III. Concern for the suffering of animals.

1. Use Rule Utilitarianism to argue that human beings have a duty to treat animals humanely. Would you apply this argument to all species of animals? Explain your thinking.

2. From an Act Utilitarian point of view, what reasons might someone give for being a vegetarian? Again, thinking

only of consequences, what argument might someone make for eating meat? Explain which of these positions seems to you to be more persuasive.

3. Animals are used to test vaccines and cosmetics. What reason might be given for opposing both kinds of tests? Using only consequentialist reasoning, why might someone support the use of animals to test vaccines but not to test cosmetics? Explain your answers.

WORKSHEET FOR DOING ETHICS

1) Construct an ethical presumption. *

- Describe the moral issue as a question.
- Explain how, in responding to this issue, you intend to:
    - Fulfill your moral duty to others and to other species.
    - Strengthen your character and encourage public virtue.
    - Act with empathy to sustain caring relationships.
    - Protect and realize human rights.
- State your reasoning as an ethical presumption.

2) Consider the consequences. **

- List likely consequences of acting on this presumption.
- Sort these into pro and con arguments and weigh them.
    - If the pros "win," the presumption is confirmed.
    - If not, you should challenge the presumption.
- Assess the proof needed to set aside the presumption. ***
    - Compelling evidence when asserting a human right.
    - Convincing evidence for all other presumptions.

3) Make your decision.

- If your analysis confirms your presumption, act on it.
- If not, revise your presumption before acting on it.

* Your reasoning in this process is inductive. You are thinking from your experience about what is right and good, and then constructing an ethical hypothesis as to what action you should take and how you should conduct yourself as you take this action.

** Test out your ethical presumption by considering the likely consequences of acting on it. If the pros "win"—that is, if the likely beneficial consequences (pros) seem to outweigh the likely detrimental consequences (cons) of taking this action—then your thought experiment confirms your presumption. If, however, the pros and cons seem balanced, or the cons seem to outweigh the pros, then your thought experiment calls into question the presumption you constructed. In this case, you need to clarify the burden of proof needed to set aside the presumption by deciding how substantial the facts and reasons should be to justify revising your ethical hypothesis.

*** If your ethical presumption asserts a human right under international law, then the burden of proof required to set aside this presumption should be compelling. If, however, the ethical presumption you have constructed does not assert a human right, then the moral reasoning to set it aside only needs to be convincing.

9

Making Decisions

HIV/AIDS

The bottom line in doing ethics is acting. Everything we have considered should help us do what we think is best. Our goal in the preceding chapters was not simply to learn about different ethical theories, but to see how we might apply these in making good decisions.

In this chapter we will test our ethical approach by considering the AIDS crisis. We will use inductive reasoning to create ethical presumptions that, like scientific hypotheses, state what we presume to be right. Then we will consider the likely consequences of acting on these presumptions and whether these predictions either confirm our presumptions or give us reason to question them.

In this analysis we will follow the Worksheet for Doing Ethics, which is on page 142. The annotations on page 143 explain in more detail how to use the worksheet.

You may find it helpful at this point to refer back to the diagram on page xii. The worksheet describes the approach to doing ethics that is represented in this diagram. Chapter 9 illustrates how to use this worksheet to sort out and address a complex ethical issue.

Chapters 10–15 do not explicitly refer to the worksheet, but these chapters utilize the same reasoning process to consider other ethical issues.

Therefore, while reading these chapters, it may be helpful to refer back to the worksheet and also to the diagram on page xii.

Confronting HIV and AIDS involves facing many ethical issues. We begin by identifying four of these and stating each as a question.

- Should individuals who are infected be responsible for not infecting others?
- What should those who are not infected do about the AIDS pandemic?
- What public health measures should governments take to address this crisis?
- Should pharmaceutical companies agree to generic versions of their AIDS drugs?

Our next step is to construct an ethical presumption in response to each of these questions. We do that by considering how each question might be answered in a way that would fulfill our duty, strengthen our character, sustain caring relationships, and enforce and realize human rights.

1) Construct an ethical presumption.

Our first question is: Should individuals who are infected be responsible for not infecting others?

Duty

A person with HIV may not know he or she is infected, and so may unknowingly transmit the virus. In this case there is a tragic consequence, but it is unintentional. Yet, it is reasonable to argue, in a society where the virus is prevalent, that each person has a duty to find out if he or she is infected. Once informed, a person has a duty to try not to infect others. We could support this assertion by quoting the golden rule, or by arguing that respecting the human dignity of others requires being careful "to do no harm."

There are various forms of transmission. An individual with HIV who intends to have sex with another person has a duty to inform that person of his condition. Also, a condom should be used. There is, however, no safe way for a drug addict with HIV to share his needle with another drug addict, so he has a duty not to (unless the other addict is also infected).

Should a mother with the virus nonetheless nurse her baby? She has a duty to provide the best care she can for her child, and her breast milk is much better for her child than formula. Yet, nursing will likely transmit the virus, unless she is receiving drugs that reduce this risk. Therefore, she has a duty to at least try to obtain the treatment that will also protect her baby.

Where HIV is prevalent each person has a duty to be tested and, if infected, to seek treatment and take precautions against transmitting the virus, and to inform other people who are at risk.

Character

Some argue that we should make the knowing transmission of the virus a crime, seeing it as a kind of assault. We argue in favor of positive reinforcement for responsible conduct that builds character, rather than relying on the negative threat of punishment.

We should expect those who are infected to fulfill their duty to others, and we should support incentives both to encourage and recognize responsible conduct.

Relationships

Economic and cultural circumstances may make it harder for couples to have safe sex. Men and women may be separated for long periods, working away from home to support their families, and in these circumstances men living where they work are more likely to have casual sex or sex with a prostitute. In addition, there may be a cultural expectation that men alone decide about sex and that condoms are not manly. As sex is largely governed by cultural and religious norms, education that informs men and women of the consequences of unsafe sex should include a discussion that draws on relevant cultural and religious teachings to emphasize committed relationships, care, and respect for others.

Sex education should combine facts about safe sex with moral reflection on cultural and religious teachings that encourage commitment and responsible conduct.

Rights

Under international law men and women have equal rights, so women have the same right as men to decline an invitation to have sex or to require the use of a condom as a condition for having sex.

Laws and public education should promote the right of both women and men to abstain from sex or, if consenting, to require that a condom be used to help protect against infection.

Editing these four statements into a single ethical presumption might lead us to affirm: *Men and women have a duty to be informed about safe sex, to be tested and, if infected, to seek treatment and take precautions against transmitting the virus, and everyone's right to abstain from sex or, if consenting, to require that sex be safe, should be respected.*

2) Consider the likely consequences of acting on this presumption.

Pro

- Encouraging responsible conduct will lead to more responsible conduct.
- More people will be tested and thus will be better informed about:
  - Their health and options for health care.
  - The danger they pose to others.
  - How they can act more responsibly.
- Promoting women's rights will increase safe sex and reduce the spread of HIV.

Con

- Local leaders will resist health initiatives seen as undermining traditional values.

- •   Voluntary compliance will be inadequate, therefore:
  - •   Testing should be mandatory.
  - •   Negligence by those infected should be criminal.
  - •   Sex with prostitutes, without using a condom, should be prosecuted.
  - •   Teaching safe sex will promote sex outside of marriage, especially among teens.

Weighing these pro and con arguments about likely consequences is difficult, as predicting consequences is always speculative. We have suggested that the burden of proof to overcome a moral presumption should be compelling, if the presumption involves a human right.

The ethical presumption we have constructed affirms the equal rights of women and men to decide about having sex, and equal rights for men and women is an assertion of human rights under international law. At least in this respect, to justify setting aside the moral presumption, the argument that the cons outweigh the pros should be compelling. We think the arguments against the presumption do not meet this burden.

What about the assertion that an infected person has a duty to become informed about safe sex, to be tested, and, if infected, to seek treatment and to protect against transmitting the virus? The golden rule would seem to support these moral presumptions, and doing our duty means respecting ourselves as well as others. Being careful not to transmit the virus, however, involves more than using a condom while having sex. HIV may be transmitted by infected drug addicts who share needles, or by mothers with HIV who nurse their babies.

As there is no human right not to be infected by someone else with a disease, only a *convincing* burden of proof is required to set aside these moral presumptions. In this case, do the cons outweigh the pros? We think not.

3) Make your decision.

We conclude that the predicted consequences do not meet the burden of proof to overturn our ethical presumption, and some may even argue that the pros confirm this presumption. As we have reasoned that our presumption states the best course of action, we should take it.

We now consider the second ethical question we raised concerning AIDS: What should those not infected do about the AIDS pandemic?

1) *Construct an ethical presumption.*

Duty

What duty do those not infected have for those who are infected? A parent not infected would have a duty to care for an infected child, as parents have a duty to care for any of their children. A healthy spouse would have such a duty for an infected spouse, and we might say a healthy person would have a duty to assist any infected relative. These duties come from our roles in society, as members of families.

This means, of course, that we do not have the same duty to those who are not members of our family. Do the citizens of a country have a duty to help other citizens? We tend to leave such a duty to the government, merely defining our duty to support the government's care for the general health and welfare of all its citizens. We also may volunteer with non-governmental organizations (NGOs) to help relieve suffering.

Do the citizens of one country have a duty to care for the citizens of other countries? If we say yes, how would we define this duty? The silver rule affirms that we have a duty not to harm others. Kant's categorical imperative and the golden rule seem to suggest that we have a duty to help all other people in the world. Specifically, in the case of the AIDS pandemic, do we each have a duty to provide, say, a portion of our income, to help purchase the drugs needed by those with AIDS?

It seems reasonable to assert that everyone has a duty to respect the human dignity of each other person by supporting the enforcement of human rights for every person in every nation. If we claim a human right for ourselves, then we have a duty to ensure that all others enjoy this same right. This would include the right to health care. Under international law, however, this does not mean a duty to fund equal health care everywhere, as enforcing the right to health care is largely left to each nation and varies according to its economic development. So, we suggest that:

Each person (including everyone who is healthy) has a duty to support health care as a human right, which means supporting international initiatives to assist national governments in meeting their obligations under the International Covenant on Economic, Social and Cultural Rights to achieve the progressive realization of "the right of everyone to the enjoyment of the highest attainable standard of physical and mental health." (ICESCR, Article 12)

Character

What sort of people should we, who are not infected with HIV, be? We could simply be grateful that we have been lucky, or that we were not born in a country where AIDS is rampant. Or, we could be a bit smug, because we have avoided dangerous sex.

If we accept that our purpose is to flourish and to be virtuous not only as individuals but also as a society, then we can hardly turn away from the suffering of people with AIDS. Thus, we may assert as a goal:

Those not infected should aspire to respond with compassion by providing financial support, as they are able, to address the AIDS crisis.

Relationships

Do we have a moral responsibility for relationships that extend beyond our duty to our relatives? Many feel drawn to help others, because they feel related by religion, culture, nationality, or gender. This sense of relationship inspires compassion.

People also respond with compassion to the suffering of persons with different religious and cultural backgrounds. The global outpouring of support for the victims of the Asian tsunami in 2004 reflects the power of this moral appeal, and is a reminder that we should not discount the capacity of human beings to respond to strangers in need.

People who are not infected with HIV may discover a sense of relatedness with those who have AIDS that will move them to support charities and the allocation of tax revenues by their government to care for those with the disease.

Rights

We have already identified a duty to support the human right to health care. There is nothing selfish about claiming this right for ourselves as long as we accept our duty to support it for everyone.

Everyone, whether ill or healthy, has a duty to support the human right to health care.

Editing these four statements into a single moral presumption might lead us to affirm: *Each person has a duty to support health care as a human right, and those who are healthy should encourage one another to support charitable giving, NGO initiatives, and government programs to care for the ill.*

2) *Consider the likely consequences of acting on this presumption.*

Pro

- Governments will ratify the ICESCR and act to realize the right to health care.
- Funds will be raised for charitable relief and NGO programs for those with HIV and AIDS.
- Governments will give greater priority to the fight against the AIDS pandemic.

Con

- Advocacy for ratification of the ICESCR will generate opposition in the United States.
- More charitable funds may discourage responsible conduct by those with HIV and AIDS.
- Government spending on AIDS may decrease spending for other priorities.

As always, predicting consequences is full of uncertainty. Some would argue that responding to the AIDS crisis should not be linked with arguing for health care as a human right, as this will likely weaken the appeal to many Americans. Others may argue that government programs to fight AIDS should promote more democratic decision making and also greater protection for the equal rights of women.

Because of the human rights issue in our ethical presumption, our burden of proof for setting aside this presumption needs to be a compelling argument that some other course of action would be better. This might well be argued by those opposed to the International Covenant on Economic, Social and Cultural Rights, because they believe that it merely labels as "rights" what more accurately are described as human needs.

If we took support for the International Covenant on Economic, Social and Cultural Rights out of our moral presumption, then the burden of proof to overturn the presumption would only be a convincing argument. The issues primarily involve how health care resources should be distributed in a fair manner that is also effective in addressing the AIDS pandemic.

Those opposing sex education that endorses the use of condoms have argued that this awareness program encourages sexual promiscuity with all its dangers. In response to this concern the US government required in 2006 that a third of its funds to prevent AIDS globally be used for promoting abstinence outside of marriage and fidelity within marriage. There is only anecdotal evidence, however, that this use of funds is more likely to prevent the spread of AIDS than promoting the more inclusive ABC approach to sex (Abstain, Be faithful, or use Condoms).

3) Make your decision.

Arguments asserting duty and rights may only substantiate a general response, whereas a concern for character and relationships is more likely to move people to support specific actions. In considering the possible consequences, however, we must recognize that the con arguments seem to be very persuasive, as the response of the affluent nations to the AIDS crisis is far from comprehensive or even generous.

Therefore, we might well consider whether or not there is a more effective course of action. Some have suggested that the money being spent on alleviating suffering would be better invested in research to develop a vaccine.

This is essentially a consequence debate about which use of money would generate the better result. We think it is impossible to say over the long term, but would note that using charitable and governmental funds primarily for vaccine research would mean spending most of this money in the short term within affluent countries. We think money for AIDS should largely be used to provide direct assistance for those who are infected—to alleviate their suffering and to support efforts in their communities and countries to slow the spread of the virus.

Another suggestion might be using the money now being spent on AIDS to fight poverty. Affluent countries have found ways to check the spread of AIDS and treat people who are HIV-positive, so investing in the economic development of poor countries might be a way of enabling these countries to provide their own solutions, rather than depending on foreign assistance.

We will argue in chapter 14 for a moral presumption to fight global poverty, but we cannot agree that AIDS is a problem that support for economic development will quickly resolve, at least not in nations with high rates of infection. Moreover, there is no evidence that investing large sums of money in developing countries will help them quickly overcome their poverty. Even with good intentions, foreign investment in poor countries often results largely in political and economic benefits for the industrial nations and multinational corporations that control the terms of the investment.

Therefore, we acknowledge that the consequence arguments are unclear, but we reaffirm our ethical presumption and urge that all of us who do not have HIV consider how we may take responsible action.

We now take up the third ethical question we raised about AIDS: What public health measures should governments take to address this crisis?

1) *Construct an ethical presumption.*
Duty
No legitimate government would deny that it has a duty to assist its citizens who have AIDS, but governments will differ in defining this duty. National

governments that have ratified the International Covenant on Economic, Social and Cultural Rights have an explicit duty under international law to take steps to realize, progressively, the right to health care, which certainly includes care for those suffering from AIDS.

This general duty, however, involves all health issues, and the budgets for public health of many countries are already insufficient to deal with a host of debilitating and deadly diseases. AIDS may be given priority, but every public health program will have to consider how best to allocate limited funds not only for various diseases, but also for training health care professionals, supporting the delivery of health care services, and health care education.

The choices are difficult. In Kenya, for instance, sufficient nurses are being trained, yet the government cannot hire them because, in order to receive aid for economic development from the World Bank and the International Monetary Fund (IMF), it has pledged to reduce its civil service costs. Yet, hospitals in Kenya have a nursing ratio of over forty patients per nurse, and rural clinics are being closed because nurses are not being hired to staff these primary care facilities.

The Clinton AIDS Foundation has made a commitment to provide funds to the government of Kenya for 3,800 nursing positions, but to fulfill its obligations to the World Bank and the IMF the Kenyan government will only be able to offer temporary contracts to these nurses.

Because Kenya trains more nurses than it can afford to hire, Kenyan nurses are being hired to work in other countries. This is a financial boon for Kenya, as about 8 percent of its national wealth comes from Kenyans who work outside the country and send money home to help support their relatives. To increase its revenue from exporting nurses, the Kenyan government has set up a profit-making agency to help Kenyan nurses find jobs in the United Kingdom and the United States, as both countries do not educate a sufficient number of nurses to meet their needs.[1] (Despite trying to check immigration, the US Congress recently made an exception for nurses trained elsewhere.)

National governments have a duty under the International Covenant on Economic, Social and Cultural Rights to promote economic development, because greater income is needed to realize the economic and social human rights that are necessary conditions for human dignity. Nonetheless, the way this is being done in Kenya reveals some of the problems with economic globalization. (We will address the ethical issue of economic justice in chapter 14.)

Botswana offers a more encouraging example than Kenya. In 2004 the president of Botswana acted to fulfill his government's obligations to provide health care by directing that every person going to a hospital or clinic in Botswana be given an HIV test, unless the person refused. At that time less than one in twelve citizens had been tested, but six months later the number had quadrupled. Testing has led to earlier intervention for many with HIV people, which has meant more people recovering from AIDS, as the government of Botswana has pledged to provide free drug treatment to everyone needing it. In a country where 40 percent of the adult population is infected, Botswana nonetheless expects by 2009 to offer drug treatment for all those with AIDS.[2]

In countries with high rates of HIV infection, we suggest that:

Governments should give priority to funding: 1. Health care staff providing education and treatment; 2. HIV testing for everyone; and 3. Effective drug treatment for everyone with HIV and AIDS.

Character

This moral concern is exemplified primarily in virtuous conduct, so strictly speaking it would only apply to individuals and not to governments. Yet, it is reasonable to speak of the "character" of a government (or other institution), and in a positive sense this generally means that leaders have acted responsibly to ensure that government actions will be transparent and worthy of praise.

In her book *Lying*, Sissela Bok argues that a government is responsible for the "climate" of its actions concerning the public trust. She urges officials to maintain the integrity of their government's decision-making process, to promulgate and enforce laws that prohibit fraud and perjury, and to ensure that laws and rules do not encourage deception.[3] We should expect no less of AIDS programs administered by governments.

Government initiatives to address AIDS should be exemplary in transparency and accountability.

Relationships

Decisions by governments should always seek to strengthen the relationships within a society as well as meet the particular objective of the action that is taken. We suggest that a government conceive of its decision making in the way that health care professionals now obtain informed consent from their patients. Doctors must explain to their patients the choices for treatment, and the pros and cons of each choice, so patients may reasonably exercise their right to consent. For the same reasons, elected officials should inform their constituents and listen to their concerns and suggestions, before deciding what policy or program should be promoted.

Governments should inform their citizens and make decisions in ways that instill greater trust.

Rights

A government does not have rights, as such, but has a duty to protect and realize the human rights of its people. So, we will not suggest an ethical presumption for this approach to ethics.

Editing the three moral presumptions we have drafted into one statement might lead us to affirm: *Governments should promote HIV testing and drug treatment for everyone through a decision-making process that involves citizens, is transparent, and fosters greater trust.*

2) Consider the likely consequences of acting on this presumption.

Pro

- Testing the population for HIV will increase effective treatment.
- Providing low-cost or free drugs will lower the death rate.
- Citizen involvement will increase support for AIDS prevention.

Con

- Mandating HIV tests may shift expenditures from treatment to testing.
- Providing cheap drugs may reduce the incentive to act more responsibly.
- Citizen involvement may be divisive and thus delay important decisions.

The smaller the percentage of a population that has been tested, the more important it is to require testing, while allowing individuals to refuse testing if they so desire. Providing free drugs is a higher priority when the population with AIDS is largely destitute, and payments may be set to reflect the income of those who are ill so all who need the drugs can obtain them. Citizen involvement may result in a divided public, but if differences are not dealt with before an AIDS initiative is begun, those who disagree with the policy are likely to resist it.

The ethical presumption does not involve a human right, so only a convincing argument should be required to set the presumption aside.

3) *Make your decision.*

If the reader is convinced that the cons outweigh the pros or that there are other good arguments to oppose this presumption, then the reader should formulate an alternative that seems to offer better results. The authors think that the cons do not offer a convincing argument against the ethical presumption, so we recommend acting on this presumption.

Finally, we consider the fourth ethical question about responding to AIDS: Should pharmaceutical companies agree to generic versions of their AIDS drugs?

1) *Construct an ethical presumption.*

Duty

Patent laws allow companies to protect the investment made in research and development to develop a new product. Without patent protection, competitors would be able to copy a successful drug and sell a generic form of it at a much lower price, because these companies would not have to recoup any research or development costs in their selling price.

In the case of AIDS drugs, however, the price that pharmaceutical companies charge is too high for these drugs to be widely used in poor countries where AIDS is rampant.

As corporate leaders have a duty to the stockholders of a company to maximize its profits, it is hard to argue that pharmaceutical companies have a duty to allow a competitor to disregard the patent laws and produce a lower-cost, generic version of its patented drug. Therefore, our moral presumption concerning duty is that:

Pharmaceutical companies do not have a duty to agree to generic versions of their drugs.

Character

The importance of character in ethics is revealed in having the courage to say at times that the rules do not encourage a sufficiently high level of moral action. The AIDS crisis, we argue, requires compassion and moral leadership that go beyond the duty of a company to defend its patents.

To organize such an extraordinary effort, the UN established the Global Fund to Fight AIDS, Tuberculosis and Malaria, which began in 2002 to fund lower-cost, generic drugs for use in poor countries. In September of 2003 the World Trade Organization (WTO) accepted that poor nations could authorize generic copies of patented drugs when there was a national health crisis. In the United States, rather than support these international efforts, pharmaceutical companies have endorsed the President's Emergency Plan for AIDS Relief (PEPFAR). PEPFAR limits the use of US funds to purchasing drugs approved by the Food and Drug Administration (FDA), and the FDA has resisted approving generic drugs produced cheaply in countries that refuse to enforce the patent protection for the same brand-name drugs.

We argue that our ethical presumption ought to support making AIDS drugs more available at lower cost so that the large numbers of AIDS patients living in less affluent countries may be treated with these lifesaving drugs. Pharmaceutical companies, although they do not have a duty to act on this presumption, would set a good moral example by doing so.

Pharmaceutical companies should support international efforts that enable the production and sale in poor countries of generic drugs that copy patented AIDS drugs.

Relationships

The UN Global Fund to Fight AIDS, Tuberculosis and Malaria seeks to foster collaboration among nations in addressing three major global threats to health. The United States has pledged to contribute one billion dollars to this fund, but intends to control the use of most of its AIDS funds through PEPFAR, which prevents the purchase of generic AIDS drugs until these drugs have been approved by the FDA.

We argue that collaboration between pharmaceutical companies and the US government should not be at the expense of funding a global UN effort to address the AIDS crisis.

Pharmaceutical companies should support shifting US funds for purchasing AIDS drugs from PEPFAR to the UN Global Fund.

Rights

Pharmaceutical companies are "legal persons" and thus have rights including the right to protect patents. However, these rights are not "human rights" and must be weighed against the human right to health care.

Article 12 of the International Covenant on Economic, Social and Cultural Rights specifies that this right involves "enjoyment of the highest attainable standards of physical and mental health." National governments that have ratified this Covenant are obliged to take steps necessary for the "prevention, treatment and control of epidemic, endemic, occupational and other diseases." (Article 12.2.c) These moral and legal principles are clearly applicable to the AIDS crisis.

The ruling by the World Trade Organization creates a limited exception to protecting the rights afforded by patent laws for the national AIDS emergency in many poor countries. Pharmaceutical companies have a right to resist the WTO ruling, and have done so by supporting limitations on US funds for drug purchases through the PEPFAR, for which the United States has pledged fifteen billion dollars.[4] Buying AIDS drugs through PEPFAR means paying the consumer price for the drugs, which would yield greater profits for the pharmaceutical companies, but also would result in purchasing fewer drugs with the available funds for those who need them in poor countries.

It is important, however, to consider that corporations not only have legal rights, but also derive significant benefits from the governments that grant them legal status. Therefore, corporations have ethical as well as legal responsibilities to governments as well as to the societies in which they operate. It seems reasonable in a time of crisis to ask that pharmaceutical companies accept a less profitable arrangement than would otherwise be expected in order to support an important public purpose.

Thus, for the sake of the health care of tens of millions of poor people, we urge pharmaceutical companies to support the production and use of generic AIDS drugs in less developed countries and the use of US funds to purchase these drugs at discounted prices.

Pharmaceutical companies should accept a limited exception to the right to protect their patents that allows the development and use of generic AIDS drugs in poor counties.

Editing these four statements into a single moral presumption might lead us to affirm: *Pharmaceutical companies should support international decisions that enable lower-cost generic AIDS drugs (which copy patented drugs) to be made and used in poor countries.*

2) Consider the likely consequences of acting on this presumption.

Pro

- Treatment for AIDS patients in poor countries would increase.
- International cooperation would be strengthened.

- The moral climate for addressing public issues would improve.

Con

- Pharmaceutical companies would have less money for research and development.
- Generic drugs would not necessarily meet stringent FDA requirements.
- A precedent would be set that weakens the protection of patent laws.

The least tangible of the pro arguments is that acting on the ethical presumption we have constructed would improve the moral climate. Clearly, however, the use of generic drugs will make the funds available for AIDS drugs go much further in providing care, and the UN Global Fund offers the most cooperative way to distribute drugs.

All of the con arguments are intangible. Most likely pharmaceutical companies will invest in drug research that offers the greatest potential profit, which would be drugs for sale within affluent countries for affluent consumers. Therefore, research on AIDS, malaria, and tuberculosis—the diseases targeted by the Global Fund—is not likely to be funded by pharmaceutical companies in any event.

There are good reasons for supporting FDA testing requirements including the danger that generic drugs, if made without proper care, could result in strains of HIV that are resistant to the patented drugs. Yet, the World Health Organization has tested generic AIDS drugs to ensure that they are safe, and the FDA has considerable influence over the development of WHO protocols, which seek to minimize these risks.

The WTO ruling allowing the production of generic drugs in poor countries because of the AIDS crisis does set a precedent, but one that is limited in scope to national public health emergencies. This does not seem to undermine the general protection of patent rights.

As the human right to health care is at issue, we should require a compelling argument before setting aside the ethical presumption we have constructed. Yet, knowing that the United States does not recognize health care as a human right, we suggest that the likely consequences anticipated by those opposing our moral presumption do not meet even a convincing burden of proof.

3) *Make your decision.*

We urge pharmaceutical companies to accept international decisions that facilitate funding for the development and use of generic AIDS drugs in poor countries.

We have considered only four ethical issues involving our response to the AIDS crisis, using the *Worksheet for Doing Ethics*, as a way of illustrating our approach to making moral decisions. If you find the Worksheet helpful, please use it to address other ethical issues. If you want to work out your own approach, we hope that you have at least found this chapter to be interesting and informative.

Our concern with duty, character, relationships, and human rights could be applied to the many other ethical dilemmas posed by HIV and AIDS. In this chapter we have merely tried to show how constructing presumptions may be helpful in considering what response to a moral problem would be best. In subsequent chapters we will apply this approach to several other pressing ethical issues. We hope in this way to clarify our thinking about doing ethics and also to increase our understanding of these issues.

DOING ETHICS TOGETHER

I. Individual responses to AIDS.

1. Give an argument for, and an argument against, prosecuting someone who has AIDS for having sex without informing the other person and without using a condom.

2. Give two reasons why someone not infected with HIV has a moral responsibility to support charitable and governmental efforts to prevent the spread of the virus.

3. Make an argument that each person, whether healthy or not, should support the recognition and realization of health care as a human right. Give one reason opposing this argument. In these two arguments, do you emphasize duty, character, relationships, rights, or consequences? Explain why you chose the ethical approach that you used.

II. The responsibility of governments.

1. How would you argue that governments have a moral responsibility to ensure that citizens are able to access the highest attainable level of health care?

2. Should a national government of an affluent country ensure that enough nurses are trained to meet the society's health care requirements? Or should it simply import nurses trained in other countries? What ethical issues are at stake in this debate?

3. What should be the priorities for government spending in poor countries to address the AIDS crisis? What ethical approach are you using to make this argument?

III. The responsibility of pharmaceutical companies.

1. Give a reason supporting the WTO ruling that permits making and using generic drugs in poor countries when there is a national health care crisis. Raise an ethical objection to this ruling.

2. Defend the restrictions on purchasing drugs that limit the use of US funds in the President's Emergency Plan for AIDS Relief (PEPFAR). Raise an ethical objection to these restrictions.

3. Why should pharmaceutical companies agree to the use
    of generic copies of their patented drugs in poor coun-
    tries? Give an opposing argument. For each argument,
    identify the ethical approach are you emphasizing.

PART IV
Applying the Approach

Ethical issues are personal for those who face them, and some of these are also issues of social ethics. In chapter 10 we use the rule of law as a starting point to assert a moral standard for society and then explore the debate about this standard. Public morality includes agreeing on the law, protecting the right to dissent, and aspiring for the common good. To explore what it means to pursue public morality, we will construct ethical presumptions to consider the issues of abortion, same-sex marriage, and capital punishment.

Chapter 11 addresses health care issues. Health care professionals have a duty to ensure that patients are fully informed so patients can exercise their right to consent to their treatment. Our social agreements and our laws assert moral presumptions concerning organ donations and transplants, stem cell research, and access to health care. We consider what our ethical approach (and the law) should presume about allowing a physician to assist in a patient's death when the patient asks for help so she can have a comfortable, dignified death.

Chapter 12 describes how making decisions about sex are now, by law and social mores, largely left to the conscience of consenting adults. Prostitution is an exception, as it remains illegal in most places, perhaps because people want sex to be more than a commodity. We suggest that the challenge of sex education is not merely to explain the law and warn of the consequences of careless sex, but also to help young people see that having sex is an ethical decision requiring mutual respect.

In chapter 13 we reflect on the war against terrorism. To understand the ethical issues raised by this new kind of war, we look first at the just war tradition and what we mean today by terrorism. This chapter also applies the standards of international law to the security measures that the US government has pursued since 9/11. If terrorism is evil, and not merely bad, we suggest that the ethical battle can only be won by doing what is right: defending the rule of law, and seeking truth and reconciliation as well as justice.

In chapter 14 we consider the issue of economic justice and a caring economy. We suggest that the debilitating poverty of more than a billion people is evidence that global policies are contributing to an unfair distribution of economic benefits and burdens. Our moral presumption should be otherwise, and this means both changes in the law and raising our aspirations for a more just system of trade. Our goal should be to support political and economic decisions necessary for sustainable economic development, and also the progressive realization of economic human rights.

Chapter 15 concerns our environmental crisis. We urgently need public policies that will protect our ecosystems, yet these policies will not be possible without a much greater commitment by citizens and corporations to reduce pollution, increase recycling, and transform our expectations from economic growth to a sustainable way of life. We have to accept our place in nature if we are to live more ecologically. We also must ensure that governments enable communities affected by economic development to participate in these decisions, as well as hold investors accountable for the environmental damage caused by their use of funds.

10

Public Morality

SEEKING THE COMMON GOOD

All our moral convictions are private, until we make them public. Once we openly express a position on an issue, then we have joined the debate about our public morality. Robert Kane reminds us that entering into public debate means agreeing to disagree: "Public morality is what you owe to others, *even if they do not agree with your private morality.*"[1] We owe all others a duty of respect.

Divisive moral issues put every ethical approach we have discussed to the test. In this chapter we consider three such issues. Is abortion ever right? Should same-sex marriage be allowed? Does justice require capital punishment? There is no single moral philosophy or set of rules that will answer these questions to the satisfaction of everyone. Therefore, in doing ethics we use inductive reasoning to construct moral presumptions (hypotheses) about what is right (or good or fair), before testing these presumptions by considering the possible consequences of acting on them.

We will rely on the rule of law to begin our consideration of public morality. Our goal in doing ethics—and we would say the goal of public morality as well—is to clarify our legal presumptions, protect the right to dissent, and aspire to higher ethical standards.

ABORTION

The 1973 *Roe v. Wade* decision by the US Supreme Court, which legalized abortion to protect a woman's right to privacy, reflects a significant change in public morality. The court held that state legislatures may not restrict a woman's right to an abortion during the first trimester of her pregnancy, but can regulate the procedure during the second trimester "in ways that are reasonably related to maternal health."[2] In the third trimester, the state can restrict or even proscribe abortion under most circumstances, because of the viability of the fetus, but must protect a woman's health by allowing for abortion when her life is threatened.

State legislatures have yielded to the lobbying efforts of those morally opposed to the *Roe* standard by passing laws that limit the effect of this ruling. In *Webster v. Reproductive Health Services* (1989) the US Supreme Court upheld a Missouri law prohibiting the use of state funds, facilities, and employees to perform abortions, except where a woman's life is in danger.

In *Planned Parenthood v. Casey* (1992) the US Supreme Court overturned a law requiring a married woman to notify her husband of her intention to have an abortion. Nonetheless, *Casey* held that laws placing restrictions on a woman seeking an abortion were permissible, as long as the restrictions do not impose an "undue burden" on a pregnant woman by placing a "substantial obstacle in the path of a woman seeking an abortion before the fetus attains viability."[3]

The *Roe* and *Casey* rulings define the present moral presumption of US law. This presumption protects the *right to privacy* of a woman in the first two trimesters of her pregnancy. It also implicitly recognizes the *right to life* of the fetus in the third trimester of a woman's pregnancy when the fetus becomes an "unborn child" by being viable.

In many other countries abortion is also recognized as a limited right. In China[4] and India[5] a woman may choose an abortion early in her pregnancy, but may not ask to determine the gender of her fetus before requesting an abortion. These two countries have a long history of killing female newborns. The continuing population imbalance of men and women in both countries suggests that *abortion* is now being used for gender selection.

Duty

As we affirmed in chapter 4 our duty is to respect others in order to uphold their dignity as autonomous human beings. One way we fulfill this duty is by obeying the laws of our society, and thus we have a duty to obey the law allowing abortion. If we disagree with the law, we are free in a democratic society to protest and try to change the standard of public morality.

If we believe a law is so wrong that we cannot support its legal enforcement, then we may conclude that we have an ethical duty to resist it by committing an act of civil disobedience. Such an act is "civil" when those resisting a law do so openly, explain their moral reasons, act without violence, show respect for the rights of others, and accept the punishment that the law imposes for their disobedience.

This notion of public morality requires a high level of tolerance for conflicting convictions. We have a duty to respect the rights of others, even if we find their opinions distasteful or their conduct repugnant, as long as in exercising their freedom they do not violate the rule of law.

In this regard freedom of the press is crucial. It is no small matter that we encourage open discussion of ethical issues, for we affirm that the laws in our society only approximate the good and must be tested by critical debate. In this way the rule of law encourages citizens to aspire to higher standards of public morality.

Character

In chapter 5 we suggest that humility and compassion, among other virtues, are character traits that may be easily ignored in a time when assertiveness is greatly encouraged. In considering the issue of abortion, perhaps we need to reaffirm these traditional virtues, as many people arguing about this issue today are quick to judge and condemn.

Most of those who oppose the current law protecting a woman's right to choose to have an abortion claim that the law should reflect a higher standard of character by protecting the right to life of a "child" from the moment of its conception.

Those who support the *Roe* and *Casey* standard also express a concern for character by affirming that the decision of continuing a pregnancy is best left to the conscience of the pregnant woman. Yet, many defending the right to abortion believe women should not abuse this right by being careless about protecting themselves against pregnancy, just because they can always have an abortion if they become pregnant. They believe a woman's *character* is tested when she discovers she is pregnant and does not want to be.

Relationships

In chapter 6 we argue that an emphasis on relationships would mean a careful consideration of who should be involved in making an ethical decision. The crux of this approach is greater awareness of the relationships that make us who we are, so we may resist the temptation to see ourselves simply as autonomous individuals.

Those who support the *Roe* and *Casey* standard emphasize the individual right of a woman, whereas those opposed to the present law focus on the responsibility of a pregnant woman for the life within her womb. "Pro-choice" advocates do not deny the significance of personal relationships, but argue that weighing the impact of a pregnancy on family and friends should be left to the pregnant woman.

Advocates for the right of the fetus often show little empathy either for the pregnant women seeking an abortion or for the doctors and nurses who provide safe health care for these women. Having judged abortion to be a crime, these "pro-life" proponents dismiss the economic, emotional, and ethical difficulties that many pregnant women must face. Equally harsh is the moral assertion by some who defend abortion; that a woman has the right to make decisions about what happens to her own body, as if this right were absolute and should obviously determine the morality of terminating a pregnancy.

Concern for relationships may also include a sense of responsibility to God or to the teachings of a religious community. For a woman who believes each conception of life is a gift from God, considering an abortion is a spiritual as well as an ethical issue.

Rights

In chapter 7 we argued that all governments should act to secure the necessary social conditions for human dignity, and that this means protecting a patient's right to informed consent in receiving health care. These legal presumptions are reflected in laws that permit abortion under certain circumstances.

The *Roe* decision gives women in the United States a limited right to an abortion. Opponents of *Roe* assert that the fetus has a more fundamental right to life. Both legally and morally, the issue of abortion involves a conflict of rights.

International human rights law does not speak directly to the issue of abortion. The right to life is a human right, but there is no international standard defining when life begins or when the right to life should be given priority over a woman's right to privacy. Laws vary considerably from country to country, reflecting the strength of religious and cultural traditions.

International human rights law clearly affirms that women and men should be treated equally, and this argument may be used to support the moral presumption in China and India that prohibits abortion for the purpose of gender selection.

Consequences

Opponents of abortion argue that the consequences of permitting abortion are so horrendous that the practice should be illegal, as it once was. In the United States alone, they remind us, more than a million abortions are performed each year. Many pro-life advocates believe that permitting abortion is changing the *character* of our society and that the *consequences* will include a less caring response to the health needs of impaired newborns and the elderly.

Advocates for legal abortions assert that the consequences of criminalizing abortion would be even worse, as hundreds of thousands of women would have illegal abortions that would put their health at risk. In addition, health professionals who helped these women would be subject to criminal penalties, and the respect that people have for the rule of law would decline. In countries such as China and India that have difficulty feeding their people, pro-choice advocates add that abortion is needed to limit population growth.

In the controversy over abortion it seems reasonable to place the moral burden of proof on those who oppose existing laws, which state the present presumption of our public morality. In the United States this means those opposing abortion bear the burden of overturning this presumption. In countries in Latin America that prohibit abortion, however, pro-choice advocates have the burden of arguing that allowing abortion at least in some circumstances would result in more ethical consequences. Given that the right to have an abortion is not asserted as a human right under international law, we suggest that the evidence needed to overturn a moral and legal presumption need only be *convincing*.

We recognize that there are cases where either the pro-choice presumption, or the pro-life presumption, might be set aside, because of the possible dire consequences of acting on it. For instance, Catholics agree that a woman who is three months pregnant and has uterine cancer may morally choose to have the surgery that will save her life, even though this surgery will end the life of the fetus within her uterus. In the natural law tradition of ethics taught by the Catholic Church, the purpose of an action (saving a woman from cancer) and the action (surgery) must be morally good or indifferent. If there is a bad consequence (the death of the fetus), this must be unintended. Moreover, the good consequence (saving the woman's life) must be at least as important as the bad consequence (ending the life of the fetus). In ethics this is the principle of "double effect."[6]

Similarly, the right to abortion in the United States is a limited right, and the burden of proof to have an abortion in the third trimester of a woman's pregnancy is hard to meet. Conditions that some believe justify such an abortion include:

- When a pregnancy threatens the life of a woman.
- When a fetus has developed a severe defect.

- When the pregnant woman is a teenager or is using drugs.

In the third trimester the moral presumption under the law shifts to favor the life of the unborn child, and so the burden of proof to overturn this presumption must be met by the woman and her doctor.[7]

SAME-SEX MARRIAGE

Historically, marriage has been a socially sanctioned relationship between a man and one or more women. Polygamous relationships were permitted in ancient Israel, but the descendants of the Israelites, who we know as Jews, turned to monogamy. Christians have always opposed polygamy. Muslims, however, allow polygamy, as the Qur'an permits a man to marry up to four women as long as he treats each of his wives equally.

Throughout the world today, the moral presumption is that marriage is between a man and a woman. This is the view held by all religious traditions and is also the law in most jurisdictions. Now, however, there is a challenge to this presumption, primarily in Western societies. Some argue that to avoid discrimination and to provide equal rights under the law, same-sex marriage should be legalized. While we should expect a vigorous defense of traditional marriage, we should also listen carefully to those who assert that the standard of our public morality in this respect is not as high as it should be.

Duty

We affirm that each person has a duty to respect the human dignity of every other person. We need to consider what this might mean in the current debate over same-sex marriage.

Recently, Canada, the Netherlands, Belgium, and Spain[8] have changed their laws to permit same-sex marriage. The primary argument in favor of same-sex marriage is that excluding lesbian and gay couples from the legal benefits, as well as the legal and moral responsibilities of marriage, is discriminatory. Those who want the law to recognize same-sex marriage argue that everyone has a duty to ensure that our laws protect equal rights and promote nondiscrimination.

Those who oppose same-sex marriage claim a duty to defend the traditional understanding of marriage, arguing that it protects the sanctity of the family and also promotes a high standard of public morality.

Character

We have seen that the natural law and Tao traditions find the standard for public morality revealed in the way things actually are. Advocates for same-sex marriage make an analogous argument by relying on scientific evidence that sexual orientation is a genetic predisposition. If gay people are gay by nature—and are not simply making a choice—then the claim that same-sex couples should have equal protection is much stronger.

Some opponents of same-sex marriage argue that the law can provide for civil unions between gays and lesbians, which will fully protect their rights. So, there is no reason to change the legal definition of marriage. Proponents of same-sex marriage, however, assert that a civil union will not actually be recognized as equal to marriage, and thus will not solve the problem of discrimination against same-sex couples.

Relationships

David Brooks, a columnist for the *New York Times* who opposes homosexuality on the grounds that it violates biblical teachings, nonetheless supports laws that would allow homosexual couples to marry. "We should regard it as scandalous that two people could claim to love each other and not want to sanctify their love with marriage and fidelity."[9] The public should, he argues, not just tolerate same-sex marriage, but insist on it.

In stark contrast to his conservative colleagues, Brooks urges that the virtue of making and keeping our promises to one another, which is crucial for a high standard of public morality, should be expected of homosexual as well as heterosexual couples. He believes that changing our ethical presumption, by expanding the legal definition of marriage to include same-sex couples, would be best for our society.

Others disagree, claiming that such a change in the law would weaken the promises made and confirmed legally by the men and women who marry. This argument is also bolstered by religious traditions that claim marriage is a covenant with God as well as a covenant between a man and a woman.

Rights

International law assumes that marriage is between a man and a woman and deserves protection because of the human dignity of each person. Yet, nothing in international human rights law prohibits redefining marriage to include same-sex couples. International law defends the equal rights of women and men, and the right of parents to determine the religious training and education of their children. Legalizing same-sex marriage would not compromise either of these protections.

The legal status of marriage in the United States and most countries entitles a man and a woman to be married and to enjoy the rights and responsibilities of being spouses. These include tax benefits, inheritance rights, and the right to make medical and other legal decisions for a spouse who is incapacitated.

By the end of 2006, twenty-seven states in the United States had passed constitutional amendments prohibiting same-sex marriage. On the other hand, legislatures in the states of Vermont, Connecticut, and New Jersey have authorized civil unions—which provide the same rights as marriage—for same-sex couples.[10]

Consequences

Both those who are for same-sex marriage and those who are against it believe that consequence arguments support their positions. Supporters predict not only equal rights for same-sex couples, but also greater social acceptance of gays and children raised by same-sex couples. Opponents of same-sex marriage believe that the social institution of marriage will be undermined if same-sex marriage is accepted.

The moral presumption and social norm has long been that marriage is between a man and a woman, so it seems reasonable to claim that those who argue otherwise bear the burden of proof required to overturn this presumption. Yet, in 2003 the Massachusetts Supreme Judicial Court set aside this presumption by ruling that government attorneys failed to identify any adequate reason in the Massachusetts Constitution for denying same-sex couples the same rights guaranteed to married couples. The court said that denying same-sex couples the right to marry "is incompatible with the constitutional principles of respect for individual autonomy and equality under law."[11]

The present presumption that the state should only allow marriage between a man and a woman does not assert a human right, as defined by international law. Therefore, the burden of proof need only be *convincing* evidence that allowing same-sex marriage would strengthen rather than weaken our public morality. Given our society's commitment to nondiscrimination, our moral presumption should at least support a legal status of civil union with all the rights of marriage. As the human right to nondiscrimination is at stake, those who oppose the status of civil union for same-sex couples must show with *compelling* evidence that it would lead to more harm than good.

If the consequences of legalizing civil unions verify that same-sex couples actually have unequal rights, then we should change our moral presumption to support same-sex marriage. Granting same-sex couples the right to marry does not take away the right of a man and woman to marry, therefore expanding the moral presumption of marriage to include same-sex couples only requires a *convincing* burden of proof.

CAPITAL PUNISHMENT

Our approach to public morality asserts ethical presumptions and protects the right to dissent, because it affirms that our ethical presumptions are approximations of what is right and wrong, and so should be reviewed and perhaps revised as we weigh additional evidence and new arguments.

Retributive justice requires fair punishment, and the moral presumption is that fair punishment must be proportional to the crime committed. For premeditated murder, the death penalty continues to be seen by many as fair, and the US Supreme Court has ruled that capital punishment does not in and of itself violate the constitutional prohibition of "cruel and unusual punishment," if it is used only for the most heinous crimes. Most countries, however, have outlawed capital punishment, because it is widely believed that retributive justice does not require the death penalty and affirms a higher moral standard without it.

Duty

Proponents of the death penalty claim the government has a duty to protect society and to punish those who commit murder. Capital punishment is said to be a deterrent to crime—although there is no convincing evidence that this is so—but more importantly capital punishment is seen as just retribution for people who have committed murder. Supporters of the death penalty also argue that capital punishment is required to provide the justice that the victim's family and friends deserve.

While not prohibiting the death penalty, international law asserts that governments have a duty to restrict its use. The International Covenant on Civil and Political Rights states that capital punishment may be imposed only for the most serious crimes and prohibits the use of the death penalty on pregnant women and people who committed their crimes when they were less than eighteen years old. In addition, a government can only put a person to death after a final judgment by a competent court, and anyone sentenced to death has the right to seek a pardon.

Those opposed to the death penalty claim the government has a duty to ensure that no innocent person is put to death, and that there is no discrimination in the sentencing of those convicted of capital offenses. Citing evidence that innocent people have been put to death and that discrimination has existed in the US criminal justice system, opponents of capital punishment argue that only by eliminating the death penalty will the government be able to fulfill its duty to protect innocent life.

Our ethical commitment to do our duty reflects a profound respect for the dignity of others. This respect must be clearly reflected in our laws and social institutions, and especially in our prisons and the criminal justice system, where administering retributive justice requires taking away the liberty of those who are convicted of serious crimes.

Character

We have seen that acting with the virtue of compassion, and not merely enforcing a just punishment according to the law, is often a way of expressing a higher moral standard. This is why the Catholic Church opposes capital punishment. Although many other Christians do not share this view, the image of Jesus being unjustly put to death on a cross is a powerful reminder that capital punishment may result in the execution of an innocent person.

Helen Prejean, a Catholic sister, began writing in 1982 to a convicted murderer on death row. She was repelled by his crime but believed in having compassion not only for the victims of violent crimes and their families, but also for those who commit these crimes. She did not have a *duty* to write to a man on death row, but chose nonetheless to offer him her friendship. He responded, and she discovered that he was not only a heinous criminal, but also a vulnerable human being.

That experience led her to write the book *Dead Man Walking*, which was later made into a Hollywood movie, and also to launch a campaign calling for a moratorium on all executions. Because of her private experience and her religious faith, she became a public advocate for legal reform. She writes:

> I have no doubt that we will one day abolish the death penalty in America. It will come sooner if people like me who know the truth about executions do our work well and educate the public. It will come slowly if we do not. Because, finally, I know that it is not a question of malice or ill will or meanness of spirit that prompts our citizens to support executions. It is, quite simply, that people don't know the truth of what is going on. That is not by accident. The secrecy surrounding executions makes it possible for executions to continue. I am convinced that if executions were

made public, the torture and violence would be unmasked,
and we would be shamed into abolishing executions.[12]

Helen Prejean appeals to the *character* and dignity of other citizens, who
would respond with the virtue of compassion, she believes, if they were to
have the same personal awareness that she has of what capital punishment
actually means.

Relationships

Under apartheid in South Africa the police and the army killed many innocent people, often after torturing them. Yet, instead of prosecuting those
charged with these offenses and seeking the death penalty for those found
guilty of crimes against humanity, the new government of South Africa
embraced a higher standard of public morality.

The new government established a Truth and Reconciliation Commission to carry out three tasks:

- A committee investigated the human rights abuses that
  had occurred under apartheid and verified the claims of
  victims to ensure that there was sufficient evidence to
  pursue any criminal charge.
- A second committee made recommendations for public
  policies and for restitution to victims and their surviving
  family members.
- A third committee heard requests for amnesty, which
  was offered to those who publicly admitted violating the
  human rights of others and expressed remorse for their
  actions.

This was a remarkable attempt to discover the truth and foster reconciliation between those who had supported apartheid and their victims (and the
families of their victims). The commission acted on the moral presumption
that retributive justice, for all those guilty of enforcing apartheid laws, was
less important in the new South Africa than seeking truth and reconciliation.

The commission recognized that at least some of those who supported the government's policy of apartheid were not evil persons, but had acted unjustly because they feared for the future of their families and their society. The commission acted on the moral presumption that many of these individuals were capable of repentance, and also of being reconciled to those they had previously seen as enemies.

In addition, the commission encouraged the families of those who were tortured or killed under apartheid not to demand vengeance, but to honor their loved ones for their righteous suffering by supporting a public process of healing. The commission asked black South Africans to waive their right to demand retribution for their losses, including the death penalty for murder, in order to try to reconcile black and white South Africans.[13]

The initial results of this experiment in public morality have been remarkable, and South Africa has been able to move forward under the leadership of the African National Congress without the bloodletting that has followed most other social revolutions. Yet, we will not know the full consequences of this experiment for at least several decades.

Rights

All people have the right to expect not only that the government will try to prevent a violation of their security, but also that the government will punish those who commit such a violation. The victims of crime and their loved ones have a right to demand a lawful penalty for those held responsible.

Just retribution is punishment that is proportional to the crime committed. Punishment that is too severe would be considered an act of vengeance, and both procedural and substantive rights afforded the accused by law are intended to prevent such excessive punishment.

Punishment that is too light with respect to the wrong done may undermine the authority of the government and lead to vigilante acts by those who believe justice has not been done. Supporters of the death penalty argue that any punishment short of death for murderers fails to satisfy the society's proper demand for *just* retribution.

Yet, the experience of South Africa is evidence that a higher standard of public morality is possible. After the end of apartheid the new government in South Africa choose to pursue a reconciled society by urging the victims of apartheid to forego their right to seek retribution—at least for those individuals who confessed to their wrongdoing and expressed remorse. Without the support of a majority of South Africans, the efforts of the Truth and Reconciliation Commission would have been impossible.

Helen Prejean argues that making *truth* our goal, and not only just punishment, would increase support for ending the death penalty.[14] We add that truth should also be our goal, as we try to understand the reasons for criminal conduct and how best to help offenders live more responsibly after they complete their sentences and are released from prison.

Consequences

Those who continue to support capital punishment claim that prohibiting it would have adverse consequences, as this change would remove a major deterrent to premeditated murder.[15] There is no convincing evidence, however, for this claim. The counterargument is that a well-informed public would no longer demand the death penalty, but instead would accept as fair punishment either life in prison without parole or even a long prison sentence. Greater awareness of the causes of crime and more effective assistance for those recently released from prison, as they reenter society, may result in reducing both crime and recidivism. All these claims, however, remain unverified.

Which side of this argument should bear the burden of proof? US law allows the moral presumption that the death penalty may be a proportionate punishment for the crime of murder. As this issue does not involve setting aside a human right under international law, only *convincing* evidence would be required to change this moral presumption. In the United States those opposed to capital punishment should accept that they have to meet this burden of proof.

In most other nations, the law prohibits the use of the death penalty. In these countries advocates for capital punishment must show with convincing evidence that reintroducing the death penalty would result in a more just society.

RAISING OUR STANDARDS

The rule of law is the means by which we agree to disagree. It asserts moral presumptions, protects dissent, and encourages open debate about improving the moral standards of the law.

As no one is above the law, no one should have the power to put an end to public advocacy. Therefore, our ethical debate takes place in political contests, in the freedom of religious communities to promote their moral positions, in lobbying elected officials, in the freedom of the press to search out and publish information, and in the courts that enforce the law. We all have a duty to ensure that each citizen has an equal opportunity to exercise these rights, for this is how we maintain and try to raise our standards of public morality.

We have reviewed arguments about abortion, same-sex marriage, and capital punishment to see how the presumptions of public morality are affirmed, resisted, and may be revised.

As long as abortion is legal, it is important that a pregnant woman consider the ethical implications of abortion as well the legal options available to her, so that she is well informed if she chooses, in good conscience, to seek an abortion. Also, the life of a woman must be protected when her pregnancy is life threatening.

The ethical presumption that marriage is between a man and a woman should not easily be set aside, as it is rooted in centuries of history and also is supported by the teachings of several major religious traditions. Yet, our commitment to the human right of equal opportunity, and also the clear evidence that our present marriage laws discriminate against gay and lesbian couples, suggest that we have a duty to make a change in our public morality.

In addition, we should encourage young people, whether straight or gay, to enter into committed relationships, to solemnize these publicly, and to be faithful in their vows. Keeping promises is good not only for couples, but also for the entire society.

Therefore, either we should support legalizing a civil union with the same rights and responsibilities as marriage, or expand the legal definition of marriage so a same-sex couple has the same right to marry as a man and a woman.

Evidence that a number of people have been unfairly or mistakenly sentenced to death and executed weighs heavily against the use of the death penalty. Moreover, the need to encourage rehabilitation and not only punishment for crimes is a good reason for ending capital punishment and applying our resources to crime prevention, job training, and programs to help those who have paid their debt to society return to our communities.

Therefore, dissent against capital punishment, especially when it is motivated by a commitment to achieving greater truth and reconciliation in society, seems worthy of our support.

DOING ETHICS TOGETHER

I. Is abortion right?

1. State the moral presumption of US law under *Roe* and *Casey*. Give a reason in support of this presumption, and also a reason for opposing it.

2. The law as defined by *Roe* and *Casey* does not distinguish between a woman who is pregnant because she was raped and a woman who is pregnant because she did not use a contraceptive. Are there reasons for distinguishing the moral choices in these two instances? Explain your thinking.

3. Give a moral argument supporting laws in China and India that prohibit informing a pregnant woman of the gender of her fetus. Would this restriction on abortion be legal under the standard of *Roe* and *Casey*? Explain your answer.

II. Should same-sex marriage be allowed?

1. A student of one of the authors wrote on an exam: "Marriage is a private decision, so it shouldn't matter whether a couple is straight or gay. The government should butt out." How would you explain that the government has a duty with respect to marriage?

2. Give one reason for opposing same-sex marriage and another reason for supporting it. Argue for or against creating the legal status of civil union as an alternative to legalizing same-sex marriage.

3. Public morality requires tolerance for different views. When a society is deeply divided over a moral issue, what expectations should we have for the rule of law?

III. *Does justice require capital punishment?*

1. Give a reason for supporting the moral presumption that the death penalty should be abolished, and a reason for continuing its use. If a person commits a capital crime, but expresses profound remorse before being sentenced, should this affect the sentence? Explain your thinking.

2. How do you assess the possible consequences of continuing to use the death penalty in the United States? Of abolishing its use? How would you weigh these possible consequences?

3. Which side of the debate over capital punishment should have the moral presumption? Explain your thinking.

11

Health Care

LIFE AND DEATH

Health care is fraught with moral issues. Is prenatal care for pregnant women adequate and accessible? Should organs be harvested after death and, if so, how are these scarce resources to be allocated among those who would benefit from them? How are we to pay for the health care we want and need? And who is to decide?

In the voting booth we make ethical decisions about health care, because elected officials have considerable control over our hospitals, clinics, and government-supported health care programs. Everywhere politicians are embroiled in contentious debates about the priorities for health care, the use of public resources, access to health care facilities, etc.

With few exceptions, issues in health care concern *distributive justice*. As health care is usually expensive, we must decide not only who will receive what care but also how the cost of this care is to be distributed within our society.

To ensure distributive justice we should abide by the rule of law, act on our duty, aspire to be virtuous, make decisions with others, and safeguard human rights. Health care professionals have a duty to do no harm as they seek to provide the best care they can. We also expect health care providers to act in a caring manner, as effective health care requires a trusting relationship between patients and those caring for them.

In an effort to meet these ethical expectations, the American Nurses' Association promotes a *Code for Nurses* that includes the following presumptions:

- The nurse in all professional relationships, practices with compassion and respect for the inherent dignity, worth, and uniqueness of every individual, unrestricted by consideration of social or economic status, personal attributes, or the nature of health problems.
- The nurse promotes, advocates for, and strives to protect the health, safety, and rights of the patient.
- The nurse owes the same duties to self as to others, including the responsibility to preserve integrity and safety, to maintain competence, and to continue personal and professional growth.[1]

To construct presumptions concerning distributive justice in providing health care, we first consider what duty requires, what our character aspirations should be, how relationships can be sustained and even strengthened in providing health care, and what human rights should be protected and promoted. Then we weigh the likely consequences of acting on our moral presumptions.

INFORMED CONSENT

Until quite recently, traditional health care left all the decisions to the doctor. After all, the doctor was the expert and had a clear professional duty to provide the best health care available to every patient.

Now, however, a doctor must adequately inform a patient about the recommended treatment, as every patient has the right to give informed consent.

Medical experiments on prisoners conducted by the Nazis during World War II were judged as war crimes by the Nuremberg Military Tribunals held after the war, and out of this public legal process came a set of princi-

ples concerning "Permissible Medical Experiments."[2] The first of these
principles requires the consent of all those subjected to medical experiments, and this principle has been extended beyond medical research to
every aspect of health care.

The right to consent implies an additional duty for health care professionals, which the Nuremberg principles also make explicit. Today, informed consent is a legal and ethical presumption in health care.
Therefore, health care providers have a duty to inform each patient of the
reasons for recommending a particular treatment and the possible risks,
dangers, and side effects of the recommended treatment. The health care
provider is also required to discuss other ways of treating a patient's condition. A patient has the right to be adequately informed in this way so he or
she can voluntarily consent to the recommended treatment, or another
treatment option altogether.

This is a profound change from the paternalistic presumption that doctors should simply provide the care they believe is best, and it reflects the
growing emphasis in contemporary public morality on personal autonomy. Pluralistic and democratic societies not only give voters the right to
choose their leaders, but also presume that people have the right to make
decisions about what forms of health care are in their best interests.

The case of Donald Cowart powerfully illustrates this transformation in
medical ethics. Severely burned in 1973 by an exploding propane transmission line, Cowart refused treatment for his burns because the treatment
caused excruciating pain. The right to informed consent, however, was not
yet widely recognized, and his doctors did not listen to him. They believed
it was their professional duty to treat his burns. Were Cowart to be injured
today, as he was in 1973, the doctors treating him would have a duty to obtain his informed consent in order to treat his injuries.

To verify the ethical presumption of informed consent we might ask
whether this principle is supported by the concerns we have addressed
with respect to character and relationships. Trusting patients to make
their own choices encourages them to be more responsible for their own
health and requires humility on the part of physicians. It recognizes the

autonomy of a patient and also the patient's relationships. If a patient is unable to provide informed consent, family members are given the responsibility of acting on the patient's behalf.

Because informed consent involves a human right as defined in international law, the burden of proof to overcome this presumption should be *compelling* evidence that the consequences of not allowing informed consent would be much better than allowing it.

Are there consequence arguments that might meet this burden? The Cowart case offers a striking example. Although blind and disfigured, Cowart survived, received a large cash settlement, married, became a lawyer, and is now an advocate for the rights of patients. Thus, the benefits of disregarding his consent seem to outweigh the adverse consequences of ending his treatment.

Yet, Cowart maintains that the satisfying life he now enjoys does not overcome the moral and legal presumption that the patient has the right to decide, and Cowart continues to affirm that the pain he suffered was reason enough for allowing him to refuse treatment and die. He argues, therefore, that his experience does not undermine the ethical presumption that informed consent should be required for all medical treatment, but instead verifies it.[3]

RESOURCES

The demand for health care resources often exceeds the supply of these resources. More doctors and nurses can be educated, more hospitals can be built, more drugs and more equipment can be manufactured. Nonetheless, there are two reasons why the supply will likely never equal the demand. First, the more health care we have, the more we want. Second, as a society, we are unwilling to pay for all the heath care that we want.

For instance, if your kidneys were to fail, you would want a kidney transplant. Certainly, that would be preferable to being hooked up to a dialysis machine a few times each week. Of course, both procedures are fantastic improvements in health care that were unavailable to those who lived before the latter part of the twentieth century, but neither procedure is available to everyone who has kidney failure, because each is expensive.

In the United States more than three hundred thousand people are receiving dialysis paid for by Medicare, a federal health insurance program for the elderly. The cost is about one hundred thousand dollars per year per patient or more than ten billion dollars annually, which is more than four times the cost that was projected when the decision was made to cover dialysis under Medicare. Furthermore, the number of patients needing dialysis is increasing by fifty thousand a year. Transplants cost less per person, but there are not enough available kidneys for all those who need a transplant.

This dilemma is not the result of any wrongdoing, so the ethical issue simply concerns distributive justice. Health care professionals have a duty to care that includes providing dialysis or kidney transplants to patients with kidney failure. Moreover, patients have a human right to health care under international law, and where that right is not recognized legally, as in the United States, it is nonetheless asserted morally. We certainly aspire to be the kind of society that provides dialysis and kidney transplants and, as individuals, we want this not only for ourselves, if we need such medical treatment, but for others as well.

Our moral presumption, therefore, is that a scarce and expensive resource should be made available in a fair way to those who need it and will benefit from it. If the duty to provide equitable care for everyone cannot be met because of scarce resources, then a fair selection process should be used.

Transplants

With respect to selecting patients to receive organ transplants, we suggest that it would be fair to:

- Use medical criteria to create a list of potential recipients who are sufficiently healthy to survive the operation and benefit from it.

- Rank the patients on the list by a random or a first-come-first-served procedure.
- Give priority to those on the list who more urgently need a transplant.[4]

We oppose selecting recipients for organ transplants using "social worth" criteria, a process that favors patients who are deemed to be of greater value to the community, because we do not believe such a judgment can be made in a nondiscriminatory way.

Ethical issues also arise with the donation of organs. In most places, the ethical presumption is that what happens to a patient's body after death is up to the patient or, if the patient did not make this clear before dying, is up to the closest relative. In some European countries, however, the moral presumption is exactly the opposite. Harvesting organs from bodies is permitted unless, before death, a patient explicitly opts out.

We probably all agree that there ought to be a public debate about how best to harvest and distribute such scarce resources. We may also agree that a particular way of allocating organs, such as a random selection process, should be seen as an ethical presumption, which might be overcome by convincing evidence that the probable adverse consequences exceed the expected benefits.

Permitting the sale of organs would increase the supply available for transplants, however most countries prohibit this because public opinion opposes the buying and selling of body parts. The sale of organs has begun, however, in India and elsewhere, and in countries that make the practice illegal a black market is operating.

A market for organs will pressure poor people to sell their organs simply to support their families. Given our commitment to upholding the moral character of our society, we should look for a way of providing organs for transplantation without exploiting the poor.

Stem Cell Research

Stem cell research also involves ethical issues concerning the use of resources. Prior to differentiating, embryonic stem cells have the potential to become any specialized cell in the body. Once separated from an embryo, stem cells can be cultured so they reproduce. Using stem cells, scientists expect to be able to grow tissue and organs that can be transplanted.

Those who believe embryos are human persons oppose stem cell research that involves obtaining stem cells by destroying embryos. They see this procedure as a form of premeditated murder. Therefore, from their moral perspective, stem cell research raises issues of retributive justice. On the other hand, those who believe embryos are not human persons argue that medical scientists have a duty to use stem cells in research, which will likely result in better treatments for many patients. Advocates of stem cell research deny that there is any wrongdoing in obtaining stem cells from embryos that will never be implanted in a woman's uterus and will probably be destroyed.

At the end of 2006, the ethical presumption in the United States concerning stem cell research was defined by a presidential policy that restricts federal funding for stem cell research to established stem cell lines. The United Kingdom, South Korea, and several other countries have fewer restrictions, and so research in these countries on new stem cell lines is proceeding. There has been little progress on a United Nations treaty that was drafted to resolve the ethical and legal issues involved in stem cell research.

As the ethical presumption asserted by a presidential policy does not involve a human right under international law, we suggest that the burden of proof for overturning it is only *convincing* evidence that this would lead to more beneficial consequences. Those who favor putting greater emphasis on stem cell research make a consequential argument that the possible benefits far outweigh any likely adverse outcomes. Supporters of the present policy claim that even if there would be substantial benefits in health care, these would be morally tainted by the killing of embryos required in the research used to achieve these beneficial results.

ACCESS

Access to health care is more than a matter of getting to the hospital. In the United States access involves qualifying for private insurance, or qualifying for a health care program sponsored by the government, or being able to pay for health care with cash. Access to health care involves ethical issues of distributive justice.

In Canada any person can access adequate health care, because Canada recognizes health care as a human right and provides universal coverage. The cost of providing health care for everyone in Canada is paid by taxes. Ronald Munson writes:

> Various objective measures of health care show that the Canadian system has been successful. The infant mortality rate of 7.1 per 1,000 live births is superior to the US rate of 8.9. The Canadian life expectancy is 78.6 years (from 1997), while life expectancy in the United States is 76.5 years. Cost control also has been successful under the plan. In 1999, Canada spent about 9.3 percent of its national income for medical care; the United States spent 13.1 percent. In 1971, the year Canadian Medicare became universal, the proportions were 7.3 and 7.4 respectively. This suggests that the Canadians have been able to provide both universal coverage and high-quality care, while successfully controlling costs.[5]

In the United States almost a third of the population does not have health insurance, and half of those not covered are children or families with children. Taxes pay only for the Medicaid program for the destitute and the Medicare program for the elderly, and perhaps also for health care programs run by state governments to extend Medicaid coverage to more of the working poor and their children. About half of the poor in America, according to federal standards, are ineligible for Medicaid, because they have more assets than the very low level that Medicaid allows and thus do not meet the eligibility requirement for the program. Those who do not qualify for these programs must cover their health care costs either by obtaining health insurance through their employer, buying a private health insurance policy, or paying for their medical expenses out of pocket.

International human rights law defines health care as one of the necessary social conditions for human dignity, and the ICESCR requires governments to provide health services to the extent that they are financially able
to do so. Even US citizens opposed to universal health care acknowledge
that the United States should be a place where every person can obtain adequate medical treatment. Empathy compels us to support this view.
Nonetheless, the United States has yet to embody in law the ethical presumption that health care is a human right.

The present US system of health care invests more in new technology
than Canada, and therefore provides specialized medical services to a
greater number of people. The Canadian system, however, has lower administrative costs, covers people when they change jobs and locations, and
provides care for every man, woman, and child in Canada. Per capita,
Canadians spend half as much as Americans on health care. Canada has
one hundred primary-care or family-practice doctors per one hundred
thousand people, whereas the United States has twenty. US doctors' fees
are twice the fees in Canada, but nonetheless the income of Canadian doctors is about two-thirds of US doctors because the Canadian physicians see
more patients. In Canada patients do not make copayments, fill out claim
forms, or wait for reimbursement. They simply present an identification
card to access health care.

Canadians strongly support their health care system, but a poll in 2000
of three thousand Canadians found that 93 percent felt improving health
care should be the government's top priority. In another survey, 74 percent
of those polled felt introducing user fees would reduce the waiting time for
specialized services. Some affluent Canadians come to the United States to
pay cash and quickly obtain specialized services such as MRIs, chemother-
apy, hip replacements, and heart bypass or prostrate surgery. Some Americans purchase their prescription drugs in Canada to benefit from lower
prices.

Canada has ratified the International Covenant on Economic, Cultural
and Social Rights, and thus accepts its responsibilities under this covenant
to provide adequate health care for all those within its borders. The United

States has not ratified this covenant, but the *moral* argument behind international human rights law is no less compelling.

Arguments based on the *duty* of health care professionals and the human rights of patients support the moral presumption that health care should be made available to everyone, in the US and elsewhere. As Americans seek to be a caring people, a concern for *character* reinforces this ethical presumption.

Who should bear the burden of proof in this debate? Those who support a health care system more like the single-payer Canadian system? Or, those who defend the present US approach to health care?

Because health care is a human right in most parts of the world, we suggest that national health care should be our moral presumption and that the champions of private health care bear the burden of proof required to set this presumption aside. As this presumption asserts the human right to health care, the burden of proof to overturn it should require *compelling* evidence.

TERMINATIONS

In textbooks on medical ethics the word *termination* describes abortions, decisions to withhold care from impaired newborns, and euthanasia. These decisions raise questions of wrongdoing, because the care denied or given is intended to cause a patient's death. In chapter 10 we discussed the issue of abortion. Here we consider the ethical issues concerning impaired newborns and euthanasia (which, in health care debates, is generally characterized as "physician-assisted suicide").

Impaired Newborns

Impaired newborns include babies with birth defects such as Down syndrome, Spina bifida, hydrocephaly (fluid on the brain), anencephaly (without a brain), and premature infants. Fifteen years ago newborns that weighed under a pound and a half rarely survived, but new technology has raised the survival rate to 50 percent. Nevertheless, up to a third of these surviving infants have irreversible neurological damage. A study of siblings in 2000 revealed that almost 60 percent of those with normal birth weights graduated from high school, whereas only about 15 percent of their low-birth-weight siblings graduated.

The ethical issue with impaired newborns arises when either the parents or the physician believe it would be best to allow a baby to die. Arguments against allowing an impaired newborn infant to die, by withholding treatment required to prolong life, rely on two of the strongest ethical presumptions in medicine: a duty to care for every patient, and the right to life of every person.

In the 1980s in the United States the administration of President Ronald Reagan required hospitals receiving federal funds to display a poster in the pediatric ward stating that "discrimination" against handicapped infants violated federal law. In addition, the US Health and Human Services Department was required to take "immediate remedial action" to protect newborns.

This "Baby Doe" regulation was implemented as an amendment to the Child Abuse Prevention and Treatment Act passed by Congress in October 1985. The regulation prohibited "medical neglect," which was defined as the "withholding of medically indicated treatment from a disabled infant with a life-threatening condition," and mandated state child protection agencies to determine if infants were victims of medical neglect.[6]

The Baby Doe regulation created a legal and moral presumption to provide care for all impaired infants, and put the burden of proof on withholding treatment. In effect, the regulation took the ethical decision about the care of a newborn away from parents and their doctors.

In 1986 the US Supreme Court struck down the Baby Doe regulation, ruling that the federal government had no legal basis for intervening in a decision that should be left to parents and physicians. The court did not rule on what standard should be used for treating impaired infants, but left that ethical decision to those who have traditionally made it.

The ethical presumption in this Supreme Court decision reaffirms the autonomous right of parents, but recognizes as well the duty of physicians to inform parents of the options for treating an impaired infant and the likely outcome of a possible treatment.

Those who support a mother's decision to withdraw treatment from an impaired newborn often argue that the negative impact of the child on the "quality of life" of the family justifies allowing the child to die. Those who defend the right of the child to live usually argue that the decision should be based on "the best interest of the child," a standard that only considers the likely health of the child. These two approaches are variations of the utilitarian argument that looks at possible consequences to decide what action should be taken.

An alternative view asserts that newborns with profound neurological impairment are not "persons" with full rights, but instead are only "potential persons." This approach is not based on calculating consequences, but instead revises the way we assess the rights and duties involved in deciding whether to terminate treatment for an impaired infant.

Hospitals and insurance companies have also raised issues about the cost of treating impaired newborns. We may aspire to be a society that cares for every newborn no matter what the cost, but doing ethics also requires a concern for the principle of proportionality. It costs over three thousand dollars a day in a US hospital to sustain the life of a low-birth-weight infant, and often the care for a particular infant will exceed five hundred thousand dollars.

In the United States these costs for uninsured and unemployed women are paid for by the Medicaid program, which receives funds from both state and federal governments. To limit the accelerating cost of Medicaid, many states have assigned a low priority to providing intensive care for low-birth-weight newborns.

Despite their support for the right to life, Roman Catholics have not challenged such a low priority. Natural law requires only *ordinary care* and not the use of extraordinary measures. By ordinary care, Catholic ethicists mean "all medicines, treatments, and operations which offer a reasonable hope of benefit for the patient and which can be obtained and used without excessive expense, pain, or other inconvenience."[7] The Catholic position incorporates an estimate of likely consequences into its ethical presumption in support of the right to life. The intention must always be to preserve life, but the means used are limited to ordinary measures.

Euthanasia

The word *euthanasia* comes from the Greek for "good death." The ethical issues facing health care professionals concern assisted euthanasia, which is generally referred to as "physician-assisted suicide" to put the onus of the decision on the patient.

In the 1990 case *Cruzan v. Director, DMH,* the US Supreme Court held that the right to die was a liberty right protected by the US Constitution. To be consistent in upholding the right of patients to give informed consent for their treatment, patients must also have the right to refuse medical care that they do not want. Therefore, under the *Cruzan* ruling, dying patients (or families acting on their behalf) have the right to have feeding tubes and IVs removed. Furthermore, with the informed consent of a patient, physicians have the right to increase pain medication as needed by a patient, even though it may shorten the patient's life. This practice is known as comfort care.[8]

In 1997 in *Washington v. Glucksberg* the US Supreme Court reaffirmed the *Cruzan* decision, but did not rule on the constitutionality of assisted suicide. In the United States more than twenty state legislatures have passed laws prohibiting assisted suicide; only the state of Oregon has legalized physician-assisted suicide.

Two arguments are often given in support of physician-assisted suicide. The first is based on the principle of autonomy. If a patient wants to die, some suggest, isn't a physician by assisting merely carrying out the wishes of the patient? The problem with this argument is that it would apply to anyone, terminally ill or not, who asked for help in committing suicide. Under criminal law, however, such an act constitutes murder. The public morality of our society does not accept that the right of autonomy includes a right to commit suicide, or the right of a person to help someone commit suicide.

The second argument in support of physician-assisted suicide is that helping a patient commit suicide is no different than withdrawing treatment, as the consequence (death) is the same. This argument ignores the established distinction in both ethics and law between committing an act and omitting an act. For example, not rescuing a drowning person is easily distinguished from holding a person under water, even though in both cases death is the likely result. Unless ethical decision making is merely consequentialist, which the authors do not recommend, it does matter whether we cause adverse consequences or they simply happen.

The Dutch Law

In 2000 the Dutch Parliament legalized physician-assisted suicide by lethal injection. The law requires that patients who are requesting euthanasia with a physician's assistance demonstrate that they are competent, have a clear understanding of their prognosis, and have been informed of alternatives. In addition, a patient must be terminal, be suffering unbearably, the doctor must have consulted with at least one other physician, and termination must be done using proper medical procedures.

Do the consequences of the Dutch law substantiate the ethical presumption favoring physician-assisted suicide or call it into question? In 1990 about 9,000 requests for euthanasia were reported, but there were only 2,300 deaths by voluntary euthanasia using a lethal injection and 400 other cases of assisted suicide.[9] Many Dutch physicians, however, are unwilling to assist patients in taking their lives, and the Royal Dutch Medical Association has formally raised concerns. In addition, critics assert that there have been more than a thousand cases of involuntary euthanasia in the Netherlands.[10]

The Dutch law does not recognize a right to euthanasia but does protect a physician, who assists in a suicide, against criminal penalties. Physicians may choose to refuse a request by a patient, even if the patient meets the conditions established by law. In addition, the law does not cover patients suffering from dementia, as they are presumed to be incapable of giving informed consent.

Finally, because citizens of the Netherlands have universal health coverage, a decision to request assistance in committing suicide is unlikely to be influenced by economic considerations, as neither the patient nor the family stands to gain economically by an earlier death. In the United States, however, where the cost of health care may fall heavily on many dying patients as well as their families, this possibility should be considered where physician-assisted suicide is practiced, as in Oregon.

The Oregon Law

The Oregon Death with Dignity Act does not sanction lethal injection, but does allow a physician to assist in a suicide by prescribing for a dying patient medication that can cause death, and explaining how the medication can be taken to achieve that end. Two physicians must confirm that the patient has less than six months to live and is competent, and the patient must make a written request for assistance in committing suicide two weeks after making two oral requests.

In its 2006 *Gonzales v. Oregon* decision, the US Supreme Court ruled that the federal Controlled Substances Act did not give the US Attorney General authority to prosecute doctors who were prescribing drugs under the Oregon statute. The court also reaffirmed that under the federal system of law in the United States the regulation of health care is primarily a state responsibility.[11]

As voluntary euthanasia does not involve a human right, only *convincing* evidence should be required to overcome the moral presumption that physician-assisted suicide either should be permitted or should be illegal.

Critics of the Oregon law argue that it makes doctors complicit in the morally wrong act of suicide, but defenders of the statute assert that ethically it is no different than responding to a patient's request for comfort care when death is near. Citizens of Oregon who oppose the Oregon law also complain that the state has to absorb the costs of implementing the law for residents on Medicaid, as federal law does not permit payments for physician-assisted suicide. Supporters of the law point out that the statute has not led to many requests, and thus the financial impact is negligible. In 1997 a referendum on the law received the support of sixty percent of the citizens of Oregon who voted.

Comfort Care

There is broad support in most countries for the moral presumption that comfort care requested by a patient should be provided, even if it may shorten a patient's life. The American Medical Association (AMA) rejects physician-assisted suicide, but embraces the natural law position on pain management. In 1996, Lonnie R. Bristow, as president of the AMA, made the following statement:

> For most patients, advancements in palliative care can ade-
> quately control pain through oral medications, nerve blocks,
> or radiotherapy. We all recognize, however, that there are pa-
> tients whose intractable pain cannot be relieved by treating
> the area, organ, or system perceived as the source of the pain.
> For patients for whom pain cannot be controlled by other
> means, it is ethically permissible for physicians to administer
> sufficient levels of controlled substances to ease pain, even if
> the patient's risk of addiction or death is increased.[12]

Not all states have developed clear guidelines for providing comfort care, but federal court decisions make it clear that drugs administered under these circumstances do not constitute physician-assisted suicide, because the drugs are administered with the purpose of relieving pain and therefore any hastening of death is an unintended consequence.

The position of the AMA is that allowing physician-assisted suicide will lead to dire consequences. The New York State Task Force on Life and the Law came to a similar conclusion, because "[a]ssisted suicide and euthana-sia will be practiced through the prism of social inequality and prejudice that characterizes the delivery of services in all segments of society, includ-ing health care."[13]

These same dangerous consequences, however, are not attributed to comfort care. Bristow affirms that: "The physician has an obligation to provide for the comfort of the patient. If there are no alternatives but to in-crease the risk of death in order to provide that comfort, the physician is ethically permitted to exercise that option."[14]

The moral presumptions concerning health care that we have consid-ered in this chapter include the following.

Health care professionals have a duty to:

- Do no harm and to provide the best care they can.
- Inform patients adequately of their health care options.
- Have compassion and respect for their patients.

Patients have a right to:

- Health care where the ICESCR is enforced.
- Be adequately informed in order to give informed consent for their care.
- Determine, as parents of an impaired newborn, the level of health care.
- End, when near death, any artificial means of keeping them alive.
- Receive, when dying and in pain, the comfort care they need and request.

———————

DOING ETHICS TOGETHER

I. *Resuscitating impaired infants.*

1. Give a reason for or against allowing the parents of an impaired infant to decide whether or not to resuscitate the child. Do you think the hospital should have a policy that presumes infants are not to be resuscitated when their prognosis for survival is only 50–50? Explain your reasoning.
2. Should "the best interest of the child" or the "quality of life" standard be used to decide if an impaired infant should be resuscitated? Explain the main difference between these two standards.
3. Should the federal government promulgate rules that would mandate when a newborn infant should be resuscitated? Why or why not?

II. *Organ donations for transplantation.*

1. If the demand for organs exceeds the supply, what decision-making process would you recommend to ensure that organs are fairly distributed?
2. Explain why in most countries it is against the law to sell a harvested organ. Do you find this ethical argument persuasive?
3. Should the law presume a person's organs are available for harvesting if the person who dies has not indicated otherwise? Or, should it presume organs are not to be harvested unless a person has authorized the donation? Explain your thinking.

III. *Access to health care.*

1. Give three reasons for arguing that the Canadian health care system is better than the US system. Explain your thinking.
2. Explain why the cost of medical care poses an ethical issue. In the United States who should make decisions about distributing health care fairly? Hospitals and Health maintenance organizations? Health insurance companies? State legislatures? Congress?
3. Is it fair to have programs like Medicaid and Medicare that involve federal spending on health care for some but not all Americans? Explain your reasoning.

IV. *Should voluntary euthanasia be a criminal offense?*

1. Identify three conditions in the Dutch law allowing physician-assisted suicide that guard against its abuse.
2. What does the Oregon Death with Dignity Act allow a physician to do? Give an argument supporting this law,

and an argument opposing it. Is either argument based on likely consequences?

3. Why is comfort care for a dying patient an ethical issue? Explain why the Catholic Church supports comfort care.

12

Sex

CONSENT PLUS WHAT?

Sex is part of our nature, but culture determines the legal and moral bounds of our sexual expression. In our pluralistic society there is more freedom than ever before, yet public debate about the morality of sexual expression continues.

At stake are laws and regulations concerning marriage, criminal acts of rape and harassment, the availability of birth control, gay sex, the limits of free expression in all the media, public funding for the arts, restrictions on pornography, social policies concerning prostitution, and sex education in public schools.

In this chapter we will consider sex primarily as an issue of public morality. What we say will concern private acts involving sex with others, but our focus will be the social impact of private conduct and arguments concerning public policy and the law.

Again, we begin by describing the norms of our public morality and the moral presumptions of the law, before asking if we should have higher moral aspirations.

RELIGION AND CULTURE

We are all shaped by our culture, and our culture is influenced by religious and moral traditions. In many traditional cultures, including the cultures in which the Jewish, Christian, and Muslim scriptures were written, marriage has been understood as a divinely sanctioned agreement between two families, not a personal decision made by a man and a woman. In most traditional societies marriage precedes sex and then, perhaps, is followed by love.

As the rights and feelings of individuals became more important in Western culture, the order changed to love, marriage, and then sex. Today, however, the order for many couples is sex, love, and then, perhaps, marriage. Moreover, about half of those who marry will later choose to divorce.

In addition to changing beliefs within various religious and cultural traditions, recent immigrants have brought diverse religious and cultural practices about sex and marriage into our Western societies. Today, the view of sex and marriage varies greatly from community to community and from individual to individual within our cities and on our university campuses.

No one disputes that moral presumptions about sex are in flux, but there are conflicting views as to what this means. To sort out the ethical issues concerning sex, we consider moral presumptions that reflect our duty, character aspirations, relationships, and rights before predicting the consequences of acting on these presumptions.

In most religious and cultural traditions the moral expectations about sex are expressed in the language of *duty*. A man and woman to be married have a duty first to their families, and then a duty to one another. Sex is one of the moral obligations of marriage, for a new marriage is to produce offspring for the extended family. Within marriage, men and women may be required to refrain from sex at certain times, such as when a woman is having her menstrual period or on particular holidays.

Those who are not married in most traditional societies have a duty to refrain from sex. Catholics and Buddhists also endorse communal forms of spiritual life, such as religious orders, monasteries, and convents, that impose a duty on participants to abstain from sex.

The sexual roles of men and women living in traditional societies are not only defined by duty, but by *character* expectations. Therefore, cultural changes liberating women (at least in some ways) from roles imposed on them in patriarchal societies have had an enormous impact on sexual relations. Nonetheless, the exploitation of women in advertising, pornography, and prostitution is evidence that patriarchal structures and attitudes in our pluralistic society continue to shape our conduct.

With a greater recognition of personal autonomy, the normative ethical presumption concerning sex has swung from affirming a duty to our families to assertions of our individual rights. In some societies this has been a moral revolution. Most Jews and Christians continue to affirm the last of the Ten Commandments, which forbids adultery. Yet, in Western societies there is no longer any legal penalty for those who engage in adultery.

Therefore, if the law is taken as stating the present ethical presumption about sex in Western pluralistic societies, our moral presumption seems to be that sex is a personal choice for individual men and women whether they are married or not.

Those who resist these revolutionary changes in sexual morality often do so not merely by defending tradition as expressing the commandments of God, but also by predicting the dire consequences that will follow the loss of patriarchal authority and its control over the rules governing marriage. Others, who have been empowered by laws guaranteeing their personal freedom, argue that the benefits of this change far outweigh any negative consequences.

Given the law, we suggest that those who argue for greater moral restraints on sex bear the burden of showing that the consequences of our present presumption favoring autonomy are more adverse than good, and sufficiently detrimental that our personal freedom should be restricted. As this moral presumption does not involve a human right under international law, the level of proof that these advocates must meet is merely *convincing* evidence.

CONSENSUAL

In our pluralistic and democratic societies we believe that sex must be consensual to be right. Even those who disagree about the morality of sex outside of marriage agree with the ethical presumption that nonconsensual sex is wrong.

Therefore, sexual ethics involves questions of retributive justice. Rape is a crime punishable by imprisonment, because it is nonconsensual sex. The law also holds an adult accountable for committing rape if he or she has sex with a child, for the legal presumption is that children cannot give consent to sex. Statutory rape laws define this crime by specifying the age below which a person is legally a child.

The emphasis on consent in sexual ethics is akin to the contemporary requirement for informed consent in medical ethics. Reasoning by analogy we may argue that if consent is required before a person entrusts his or her body to a physician for health care, then consent should be required before a couple engages in sex. The law in our pluralistic societies respects personal autonomy by protecting the right of adults to entrust their bodies to each other in sexual intimacy.

Given this moral presumption in pluralistic societies, the use of birth control, which was once proscribed by law, is now left to the discretion of individuals. In some countries, however, particularly where Muslims or Catholics are the majority of the population, there continue to be restrictions on the distribution of contraceptives and information about sex to minors.

Catholic Teaching

The Catholic Church is the most prominent advocate of the ethical presumption that opposes all forms of birth control, other than abstinence during the time a woman is fertile. The Catholic Church argues that artificial means of contraception violate natural law, because such methods are contrary to the divine purpose reflected both in the nature of human beings to procreate and in the institution of marriage revealed by God to the church.

In Catholic teaching married couples may refrain from sex to limit the number of children they have, according to their conscience; but husbands and wives have a duty to God, and to one another, to have sex in order to have children, "God willing."

Although the Catholic Church teaches that only consensual sex may be ethical, the church does *not* agree with the secular presumption that consent alone makes sex ethical. The church maintains that sexual intercourse is only ethical when it involves a married man and woman who consent, do not use methods of artificial contraception, and believe that sex is an expression of love.[1]

Act of Conscience

Many Jews and Muslims—as well as Christians other than Catholics and people from other religious traditions—agree that marriage is required for sex to be moral. Marriage manifests personal commitment, the consent of each person, and public recognition of their relationship. In addition, within these religious traditions marriage is celebrated as a divine institution and some of those who are religious affirm that sex within marriage is a spiritual as well as a physical act.

Of course, we do not have to be religious to believe that sex is more than a human need or a biological drive. Many of us know from experience that sex may offer a profound experience of intimacy and wonder. This is why we distinguish "casual sex" from "making love." Our moral presumption for making love is a much higher standard than for casual sex, as we expect not only consent but also mutual respect and personal commitment.

In this sense, whether we limit this expectation to marriage or not, our moral presumption ought to be that because sex is so significant, a person should be careful (in the sense of being full of care) in sharing this act of intimacy with someone else. Sex should be an act of conscience and a sharing of mutual respect and affection, not simply a "one-night stand."

The ethical presumption that consent is necessary for sex asserts a human right to protection under the law against bodily assault, so *compelling* evidence must be shown before setting this presumption aside. The added presumption that to be moral sex should be an act of conscience does not assert a human right under international law, but instead states an aspiration concerning our character and relationships. Therefore, in our approach to doing ethics, only *convincing* evidence of a better alternative would be required to overturn this presumption.

Consequences

As our moral presumption permitting access to contraceptives does not involve a human right under interenational law, the burden of proof to overturn it need only be a showing of *convincing* evidence that acting on another moral presumption would have more advantageous consequences. Those who promote abstinence outside of marriage and restricting access to birth control, at least among young people, argue that they can meet this burden of proof, but the evidence given to support this claim is not very convincing.

Of course, one can recommend abstinence outside of marriage and also support making contraceptives available to those who choose not to abstain, for there is no inconsistency in holding both positions. In fact, many Christians support the ABC approach to sex education, which promotes Abstinence, Being faithful, and then information on Condoms.

GAY SEX

A generation ago homosexual relations were illegal in most places, as public morality clearly reflected a consensus condemning homosexuality on the basis of religious teachings.

Jewish and Christian Scripture

Jews and Christians look to the beginning of their scriptures and find God creating a man and a woman as the first family. Genesis 1:27 reads: "So God created humankind in his image, in the image of God he created them; male and female he created them." Then, in Genesis 2:18 God is reported as saying: "It is not good that the man should be alone; I will make him a helper as his partner."

After making all the animals, the story relates, God discovers that none of them is "a helper" fit to be man's partner. So, God puts the man to sleep, takes from him a rib, and from this rib makes a woman. Genesis 2:24 concludes: "Therefore a man leaves his father and his mother and clings to his wife, and they become one flesh." In this passage Jews and Christians see the first man and woman becoming the first husband and wife.

In contrast to this biblical norm, homosexual relations are portrayed in scripture as unnatural and immoral. Leviticus 18:22 explicitly condemns sex between two men. "You [masculine in the Hebrew text] shall not lie with a male as with a woman; it is an abomination." Leviticus 20:13 asserts that the retributive justice for such an act is death. "If a man lies with a male as with a woman, both of them have committed an abomination; they shall be put to death; their blood is upon them."

In the New Testament of the Christian Bible, Paul writes in Romans 1:26–27 of the consequences of immorality: "For this reason God gave them up to degrading passions. Their women exchanged natural intercourse for unnatural, and in the same way also the men, giving up natural intercourse with women, were consumed with passion for one another. Men committed shameless acts with men and received in their own persons the due penalty for their error."

Paul, the most successful Christian missionary of the first century, assumes that homosexual acts between men or between women are wrong because homosexuality, he believes, is both unnatural and an act of lust.

Christians who claim to read the Bible as the literal word of God must be asked if they support enforcing all the laws of the Old Testament. Deuteronomy 13 commands that homosexuals be put to death, and Deuteronomy 22 orders that those who commit adultery be stoned. Prostitution is not proscribed, but taken for granted in Genesis 38:12–19 and Joshua 2:1–7. Furthermore, the Old Testament reveals that polygamy and concubinage (an unmarried woman living with a man) were common in ancient Israel.

Interpreting Scripture

Therefore, to be consistent, a Jew or a Christian who reads these scriptures literally should support capital punishment for male homosexual acts and for adultery and should support laws that allow prostitution, polygamy, and maintaining concubines. Many Jews and Christians, however, read their scriptures contextually, and thus interpret these texts as reflecting the knowledge and mores of an ancient society rather than as recording the literal word of God.

This is the approach taken by Reform, Conservative, and Reconstructionist Jewish groups in the United States. All three accept rabbis who are gay and sanction Jewish rituals for same-sex partnerships, but do not describe these as marriages. There is opposition to these moral presumptions, but synagogues are permitted to choose whether or not to accept gay rabbis and allow same-sex commitment ceremonies.[2]

In the United Kingdom the Orthodox Jewish community also condemns homosexuality, but Liberal Jewish congregations in the UK include four lesbian rabbis and two gay rabbis. Furthermore, after the British Parliament passed the Civil Partnership Act in December 2005, Liberal Jewish congregations authorized their rabbis to celebrate committed same-sex partnerships.[3] Orthodox Judaism everywhere continues to condemn homosexuality.

Christians, who read the Bible contextually, interpret all scripture by the New Testament witness to God's forgiving love and the commandment of Jesus to love God and our neighbors. This rule of love is applied even to teachings attributed to Jesus by New Testament writers. Although the Torah allows divorce (Deuteronomy 24:1–4), in the New Testament Jesus forbids it. (Mark 10:1–12, Matthew 19:9) The plain meaning of these texts allows no fudging, if they are to be read literally, and this was the doctrine of the church for centuries.

In our time, however, many Christians have come to see marriage differently. Wives and children are no longer property, sex within marriage is understood as intimate sharing and not merely as justified by procreation, abuse of a spouse or a child is reason for legal intervention in the family to protect the victim, and ending a marriage that lacks love is widely accepted.

Writing two millennia ago, Paul assumed all homosexual acts were unnatural acts of lust. Today, there is strong evidence that a significant portion of the population has a homosexual orientation, and this is understood to be a result of both nature and nurture, as with a heterosexual orientation.

Constructing a Presumption

Sex between a man and a woman, or between two persons of the same gender, may be more or less committed, more or less mutual, more or less fulfilling. Certainly, there is considerable evidence that love between two men or between two women may have the same character of care and commitment that Jews and Christians hope will bind a man and a woman in marriage.

The argument that love shared by two men or two women may be as committed as love between a man and a woman is persuasive for many in Europe and North America, whether or not they are Christian, which is why Canada and several European countries have sanctioned same-sex marriage. This shift in public morality has yet to occur in Africa, Asia, the Middle East, and most of South America, and may not, as in countries where Muslims and Catholics predominate, homosexuality is condemned.

When India was under British rule, a law prohibiting homosexuality was added to the penal code. Today, gay protesters there claim that this law is inconsistent with the tolerant Hindu tradition toward homosexuals. The Indian Supreme Court is presently reviewing the law.[4]

There is no human right to be gay under international law. Yet, even as the US Supreme Court derived a right of privacy from other explicit rights in the Constitution, we may argue that the provisions in international human rights law against discrimination based on social status can reasonably be interpreted as protecting the civil rights of homosexuals. We should oppose discrimination against homosexuals as we oppose discrimination based on race, religion, or gender.

Our legal presumption, therefore, is that homosexuals should enjoy the same sexual right of privacy as heterosexuals. It would seem that our ethical presumption should be the same. We acknowledge, however, that many oppose this standard of public morality, because they believe it violates the ethical traditions derived from the Jewish, Christian, and Muslim scriptures.

As our presumption asserts the human right to nondiscrimination, *compelling* evidence of better consequences is necessary to set it aside in favor of an alternative moral standard.

PORNOGRAPHY

Traditional and religious societies ban images, stories, and actions involving sexual practices that violate the moral consensus. In pluralistic societies, however, ethical debate about pornography has declined, now that we presume consensual sex does not involve wrongdoing. The general legal view today, which reflects our largely secular public morality, is that those who view pornography have a right to do so.

Our consensual approach to sexual conduct emphasizes our individual rights to privacy and freedom of speech and expression. In contemporary secular culture our moral presumption is that adults have the right in private to enjoy consensual sex in whatever way they wish, as long as they do not interfere with the rights of others.

We need to ask, however, if there are good reasons for limiting pornography. Do we have a duty to regulate the public display of sexual images to protect the rights of those who find such material offensive? Do we also have a duty to impose some public standard to guard against a general lowering of morals? Most contemporary societies accept some duty in both respects, and the authors agree.

Two Presumptions

Therefore, our commitment to protect individual freedom involves at least two ethical presumptions. First, we presume society should permit free speech and expression, even when a minority finds the exercise of this right to be offensive. The right to free speech is not only necessary to protect our autonomy, but also is essential for public debate about changing and raising our moral standards.

Second, our understanding of the rule of law presumes that a government may regulate free speech and expression so that it is reasonably avoidable by those who may be offended.[5] Under US constitutional law, this is may be done by regulating free speech with respect to the time, manner, and place of its expression.

For instance, we have a duty to protect children, not only from being exposed to pornography, but from being exploited in the creation of pornography. The criminalization of child pornography is based on the moral presumption that children are unable to consent to sex, which means it is wrong for adults to use children in creating pornography for adults. Laws against child pornography mark one of the boundaries between what is permitted and what is prohibited in pluralistic societies.

Public Standards

Some people argue that we have a duty to resist the sexual exploitation of women, even if individual women, for financial or other reasons, consent to their own exploitation. Many believe that we are all degraded morally by the promotion of sex throughout our society on the Internet, by e-mail, on television, in magazines, and in films.

These concerns pose difficult questions. Do we have a duty to try to raise our public moral standards? Is pornography now undermining our character and the loving relationships we believe are crucial for maintaining a just as well as free society?

Instead of concluding that the display and publication of sexual images is permissible as long as only consenting adults are involved, we might argue for the moral presumption that a reasonable assessment of community standards should be used to regulate the public expression of sex among consenting adults.

In the United States this issue has recently been raised by those who argue that the Federal Communications Commission (FCC) issue new guidelines for the television industry that would restrict nudity and offensive language. The baring of a breast by pop singer Janet Jackson on prime-time television during the half-time program of the 2004 pro football Super Bowl triggered widespread support for greater regulation by the FCC.

Nudity and sexual images that are offensive to many may be expected in an R-rated film and are protected as free speech. Yet, these "speech acts" need not be permitted in television programs broadcast on major channels at times when children are likely to be watching.

In a pluralistic society our moral presumption is that we have a duty to protect our right to freedom of expression, and also a duty to encourage moral character that reinforces respect for others and caring relationships.

How should images, which are not acceptable to all, be displayed in art museums? Areas open for viewing by all visitors should reflect community standards. In most communities traditional art, including nude images, will be acceptable for public viewing, but modern art that is intended to be shocking might best be placed in a gallery that requires visitors to leave the main hall in order to view it. Information on the nature of the art can be posted at the entrance to the gallery, so those entering are able to make an informed decision about seeing what is displayed.

We also must consider consequence arguments and what the burden of proof should be to overturn our ethical presumption with respect to pornography. A *compelling* burden of proof must be met to restrict the human right of free expression, which is guaranteed by international law and the US constitution. US courts require strict scrutiny of such restrictions, but allow regulation of the time, manner, and place of protected speech.

SEX TRADE

In most societies prostitution is a crime. Yet, prostitution has been widely tolerated, perhaps because men who felt they had to criticize prostitution in public often visited prostitutes in private. Today, when sexual ethics are presumed to be a private matter of consenting adults, it is not surprising that there is pressure to legalize prostitution. Several European countries have done this, and prostitution is also legal in a few jurisdictions within the United States.

Recently, however, tens of thousands of women from poor countries have been "sold as slaves" for the sex industry in more affluent societies, and this trade or "trafficking" in women has changed the way many view what has cynically been called the "oldest profession." It is estimated that fifty thousand women are brought into the United States each year by the criminal organizations engaged in this trade, despite the penalties established by the US Trafficking Victims Protection Act of 2000.[6]

The women being trafficked, as well as some young women on the streets because they are without a job and have no place to go, are clearly not engaging in what we mean by consensual sex. They are enslaved and exploited by criminal gangs that profit from their bondage. Nicholas Kristoff, columnist for the *New York Times,* writes: "Some 700,000 people are trafficked around the world each year, many of them just girls. They form part of what I believe will be the paramount moral challenge we will face in this century: to address the brutality that is the lot of so many women in the developing world."[7]

We have no difficulty judging such activity to be wrong and deserving of retributive justice, but it is much harder to know how to stop this malicious practice. Arresting and convicting those engaged in trafficking will not by itself be the solution. To stop trafficking in women, we must reduce the demand for prostitutes particularly in more affluent societies where the sex trade returns a higher profit.

Prostitution is not only about women selling their bodies, it also involves men buying sex. This demand for sex—for illicit sex and especially for sex with younger women—is what makes the sex trade so lucrative and also so morally repugnant. Our ethical imperative must require not merely retributive justice for the traffickers and assistance as well as empathy for the enslaved women. We should also try to shame and in this way deter the men who crave and pay for this kind of abusive sex.

As sex trafficking violates the human right to freedom from servitude, *compelling* evidence is required to overturn our moral presumption that it is wrong and should be resisted. It may be that women are less oppressed in pluralistic societies than in traditional cultures, but contemporary men cannot take any pride in that positive change when so many women continue to be exploited and brutalized by men.

SEX EDUCATION

Some opponents of teaching about sex in the public schools are concerned that providing birth control information will encourage promiscuous behavior. They demand that sex education in schools promote abstinence, rather than the use of contraceptives. Others argue that the high rate of pregnancy among teens and also the rapid spread of AIDS and other sexually transmitted diseases are evidence supporting the moral presumption that educators should teach students about contraception.

A survey conducted in the mid 1990s in Ontario, Canada, revealed that 89 percent of the adolescents surveyed thought it was important to receive sex education, and school was their preferred source of information. These students rated the following topics for a school-based sexual health program. These topics are listed from highest to lowest priority.

- Preventing sexual transmitted diseases.
- Sexual assault/rape.
- How to get testing and treatment for sexually transmitted diseases.
- Methods of birth control.

- Conception / pregnancy / rape.
- Building good / equal relationships.
- Making decisions about sexuality and relationships.
- Saying no to sex.
- Parenting skills.
- Talking with girlfriends / boyfriends about sexual issues.
- Peer pressure.
- Puberty.[8]

Those who differ about sex education raise largely consequential arguments. We suggest it is more helpful, at least at the beginning of our discussion, to consider our *duty*. Do educators have a responsibility to help students understand, at least, the public morality that is codified in society as law? Clearly, the answer to this question is yes. Sex must be consensual, and the law assumes children are unable to consent to sex with an adult. Students need to know that having sex with an adult is statutory rape.

Teens also need to know that any sex that is not consensual is morally wrong. Everyone has a duty to respect the rights of others. Mutual respect is at the heart of international human rights law, and this moral presumption applies whether or not we are adults or children, straight or gay.

Also, children should be encouraged to respect the ethical teachings concerning sex among the diverse religious and cultural communities in our pluralistic society. The conviction that sex outside of marriage is morally wrong is widespread among Jews, Christians, and Muslims, as well as other religious communities, and this ethical presumption should not be treated as simply old-fashioned. There are good reasons concerning health and morality for maintaining such an ethical presumption, even if many young adults today choose to ignore it.

Pornography and the sex trade should also be discussed in school. Students should talk about the moral effects of pornography on their character, as well as on the moral standards of society. Young men especially should be encouraged to be more responsible towards women. They need to understand that pornography exploits women, and that prostitution today is not just paying for consensual sex, but supports the trafficking and exploitation of women.

Our ethical presumption, therefore, is that the public schools have a duty to inform young people about all these issues concerning sex, and that students have a right to know. As sex education is not a human right, we argue that those who oppose this kind of sex education in the public schools need only provide *convincing* evidence that the consequences of such programs are less beneficial than would be the case using some alternative approach to sex education.

Sex education should go beyond information on birth control and avoiding sexually transmitted diseases. It should not merely try to frighten young people by emphasizing the terrible consequences of contracting HIV. Sex education should help young people realize that they are responsible not only for making moral choices in personal relationships, but also for confronting the exploitation of women throughout our society.

CONCLUSIONS

We have argued for the following ethical presumptions concerning sex. Each of these presumptions rests on considerations of our duty, character, relationships, and human rights.

- Nonconsensual sex is wrong.
- Children are incapable of "consensual sex."
- Homosexuals have equal rights.
- Pornography should be reasonably avoidable.
- The sex trade should be criminalized.
- Men should be encouraged to stop exploiting women.
- Sex education should teach ethics.

Our reasons for affirming these ethical presumptions are based on our duty, character, relationships, and rights, on the legal presumptions of our society, and on our aspirations for a higher standard of public morality. Those who disagree, we believe, have the burden of showing that an alternative course of action would be more beneficial.

DOING ETHICS TOGETHER

I. *What is necessary for sex to be ethical?*

1. Give two examples of sex that is consensual but illegal. Explain why consent is necessary but not sufficient for morality.

2. Construct an ethical presumption about the use of birth control and explain your reasoning. Raise an argument in opposition to your presumption. Is this a consequential argument, or does it concern duty, character, relationships, or rights?

3. What do you think is needed, beside consent, for sex between adults to be ethical? Does your reasoning involve an argument about duty, character, relationships, or rights? Or, are you making an argument about likely consequences?

II. *Gay sex.*

1. Some Christians argue that the condemnation of homosexuality in the Bible should be set aside today in favor of a new presumption allowing gay sex among consenting adults. Why? Offer an opposing argument.

2. Statements in the Torah condemn homosexual acts, yet some Jews now argue that these texts should not be applied to gay sex. Why? What argument might an Orthodox Jew make?

III. *Pornography and prostitution.*

1. If the city council were debating an ordinance banning the sale of pornographic materials, what moral argument might you make either for or against this ordinance? Does your reasoning emphasize duty, character, relationships, rights, or consequences?

2. Construct an ethical presumption about free speech and pornography that makes sense to you, and give two reasons for supporting this presumption. Explain how your presumption protects artistic expression.
3. Give a reason why we have laws that prohibit consensual sex between adults, when one person is paying the other. Give a reason for legalizing prostitution.

IV. Doing sex education.

1. To teach students the dangers of sexually transmitted diseases, do you think sex education should only promote abstinence before marriage? Or, would you endorse the ABC approach to sex education? Explain your reasoning.
2. What do you think students should be told about trafficking in women? Do you agree that men should be challenged to resist this exploitative practice?
3. What duty do we all have concerning sex? What sort of person (character) should we try to be? What kind of sexual relationship should be our goal? In answering these questions, put yourself in the role of someone giving counsel to a friend.

13

War Against Terrorism

JUSTICE AND FREEDOM

After the attack on the twin towers of the World Trade Center in New York on September 11, 2001, the president of the United States, George W. Bush, declared a "war against terrorism." Neither war nor terrorism is new, but the idea of a war against terrorism is unprecedented.

The just war tradition in moral philosophy requires warfare to have a just purpose and be fought using just means. Does the war against terrorism meet both of these tests? Contemporary international law asserts clear moral presumptions with respect to warfare and the treatment of prisoners. Do the steps taken by the administration of President Bush abide by these international human rights standards?

These are the questions we need to answer in order to decide whether the US "war on terrorism" (or "war on terror") is ethically justifiable.

In addition, we will consider the assertion by President Bush that the United States must fight terrorism not merely to protect the security of the nation and its people, but also to rid the world of evil.[1] Accomplishing this goal would seem to require preventing wrong before it is done. We should not be surprised, therefore, that President Bush has claimed that *preemptive* warfare is necessary to protect US citizens, that the United States has attacked two nations, and that the US government has detained and imprisoned suspected terrorists in several countries.

It is not clear, however, that waging war to rid the world of evil is a just purpose or, if it is, what means of warfare are justified in seeking this end.

We first review the ethical presumptions of the just war tradition and ask what these might mean for judging terrorism and our response to it. Then we summarize the moral presumptions of contemporary international law and apply these to the war against terrorism. Finally, we consider how governments and nations should respond to the threat of evil.

JUST WAR

The idea of justified warfare is ancient and, in one sense, simple. If a community is attacked, fighting to defend the community is self-defense and thus just. This notion of justified self-defense, however, does not answer the question of when, if ever, initiating a war might be justifiable.

Holy War

Religious traditions have addressed this issue. The scriptures of Judaism, Christianity, and Islam all contain passages that members of these religious traditions have used to justify going to war.

The Torah records that God told the ancient Israelites to fight the peoples of Canaan, because God wanted to take their land and give it to the Israelites. The book of Deuteronomy at the end of the Torah presents a long sermon, attributed to Moses, that includes this chilling passage:

> When the LORD your God brings you into the land that you are about to enter and possess, and He dislodges many nations before you—the Hittites, Girgashites, Amorites, Canaanites, Perizzites, Hivites, and Jebusites, seven nations much larger than you—and the LORD your God delivers them to you and you defeat them, you must doom them to destruction; grant them no terms and give them no quarter.[2]

This "holy war" is just, the Torah claims, because God is just, and God commands his chosen people to fight this war.

The Christian Bible includes the Torah in its Old Testament, so it also includes this concept of holy war. Moreover, the New Testament concludes with a vision of a cosmic battle between the forces of evil led by Satan and the forces of good led by the risen Christ. Many Christians interpret these images as symbolic, much like Gandhi interpreted the violence of the *Bhagavad Gita* as a struggle for truth, but other Christians expect God's "last judgment" will be a war to end all wars.

Despite the violent images in their scriptures, Christians were pacifists within the Roman Empire until in the fourth century Emperor Constantine converted and made defending the Empire not only a just cause, but also a Christian duty. In response to growing Islamic power Christian leaders in the eleventh century launched the Crusades, and these holy wars against Muslims continued for the next four centuries.

The Qur'an commands Muslims to embrace jihad, which means defending the truth of Islam. In a time of peace, and also within the Muslim community, jihad involves a quest for spiritual and moral purification by resisting the temptations of Satan. In a world of war, however, jihad means fighting for Islam against its enemies, and today some Muslims believe defending Islam requires such violence. As with Jewish and Christian notions of holy war, jihad is assumed to be just because it is the revealed will in the Qur'an of the one God, which is what the Arabic word *Allah* means.

Moral Principles

In an attempt to check the violence of war, moral philosophers in the West developed a notion of what might constitute a just war. The principles of the just war tradition rely on ethical presumptions, rather than assertions of divine authority. Thomas Aquinas, however, formulated these principles in the thirteenth century, and political writers used this tradition to judge the wars of the sixteenth and seventeenth centuries.

The following moral presumptions sum up the duty of a government as it considers going to war. In the just war tradition, a justifiable war must:

- Have a just cause.
- Be declared by a proper authority.

- Be based on a right intention.
- Use just means.
- Have a reasonable chance of success.
- Result in more good than harm.
- Be a last resort.[3]

At the end of the eighteenth century, revolutionary wars were fought in what would become the United States and the First Republic of France. The British government certainly did not consider the American revolt to be justified, according to the principles of the just war tradition, but instead asserted that British authority over the colonies was lawful. Likewise, the king of France did not believe the French rebels had any legitimacy. Both European governments saw the rebels as terrorists.

Yet, the American and French uprisings in pursuit of freedom and new forms of representative government were successful, not only on the battlefield, but also in securing public support for the natural rights that each rebellion affirmed. Both of these revolutions justified going to war in order to secure civil and political rights and democratic government. Today, the American and French revolutions are widely celebrated as examples of just wars.

Now the United States claims the right to defend this heritage by waging war against Muslim terrorists, who seem to believe that a violent jihad against Western society is necessary to defend Islam. To examine the ethical nature of this claim, we consider in more detail what terrorism means today.

Terrorism

All war involves terror, but terrorism is not war as such. Wars involve armies. Terrorism involves violent acts against civilians and public officials that are committed by individuals or groups in an attempt to force a government to make concessions. Both war and terrorism are political acts. Through war, armies fight to extend the power of their national governments or to defend their country. Terrorists are not strong enough to wage war, so they prey on a society in an attempt to achieve their political objectives by showing that the government is unable to provide adequate security for its citizens.

Like revolutions, terrorist acts lack lawful sanction by a government. Yet, history may conclude that terrorists, like the rebels of the American and French revolutions, had noble intentions and a just cause. Therefore, we ought not to condemn terrorism simply because terrorists are not fighting under the flag of a national government, although this is one of the principles of the just war tradition.

Instead, we should judge terrorist acts by the other principles of the just war tradition. Does terrorist violence have a just purpose and a reasonable chance of success? Will it likely result in more good than harm? Are the means being used by terrorists just? These are the crucial moral questions.

Terrorism cannot be justified simply because it seeks to right a wrong. As in war, the ethical presumption is that both ends and means must be just if warfare is to be justifiable. Moreover, in the just war tradition "the success principle" states the moral presumption that killing people is wrong even for a just cause if there is no reasonable chance of success.

In addition, the "principle of proportionality" asserts the moral presumption that the cost of a war in lives and property loss should not exceed the good that will likely be achieved. Applying these principles requires predicting the consequences of pursuing a conflict. Those supporting war (or terrorist acts) must show that the consequences of going to war (or committing terrorist acts) are likely to be more beneficial than not.

Furthermore, the requirement of "just means" in waging war supports the ethical presumption that warfare should be directed at military targets and soldiers, and not at civilians. This is one of the moral duties supporting the additional ethical presumption that war is wrong until proven right.

The burden of proof in this tradition of ethical reasoning is not on those who oppose the use of violence, but on those who claim violence is necessary. Advocates of violence must show not only that the cause and their intentions are justified, and that they have a reasonable chance of success, but also that the violent means to be used will be directed against military forces and that the use of violence is a last resort.

The just war prohibition of violence against noncombatants is the strongest moral argument against terrorism, for terrorist acts of violence generally target civilians. Because terrorists lack the strength to fight and win a war against the armed forces of a nation, they terrorize civilians to undermine the government they oppose. Terrorists hope that history will justify them, but they must meet a *compelling* burden of proof to overcome the ethical presumption that violence is not justified simply because a government has acted unjustly. Violence must be the last resort in seeking justice.

INTERNATIONAL LAW

In the second half of the nineteenth century nations began to enter into treaties to limit the devastating consequences of war, and in the twentieth century the standards of humanitarian law were raised after the formation of the United Nations.

The most recent treaties that define both the rights of people caught up in warfare and the duty of governments to protect these rights include: the International Covenant on Civil and Political Rights; the Convention against Torture and Other Cruel, Inhuman or Degrading Treatment or Punishment; the Convention on the Prevention and Punishment of the Crime of Genocide; and the Geneva Conventions. These treaties, which were written by the UN and have been ratified by most nations, assert in greater detail for our contemporary context the moral presumptions of the just war tradition.

Geneva Conventions

The Geneva Conventions are concerned primarily with the duty of governments to avoid injuring noncombatants and to provide proper health care and treatment for prisoners captured during war. The founder of the Red Cross inspired the first Geneva Convention, which was signed in 1864 to protect the sick and wounded during war. Two treaties signed in 1899 prohibit the use of asphyxiating gases and expanding bullets, and thirteen treaties in 1907 and the Geneva Gas Protocol in 1925 outlaw the use of poison gas and bacteriological warfare.

Two more Geneva Conventions in 1925 clarify standards for the treatment of the wounded and prisoners of war and, in 1949, the Hague Convention on the Protection of Cultural Property was signed and four Geneva Conventions gave humane protection to civilians and to combatants captured on the seas. The UN in 1977 added a Convention on Military or Any Other Hostile Use of Environmental Techniques, and two Protocols to the Geneva Conventions of 1949.

The Geneva Conventions and Protocols distinguish between combatants and civilians, protecting each in different ways. Military forces are prohibited from targeting civilians, and soldiers who inadvertently kill civilians may not be prosecuted for war crimes. On the other hand, civilians are prohibited from killing soldiers, and civilians who do so may be prosecuted. Soldiers are to wear uniforms, so that the distinction between civilians and combatants can be upheld.

Under the Geneva Conventions, mercenaries (defined as fighting men who are not nationals of the warring parties and are paid more than soldiers) are explicitly excluded from these protections.[4]

The Geneva Conventions seek to limit the inhumanity of warfare by appealing to the self-interest of both sides in an armed conflict. Every government engaged in warfare has a stake in requiring its military forces to abide by these rules, because each government wants the enemy to do the same. If stated as a *duty*, rather than as a consequential argument, this moral presumption is a variation of the golden rule.

By targeting civilians, terrorists clearly violate the Geneva Conventions, but this does not mean a government attacked by terrorists no longer has a duty to abide by these Conventions. One wrong does not justify another wrong. Even if terrorists have waived their right to the protections of the Geneva Conventions, the rules of international law apply to a government fighting against terrorism.

Governments have a moral and legal duty to abide by the Geneva Conventions, and it is in their best interest to do so. Both duty and the adverse consequences of abdicating that duty are strong arguments for the ethical presumption expressed in international law by the Geneva Conventions.

The *burden of proof* for overcoming this ethical presumption must rest on those arguing that the Geneva Conventions should not apply. Furthermore, given the importance of the Geneva Conventions in protecting the human rights of all those involved, overturning the presumption should require *compelling* evidence that dire consequences will result from acting on the presumption.

US Wars

The administration of President George W. Bush has argued that both just war principles and international law asserting these principles do not apply to a war against terrorism. The terrorists involved in the 9/11 attacks were, after all, not soldiers acting under the laws of a nation. They were civilians and were not wearing uniforms, but nonetheless they were combatants. So, the Bush administration argues, they are "unlawful enemy combatants" and cannot claim the protections of the just war tradition or the Geneva Conventions for civilians who are noncombatants.

The Bush administration, however, has blurred the distinction between fighting terrorists and waging a war against another country by claiming the right to attack any nation that "harbors" terrorists. The US government has taken the position that it has the right to wage war against any government that aids individuals who threaten the security of the United States and its allies.

Clearly, the burden of proof for attacking other nations rests with the US government. A nation initiating war must overcome the strong moral presumption against war, which requires that war be undertaken only as a last resort for a just cause, and be likely to succeed, with benefits outweighing the costs of lost lives and property damage. As these presumptions protect the human rights of both civilians and combatants, *compelling* evidence is required to set them aside.

The United States sought to justify attacking Afghanistan by arguing that its government was harboring terrorists who were behind the 9/11 attack, and a reasonable argument can be made that the US invasion of Afghanistan adheres to many just war principles. The purpose of the war in Afghanistan was self-defense, combatants were targeted, victory seemed likely, and noncombatants were generally protected.

The means used in the war may not always have been proportional to the danger or to the benefits of victory, but the fighting was limited. Moreover, relief and reconstruction were provided for the survivors, although the level of aid has been much less than expert observers believe is necessary to repair the damage of the war and ensure security for the people. In addition, a new government has been established through a process that allowed much of the population to express its will.

It is not clear, however, that this preemptive war was a last resort. Nor is it at all certain that the long-term benefits will outweigh the costs of the war, which include the loss of life on both sides; damage to private property, the environment, and the infrastructure of the society; and the growing Taliban resistance to the new government set up in Afghanistan.

What about the war in Iraq? The US administration has argued that Iraq's government was supporting terrorists who posed a threat to the United States. Before the attack on Iraq, however, there was no credible evidence to verify this assertion. Subsequently, the report of the 9/11 Commission confirmed that Iraq's government did not provide support for the 9/11 terrorist attacks, and also that it did not harbor any of the terrorists who were involved in preparing these attacks.

To try to justify its preemptive war against Iraq in 2003, the US administration claimed that Iraq's military posed a grave and imminent threat to the United States, which could only be checked by removing Iraq's ruler, Saddam Hussein, from power. The administration also argued that Iraq had weapons of mass destruction, although the evidence for this assertion was weak before the war and afterwards has not been substantiated.

More recently, those who have supported the war against Iraq claim that the war is justifiable because it has established a democratically elected government. It is true that many Iraqis voted for a parliament and a constitution. As in Afghanistan, however, it is not at all clear that the new government will survive as a democracy.

Furthermore, according to the presumptions of the just war tradition, to be justifiable, a war must not only have a just cause and good results, but also use just means and achieve more good than harm. Thus, to evaluate the justice of the war in Iraq, we need to consider how it has been fought and the likely costs as well as the benefits of the war.

The "shock and awe" bombing campaign in Baghdad at the beginning of the war did not target noncombatants, US leaders claim. Nonetheless, it

was foreseeable that this widespread bombing would kill thousands of innocent civilians and destroy much of the capital city of Iraq. In addition,
the bombing campaign was intended to create terror among the civilian
population, so they would surrender without fighting.[5]

An assessment of the likely consequences of the war must also consider: all those killed and injured on both sides, the suffering of the Iraqi
people due to the war, the anger and violence resulting from the occupation, the carnage of civil conflict between Sunnis and Shiites, the political
and economic repercussions of the war around the world, the environmental damage, and the hundreds of billions of dollars spent by the United
States.

Many observers argue that the negative *consequences* of the war in Iraq
outweigh the benefits of removing a murderous government from power.
Some assert that the bombing of targets in cities and the shooting and random arrests of civilians do not meet the standard of just means required
for fighting a just war, no matter what the benefits of the conflict may
prove to be.

Both the just war tradition and international law place the burden of
proof for justifying war on the nation that initiates the battle. The United
States was not attacked by either the armed forces of Afghanistan or by
Iraqi soldiers, although it was attacked by a terrorist organization that was
training and hiding in Afghanistan with the knowledge of the Afghan government. The war in Afghanistan was a response to terrorism, but the war
in Iraq was not. To justify either attack, the United States must show that:

- It was responding with good intentions to a real threat.
- Each war has a reasonable chance of success.
- The means used in these wars has been directed against
  combatants.
- Going to war in each case was a last resort.

The burden of proof on the United States in each case requires *compelling* evidence, as attacking another country places the human rights of
both combatants and civilians in grave jeopardy.

The moral debate concerning the war on terrorism and those captured in it, and also concerning the wars in Afghanistan and Iraq, has involved all three branches of the US government. The Patriot Act passed by Congress shortly after the 9/11 attacks allows the Justice Department to detain for as long as it deems necessary those suspected of involvement in terrorist acts against Americans. It also does not protect the right of those who are detained to have visits by family members, lawyers, or the Red Cross. The administration argues that these detainees are not prisoners of war, because they do not belong to the armed forces of a nation.

The administration has claimed that the Geneva Conventions do not apply to how it treats captured "enemy combatants" in its war on terrorism. It asserts, however, that if American soldiers are captured by terrorists, they must be given the protections afforded by the Geneva Conventions.

Under the Geneva Conventions, the Red Cross must be allowed during a war to make regular visits to captured combatants, and the Red Cross is obliged to communicate concerns it has about the treatment of these prisoners to the military personnel in charge of the prisons. In prisons administered by US forces in Iraq the Red Cross found a systematic pattern of beatings and humiliating treatment that constitutes torture, which is in violation of the Geneva Conventions. Moreover, the Red Cross estimated that 70 to 90 percent of the Iraqis imprisoned by US armed forces are innocent of any wrongdoing.[6]

After the Red Cross made its confidential report to the US administration in the fall of 2003, it appears that no remedial action was taken by the US government until photographs of abused prisoners in the Abu Ghraib prison appeared in the press early in 2004. These photographs prompted an investigation into actions by US personnel that, under the Geneva Conventions, would be defined as war crimes.

The US administration claims that the International Criminal Court does not have jurisdiction over acts committed by American personnel during the US war on terrorism, as the United States has not ratified the treaty constituting the International Criminal Court. Rather than submit to any international review, the US government claims the right to prosecute in its courts any alleged violations of the Geneva Conventions or any standard of international law. The Bush administration has sought to limit judicial review to military courts or special tribunals that do not have all the protections of criminal courts.

Fighting terrorists in the twenty-first century may raise ethical and legal questions that were not contemplated by those who wrote the Geneva Conventions, but these Conventions apply without any ambiguity to the war in Iraq. Moreover, the United States is obliged as a member of the United Nations to uphold and comply with the provisions of international law including the Geneva Conventions.

Torture

A major ethical issue in the war against terrorism involves claims of torture by many of those detained in prisons by the United States. Torture is clearly prohibited by just war principles, international law, and US law. Yet, the debate over torture continues as the Bush administration, Congress, and the federal courts struggle to clarify the moral and legal constraints that should apply in the treatment and interrogation of captured combatants and suspected terrorists.

The Convention against Torture and Other Cruel, Inhuman or Degrading Treatment or Punishment was adopted by a UN General Assembly resolution in 1984. The United States ratified the treaty in 1994, and a total of 141 countries had ratified it as of 2006. The convention defines torture in Article 1.1 as:

> [A]ny act by which severe pain or suffering, whether physical or mental, is intentionally inflicted on a person for such purposes as obtaining from him or a third person information or a confession, punishing him for an act he or a third person has committed or is suspected of having committed, or intimidating or coercing him or a third person, or for any reason based on discrimination of any kind, when such pain or suffering is inflicted by or at the instigation of or with the consent or acquiescence of a public official or other person acting in an official capacity. It does not include pain or suf-

fering arising only from, inherent in or incidental to lawful sanctions.[7]

The ethical presumptions asserted by this convention include the following:

- No exceptional circumstances whatsoever . . . may be invoked as a justification of torture. (Article 2.2)
- An order from a superior officer . . . may not be invoked as a justification of torture. (Article 2.3)
- No State Party shall expel . . . or extradite a person to another State where there are substantial grounds for believing that he would be in danger of being subjected to torture. (Article 3.1)
- Each State Party shall ensure . . . a prompt and impartial investigation, wherever there is reasonable ground to believe that an act of torture has been committed in any territory under its jurisdiction. (Article 12)

The convention states more precisely the rights and duties set forth in Articles 7 and 10 of the International Covenant on Civil and Political Rights, which the United States has also ratified (although with reservations limiting its assent to the standards of US law).

The Convention against Torture is not limited to the treatment of prisoners of war, so it clearly applies to suspected terrorists who are arrested and detained. The convention explicitly asserts the moral presumptions that torture and cruelty to detainees and prisoners is wrong, that governments have a duty to prevent it, and that there are to be no exceptions made to this moral and legal duty.

The United States has incorporated this presumption into its domestic laws and also into the Uniform Code of Military Justice (UCMJ, Articles 77–134). The McCain amendment to the defense spending bill, which was passed at the end of 2005, reaffirmed international and US law by prohibiting the "cruel, inhuman or degrading treatment or punishment" of anyone in US government custody anywhere in the world. This amendment also requires that procedures in the Army Field Manual be followed in the interrogation of prisoners.[8]

It would seem that nothing could be clearer than the moral and legal presumption not to torture. Yet, since 2002 the Bush administration and the US Department of Defense have ignored some of the restrictions of international and domestic law against torture in order to encourage aggressive interrogation techniques. Many military lawyers have resisted this violation of international obligations, but other voices in the administration have claimed that the president has the authority to set aside these legal obligations in order to protect American interests.[9]

When President George W. Bush signed the bill that included the McCain amendment banning torture, he attached a signing statement affirming his right, as commander in chief, to bypass the law if he felt that enforcing the prohibition against torture would jeopardize national security.[10] This statement by the president plus the treatment of prisoners in Abu Ghraib and the US prison at Guantánamo Bay are evidence that *consequence* arguments are being used by the US administration to try to justify torture.

There are, however, strong consequence arguments on the other side. Burton J. Lee III, a doctor in the Army Medical Corps who served as physician to President George H. W. Bush, articulates some of these objections to the use of torture.

> The military ethics that I know absolutely prohibit anything resembling torture. . . . Discipline and order in the military ranks depend to a large extend on compliance with the prohibition of torture. . . . In addition, military leaders have long been aware that torture inflicts lasting damage on both the victim and the torturer. The systematic infliction of torture engenders deep hatred and hostility that transcends generations.[11]

Lee also argues that:

reports of torture by U.S. forces have been accompanied by evidence that military medical personnel have played a role in this abuse and by new military ethical guidelines that in effect authorize complicity by health professionals in ill treatment of detainees. These new guidelines distort traditional ethical rules beyond recognition to serve the interests of interrogators, not doctors and detainees.[12]

To these consequence arguments, Lee adds an ethical argument based on a concern for *character* and *public virtues*: "Torture demonstrates weakness, not strength. It does not show understanding, power or magnanimity. It is not leadership. It is a reaction of government officials overwhelmed by fear who succumb to conduct unworthy of them and of the citizens of the United States."[13]

The debate over torture reveals that the war on terrorism, as it is now being waged, threatens the rule of law. Efforts by the US Supreme Court to uphold the rule of law have been resisted by both Congress and the president. In the spring of 2006 the Supreme Court twice ruled against the president's use of power to hold detainees indefinitely, without any right of appeal. Congress responded, however, by acting to legalize the actions taken by President George W. Bush.[14]

Legislation passed by Congress in late September 2006 ignores several of the moral presumptions that international human rights law asserts as necessary for the protection of human dignity and the rule of law. The new law states that:

- The president can detain indefinitely, with no right of appeal, anyone anywhere as an "illegal enemy combatant."
- The president can decide what interrogation methods may be used on a detainee and keep this decision secret.
- Detainees in US military prisons lose the right to challenge their imprisonment.
- Courts lose their authority to review any aspect of this new system, except verdicts by military tribunals.

- Coerced evidence is admissible in court, if a judge rules it
  is reliable and relevant.
- Coercion is defined in a way that exempts anything done
  before the passage of the 2005 Detainee Treatment Act,
  and anything else the president may choose to do.[15]

Early in 2007 leaders of the newly elected majority in Congress pledged to introduce legislation that would reaffirm constitutional protections for individual rights. The recent changes in US law made by the previous Congress will also be challenged in federal court on the grounds that they violate the US Constitution. We should expect as well to hear arguments that these changes in US law also fail to meet the standards of international human rights law.

This charge has already been leveled at the secret detention facilities that the United States is widely reported to be using in its war on terrorism. In a recent report the UN Committee on Human Rights said that the United States "should only detain persons in places in which they can enjoy the full protection of the law." The committee also urged the US government to "grant prompt access by the International Committee of the Red Cross to any person detained in connection with an armed conflict."[16]

The UN Human Rights Committee was reviewing US human rights practices as part of its responsibility to report on the human rights practices of countries that have ratified the International Covenant on Civil and Political Rights, as the United States has. As of the end of 2006 the US government, despite its obligations under international law, has refused to reveal the location of any secret detention facilities or to allow visits to these facilities by members of the Red Cross.

EVIL

The administration of President George W. Bush has emphasized that its war on terrorism is not only a war of national self-defense, but also a war to defeat evil. What does this mean for doing ethics?

The words *wrong* and *evil* are not generally used as synonyms. If a friend tells you a lie, you would say that is wrong, but probably not that it is evil.

Moreover, we would generally not describe even more serious wrongdoing, such as robbery and committing fraud, as evil. For by evil we tend to
mean acts that are heinous—such as murder, torture, the slave trade, and
attacks on civilians in war. Evil suggests wrongdoing that is not only inten-
tional, but also cold-blooded and brutal.

To rid the world of evil means more than applying the ethical presumptions of retributive justice to wrongdoing. Retributive justice may help to
deter wrongdoing, if punishment is sure and swift. Yet, the "evil" of a sui-
cidal attack on civilians will not be deterred by the threat of even severe
punishment.

Therefore, President George W. Bush has argued, the United States
must take preemptive action to destroy the "evildoers" before they can
harm America. He has publicly described the regimes of Iraq, Iran, and
North Korea as evil, and has sought to justify preemptive war against Iraq
as a way of preventing evil acts that, he claims, Saddam Hussein intended
to carry out against the United States.

Rule of Law

This moral argument deviates from the traditional justification for self-
defense, which allows a proportional response to a real threat or attack. To
initiate an attack on a nation that might pose a threat, by using a preemptive strike to render the nation powerless to commit an act of aggression, is
not engaging in war as a last resort.

The claim that Iraq had weapons of mass destruction and was capable
of threatening the United States with nuclear or biological weapons was
promoted as a reason for launching a preemptive war against Iraq. Yet, we
now know that the Iraqi government was unable to commit the evil acts
that were claimed to justify a preemptive strike on the Iraqi army and anyone else who resisted the ensuing American occupation.

We must conclude, therefore, that a preemptive strategy to rid the
world of evil poses a huge moral risk. In an attempt to prevent evil, we
may do evil. For if an attack against the United States by terrorists or by another nation is evil, then an attack by US military forces against a nation,
which does not pose a real and imminent threat to the American people, is
also evil.

In trying to kill terrorists before they attack us, we may kill innocent people. By imprisoning those we deem to pose a threat, we may imprison by mistake people who have done no harm. By detaining and torturing suspects that we believe are conspiring against us, we do evil to others and violate the moral presumptions of international law.

These actions are not morally justified, and we must say so. If potential terrorists have been identified, they should be arrested and charged with conspiracy to commit a crime. In this way we defend the rule of law for them, as well as for ourselves, and by using the rule of law we guard against doing evil in our efforts to prevent evil.

For the same reason, if a country is harboring terrorists or developing weapons that might pose a threat to US security, the duty of our government is to use every legal means short of war to try to find a solution to this problem. War must be the last resort, and not merely a preemptive choice.

Therefore, we suggest that maintaining the rule of law, in a time of war as well as in times of peace, is the best way to combat evil. This is the primary duty of all governments. Paul Rieckhoff, a former infantry officer in the Iraq war, writes:

> The question facing America is not whether to continue fighting our enemies in Iraq and beyond but how to do it best. My soldiers and I learned the hard way that policy at the point of a gun cannot, by itself, create democracy. The success of America's fight against terrorism depends more on the strength of its moral integrity than on troop numbers in Iraq or the flexibility of interrogation options.[17]

The US government may yet come to appreciate this, and the second inaugural address by President George W. Bush offers some hope in this regard.

Freedom and Compassion

In his address, the president turns from condemning evil to praising freedom and the rule of law. He asserts that it is "the policy of the United

States to seek and support the growth of democratic movements and institutions in every nation and culture, with the ultimate goal of ending
tyranny in our world."

"This is not primarily the task of arms," the president says, "though we
will defend ourselves and our friends by force of arms when necessary."[18]
Instead, freedom "by its nature, must be chosen, and defended by citizens,
and sustained by the rule of law and the protection of minorities."

Moreover, he promises that "America will not impose our own style of
government on the unwilling." The goal of America, the president affirms,
is "to help others find their own voice, attain their own freedom, and make
their own way."

In his second inaugural address, President George W. Bush expresses
confidence that history is on the side of freedom and justice. Instead of using fear to motivate Americans to support a policy of preemptive action
against evildoers, he appeals to their faith in freedom and in God's good
purposes. He suggests, therefore, that we may help rid the world of evil by
promoting freedom and democracy through the rule of law.

"The rulers of outlaw regimes can know," he proclaims, "that we still
believe as Abraham Lincoln did: Those who deny freedom to others deserve it not for themselves; and, under the rule of a just God, cannot long
retain it."[19] Invoking the memory of Abraham Lincoln may prompt Americans to recall Lincoln's second inaugural address, which does not cast
blame for the evils of slavery and civil war, and instead urges Americans to
act with a spirit of compassion.

> With malice toward none, with charity for all, with firmness in
> the right as God gives us to see the right, let us strive on to fin-
> ish the work we are in, to bind up the nation's wounds, to care
> for him who shall have borne the battle and for his widow and
> his orphan, to do all which may achieve and cherish a just and
> lasting peace among ourselves and with all nations.[20]

Lincoln's second inaugural address asserts a moral presumption as to
how the bitterness caused by the terrible violence of the Civil War may be

overcome by the forgiving *character* of the American people. The message is similar to that of the Truth and Reconciliation Commission, which sought after the end of apartheid in South Africa to reconcile those who were divided and to renew their commitment to the rule of law.

Fighting Evil with Good

These two inaugural addresses affirm that our ethical presumption in combating evil is to take actions that are good. If freedom, rather than preemptive violence, is the real deterrent against tyranny, then the way to rid the world of evil is not by fighting to destroy evildoers, but by creating a more just and free world order.

A more realistic and compassionate view of the world reveals that it is not simply divided into evildoers and those who do what is good. There are individuals and groups committing evil acts, but we must remember that every person and government is capable of doing evil. Moreover, we have seen that in an effort to rid the world of evil, we may unknowingly commit great evil.

A war against terrorism will not rid the world of evil, if such a war involves doing evil to innocent people. This is the wisdom of our ethical traditions that have struggled to limit the horror of war. The just war principles, the Geneva Conventions, and other international human rights treaties prohibit evil acts. The moral standards of this tradition of justice in warfare must now guide our struggle against terrorists.

There will be unintended casualties in any war, but the just purpose of a war does not justify extensive "collateral damage" to civilians and their property. Under the ethical principles of the just war tradition the means of war, as well as the cause for the war, must be just, and this requires protecting noncombatants and the rights of those who are captured and imprisoned.

Our ethical presumptions about the use of violence require using just means to ensure peace. There are many options, including a greater emphasis on homeland security measures and also policies that seek a more just world through economic development, support for international law, and greater friendship among peoples with diverse cultural and religious traditions.

Consequences

To those who say this approach will not work, we reply that there is no credible evidence that the war against terrorism (or the war in Iraq) has made the US any safer. Moreover, when we are unsure that the benefits of violence and war will outweigh the loss of life and destruction, then we have an ethical duty to refrain from violence and warfare unless it is absolutely the last resort.

It may even be that the use of evil means to fight the evil of terrorism has played into the hands of terrorists. By responding to terrorist attacks with self-righteous warfare, the United States has lost the moral high ground it once held. Many of America's friends have become critics, and the war in Iraq has become a rallying point for Muslims who fear the extension of US power in a region that for more than a millennium has been controlled by Islamic governments.

The attack on the World Trade Center and also the possibility of other devastating terrorist attacks on civilians are terrible to contemplate. Yet, these possible dire consequences do not justify setting aside our moral presumption against doing evil. Rather than continuing an endless war against terrorism, the United States and its allies should now seek a more just world order with greater respect for human rights and the rule of law. This goal can only be achieved by living and exemplifying it, despite the continuing threat of terrorist attacks.

If we want the world to choose freedom and the rule of law instead of tyranny, we must choose freedom and the rule of law instead of war to combat terrorism.

DOING ETHICS TOGETHER

I. Just war principles.

1. Make an argument either supporting the moral presumption that war, to be just, should be a last resort, or opposing this presumption.

242 13. War Against Terrorism: Justice and Freedom

2. Summarize the principle of proportionality and also the success principle.

3. Give a reason in support of the moral presumption that winning a war must be probable, and then offer a criticism of this presumption.

II. *International law.*

1. Give two examples of ethical presumptions asserted by the Geneva Conventions.

2. Does the United States have a legal and moral duty to allow the Red Cross to visit prisoners being held at Guantánamo Bay? Argue for this presumption, and then give an argument against it.

3. Summarize what torture means under international law. Give a consequence argument and also a character argument that Burton J. Lee III makes against torture.

III. *Good and evil.*

1. Explain the moral danger of trying to rid the world of evil. Does this make sense to you? Why or why not? How did Gandhi say we should resist evil? (See chapter 4.)

2. In his second inaugural address, President George W. Bush says that freedom must be sustained by the rule of law. Explain what you think this means and offer an argument either supporting or challenging this statement.

3. After the Civil War, President Lincoln urged the American people to manifest "charity for all." What sort of moral presumption is this? How might you respond to someone who argues that, to achieve justice, the Confederate leaders should have been executed?

14

Economic Justice

FAIR AND CARING?

In chapter 6 we affirmed the feminist critique that relying on rules and principles to define justice may result in ignoring the exploitation of those with little power. The laws of a society should be fair *and* caring. It is fair, for example, that everyone should have a right to representation in a court of law, but it is caring when the government provides funding to support defense attorneys for persons who cannot afford them. We are at our best when we are both fair and caring.

What does this mean for considering issues of economic justice? Those who write about ethics and the economy tend to ask: "What would a fair economic system look like?" We ask: "What would a fair and caring economy look like?" The difference is not insignificant.

We begin with the hypothesis that a proper understanding of economic justice includes acts of charity. Compassionate giving is a virtue that is worthy of praise. It is also an economic action that has economic benefits not only for those receiving aid, but for those providing the aid and also the entire society. Charity affects the economy.

We are well aware that charity is not usually included in conceptions of economic justice. This may be because charitable acts are often intended to alleviate the suffering of the poor, rather than ensure them greater justice. Yet, many charitable organizations intervene not merely to reduce suffering, but also to change unjust social and economic structures and policies. At least some international charitable organizations are as dedicated to ensuring economic justice as they are to aiding the victims of economic injustice.[1]

Charity, in this sense, is not simply compassionate giving to those in need, but also involves caring action that is intended to overcome the causes of poverty and economic exploitation.

Governments may act both to alleviate the suffering of the poor and to address the causes of poverty. In the face of an economic disaster, such as the devastating tsunami that hit the coast of Indonesia in December 2004, many governments responded with relief. In addition, these governments quickly joined with charitable organizations to fund community development projects as a way of helping the victims of the disaster renew the economic activities that are necessary for the support of their families.

When there is an economic disaster, caring that only provides immediate assistance is not sufficient as an ethical response. Resources must also be invested in economic recovery and development. In addition, the benefits provided the victims of a disaster must be distributed in a way that is fair, as well as caring.

We see this clearly in responding to a natural disaster, but much less so when considering economic policies. Yet, the consequences of our global economy are a disaster of our own making. The UN reports that: "Currently, more than a billion people live in absolute poverty—defined as subsisting on the equivalent of a dollar or less a day—while 2.7 billion others try to get by on the equivalent of between $1–2 a day. Around 11 million children die each year from preventable diseases like malaria, diarrhea and pneumonia."[2]

Most of us are enjoying affluence in the midst of an economic catastrophe. We should not simply assume that these facts are unrelated. Our moral hypothesis, therefore, is that we are responsible for doing all we can to provide relief for those who are poor and also for making the economy both fair and more caring.

DUTY: A FAIR DISTRIBUTION

Current economic theory holds that the marketplace provides the most efficient way both to allocate the resources required to produce goods and services and to distribute the income derived from this economic activity. We agree that markets are efficient in allocating resources, but assert that both human labor and natural capital are not simply "resources." Therefore, efficiency cannot be the sole standard by which we measure the success of the economy. Nor should we simply assume that the marketplace will distribute goods and services most efficiently or in a way that meets our standards for economic justice.

In chapter 15 we consider the ecological impact of global economic activity. In this chapter we focus on ethical issues involving the distribution of income resulting from economic activity.

Our moral presumption is that we have a *duty* to treat human beings as ends in themselves, not simply as means to some other end, such as achieving greater efficiency. "The economy exists for the person, not the person for the economy."[3]

The economy is not a natural phenomenon like gravity, but instead is a human activity involving government policies as well as corporate practices and individual initiatives. As with all human activities, there are choices to be made and these are not only economic and political choices, but also ethical choices. As the economy may be more or less just, our responsibility is to see that it is more just than not. This is the duty of every government, as it makes and administers economic policy, and it is also the duty of every citizen.

Government decisions affect the economy in many ways. Governments create laws that charter corporations, regulate trade, tax corporate profits, set interest rates that affect investment, charter and regulate banks, subsidize economic development, manage large tracts of land and natural resources, protect the environment, require safety standards for factories and products, set minimum wages for employees, prosecute fraud, and much more.

The ethical duty of governments in creating and enforcing these policies is to be fair and caring. Fair, because we have a right to expect that the rules of "the economic game" do not discriminate against people because of their race, religion, nationality, gender, poverty, or other social status. Caring, because a government should act to promote the good of the community it serves. Again, we see that being both fair and caring are necessary for a more inclusive concept of social justice.

Certainly, pursuing the common good includes a concern for the efficient use of resources, as we want governments to guard against extravagance and waste. Yet, government policies must also consider the impact of economic development on a community and all of its people, the poor as well as the rich and the middle class.

Agricultural Policies

To take one major example, we argue that current US agricultural policies are neither fair nor caring. These federal policies are not fair, because they favor large corporate investment and management over small family farms. Agricultural policies in the United States are not caring, because they ignore the plight of farmers who are losing both their land and their livelihood.

Federal tax policies and farm programs in the 1970s encouraged capital investment and large-scale technologies, which led US farmers to borrow heavily and expand production in order to generate the income required to repay their loans.

Similar loans for agricultural development in developing countries led to a greater supply of commodities in the 1980s and pushed down prices. Farmers all over the world, not only in the United States, were unable to pay their debts, and had to sell their land or face foreclosure. By the time the federal government increased the subsidies on agricultural products, corporations that had bought up farms were the primary beneficiaries.

Government subsidies for food have kept prices low in US supermarkets, and also allowed agribusiness to sell US-grown products in other countries at a lower price. In addition, to protect US farm products against imports, the federal government has imposed tariffs on some of these imports to make them more expensive.

This has been good for consumers in the United States and for American agribusiness, but it has driven most family farmers in the United States out of business. What have these economic policies meant for farmers in other countries?

The Institute for Agriculture and Trade Policy estimates that the federal subsidy for corn enables US growers to sell their corn in Mexico for 25 percent less than the cost of producing it in the United States *and* lower than the cost of growing it in Mexico. The Mexican government does provide a small subsidy to its farmers, but too little to enable them to sell their corn at a price lower than the corn imported from Nebraska and Iowa.

It would make sense for the government of Mexico to protect domestic production of corn with tariffs on imported corn. However, the North American Free Trade Agreement (NAFTA) prevents the government of Mexico from imposing tariffs on corn grown in the United States.[4] In an article entitled "Why Mexico's Small Corn Farmers Go Hungry," Tina Rosenberg argues: "Mexico should be helping its corn farmers increase their productivity or move into new crops," instead of merely watching as displaced farmers fill Mexico's cities and cross the border to find work in the United States. Moreover, she says, "[I]f Washington wants to reduce Mexico's immigration to the United States, ending subsidies for agribusiness would be far more effective than beefing up the border patrol."[5]

We know, of course, that immigrants from Mexico who are illegally in the United States are hired to work in the fields at very low wages. Federal policies on immigration and guest workers, as well as agricultural subsidies, ensure that corporate landowners make a profit and that consumers in the United States continue to pay low prices for food.

The US government is not alone in promoting agricultural policies that are unfair as well as uncaring. The European Union also subsidizes commodities grown in Europe, imposes tariffs on agricultural products from other countries, and uses its power to open foreign markets for European goods and services. Neither the United States nor the European Union simply supports free trade and efficiency in the marketplace.

Free Trade

National, regional, and international trade regulations are necessary, and domestic producers should receive some protection at least for products sold in the domestic marketplace. To be just, however, these trade regulations should be fair and caring for all countries. This has not generally been the case.

In 1947, in an attempt to rebuild the world economy after World War II, twenty-three nations established an international organization to promote trade and settle disputes. The result, a *New York Times* editorial asserts, was

> ... more than a half-century of unfairness in the global
> trade system. ... Over the next 50 years, that club, now
> known as the World Trade Organization, aggressively dis-
> mantled barriers against trade in industrial goods and ser-
> vices—the areas in which its members hold a comparative
> advantage. That same club dragged its feet on dismantling
> barriers against trade in agriculture and textiles, where poor
> countries have an advantage.[6]

Supporters of the World Trade Organization (WTO) argue that free trade
will benefit all countries, as each specializes where it has a comparative advantage. This economic argument holds that it will be best for all countries if
each country concentrates on the goods and services it is able to produce at a
cost lower than other countries. Neoclassical economists claim that every
country will prosper by trading for what it does not produce.

The model of comparative advantage is dated, however, because it assumes that capital in the various countries will be invested within each
country, which is no longer the case. A global economy operates on the
principle of "absolute advantage" rather than the older rule of comparative
advantage, and this means that capital will go wherever it will earn a greater
return, and jobs will be created wherever the cost of labor is lowest.

Free trade in the global economy relies on economic policies that prevent countries from exercising control over the price of imported goods
and services that undercut domestic production, and over the investment
of foreign capital that favors goods for export.

Economists Herman E. Daly and Joshua Farley remind us that:

> [I]nternational free trade is not really trade between nations,
> but rather trade between private firms or individuals resid-
> ing in different nations. Their transactions are carried out for
> the private benefit of the contracting parties, not for the
> larger benefit of their national communities. The policy of
> free trade represents the assumption that if these transac-
> tions benefit the private contracting parties, then they will
> also benefit the larger collectives (nations) to which each

party belongs. "What's good for General Motors is good for the USA," to recall a famous statement.[7]

The result is that the rich become richer, and the poor become more numerous. "In the presence of capital mobility, money will logically flow to wherever there is an absolute advantage of production."[8]

A report published by the World Bank verifies that from 1989 to 1999 the fifteen poorest countries (which had not experienced war) suffered a *decrease* in real per-capita income by an average of 3.2 percent. In this same period, however, the fifteen wealthiest countries enjoyed an average *increase* in per-capita income of 15.5 percent.[9]

Countries able to resist free trade and control foreign imports and investment, in order to protect domestic production and markets, have achieved significant economic development despite globalization. This is the path taken by Taiwan, Korea, Singapore, Hong Kong, Thailand, and Malaysia, and it is how China has so quickly become a major economic power.

Corporations

Laws that favor multinational corporations exacerbate the present imbalance of power in the global economy. Corporate lobbies in developed countries have not only maintained subsidies for commodities, but also persuaded their governments to support policies for loans to developing countries by the World Bank and International Monetary Fund (IMF), which require these countries to open their markets to multinational investment. The result has been devastating for small farmers around the world.

In an article written at the end of 2004 entitled "Supermarket Giants Crush Central American Farmers," Celia W. Dugger explains that:

> Across Latin America, supermarket chains partly or wholly owned by global corporate goliaths like Ahold, Wal-Mart, and Carrefour have revolutionized food distribution in the short span of a decade and have now begun to transform food growing, too. The megastores are popular with customers for their lower prices, choice and convenience. But their

sudden appearance has brought unanticipated and daunting
challenges to millions of struggling, small farmers. The
stark danger is that increasing numbers of them will go bust
and join streams of desperate migrants to America and the
urban slums of their own countries. Their declining for-
tunes, economists and agronomists fear, could worsen inequality in a region where the gap between rich and poor
already yawns cavernously and the concentration of land in
the hands of an elite has historically fueled cycles of rebellion and violent repression.[10]

Foreign investment in Latin America was encouraged and protected under free trade rules in order to help develop the economies of these countries. The argument was that the resulting increase in gross national
product (GNP) would have beneficial consequences for many of the
people, and not only for the shareholders, managers, and employees of the
new retailers. The consequences, however, as Celia W. Dugger explains,
have been otherwise.

As the chains' market share expands, farmers who are shut
out find themselves forced to retreat to shrinking rural markets. The changes would not be so troubling if the region's
economies were growing robustly and generating decent
jobs for globalization's losers. But economic growth has not
kept pace with rising populations. The number of people living below poverty lines in Latin America has risen from 200
million in 1990 to 224 million this year. More than 6 in 10
people living in rural areas are still poor.[11]

Poverty

Chronic poverty is a direct consequence of our present economic policies.
This judgment was confirmed in December of 2006 by the Independent
Evaluation Group of the World Bank, which reported that, despite having

a goal to alleviate poverty, the lending practices of the World Bank have been largely ineffectual in realizing this goal.

> Some of the report reads like an amalgam of the sorts of criticisms that have been leveled against the World Bank for years by activists who accuse it of an ideological bias toward market reforms and a callous disregard for the people bearing the brunt of such policies. The report chides the bank for failing to help cushion poor people against price and currency liberalizations; for focusing on the fiscal sustainability of pension systems to the detriment of the poor; for promoting the privatization of power industries without thinking enough about wiring up the indigent.[12]

The report acknowledges that the total number of people in the world living on less than a dollar a day has declined between 1990 and 2002, although it remains at about 1.1 billion, but the overall decline in poverty is largely because of the rapid development of China's economy. Unlike China, poor countries that have accepted World Bank loans and conditions requiring trade liberalization and cuts in public spending for health and education have not made progress in alleviating poverty.

The report also criticizes the World Bank for not understanding or appreciating local conditions in poor countries, and for emphasizing economic growth without requiring at the same time a more equitable distribution of the income generated from that growth. For instance, the report noted that loans from the World Bank to Georgia in support of the oil industry led to economic growth, but very few jobs. Vinod Thomas, director-general of the Independent Evaluation Group, says that the report clearly demonstrates that economic growth by itself does not alleviate poverty. "It has been a mistaken notion that you can grow first and worry about the distribution later."[13]

Reasoning inductively from the facts given in this report, we suggest that national and international economic policies must ensure a just distribution of income and not merely seek economic growth.

We agree with the philosopher John Rawls, who argues that if, before we were conceived, we didn't know what the specific conditions of our own lives would be, we would want society to be governed by two principles:

- Each person should have an equal right to the most extensive total system of equal basic liberties compatible with a similar system of liberty for all.
- Social and economic inequalities (of wealth and power) are just only if they result in benefits for everyone, especially the least advantaged members of society.[14]

All people should enjoy both personal freedom and economic benefits, and economic inequality is only justifiable if it contributes to the common good and helps the poor. This is one way of stating more precisely the moral presumption that economic justice must be both fair and caring.

Can the growing disparity between the wealthy and the poor, both in the United States and in many other countries as well, be justified as contributing to the common good and also as helping the poor? Perhaps, but we suggest that those who make this unlikely claim have the burden of proving it.

With Rawls, we conclude that economic justice requires compensatory benefits for those disadvantaged by the inequalities of our economic system. Thus, we maintain that those who would set this moral presumption aside have the burden of proving that the present global economy will achieve a greater good for a greater number of people.

As our moral presumption asserts economic and social human rights, we argue that overturning it should require *compelling* evidence. Those who support the present system bear the burden of proof to justify it, not those who demand policies that are more fair and caring.

CHARACTER: ACTING WITH INTEGRITY

Assertiveness is a character trait highly valued for success. Yet, in a society reeling from corporate scandals, our moral presumption should be that economic justice requires integrity.

It would be naïve, of course, to believe that everyone will be honest and forthright, and so we pay taxes to support a public system of retributive justice that will punish wrongdoing and may deter wrongdoing by the threat of punishment. Nonetheless, in addition to enforcing laws that punish fraud, we should expect corporate directors, business executives, and government officials to fulfill their economic and political responsibilities with integrity.

Corporate Leaders

This means we must have zero tolerance for rationalizations such as "we will do whatever it takes" to achieve greater profits. This is the view of corporate officials who have lied about earnings in order to keep stock values high, or who have hidden income in tax shelters to avoid taxes. It is also how some members of the US Congress have tried to justify public spending projects that benefit friends and contributing supporters.

When there appears to be a lack of integrity among our economic and political leaders, then we all become less trusting. This is not only disappointing, but also undermines the relationships that enable us to work together for a more just society.

If the people "on the top" of the political and economic system seem to be "on the take," then those who see themselves as being "on the bottom" of the system are more inclined simply to "look out for themselves." If our economy appears to be controlled by people without integrity, we should not be surprised to discover that many employees are stealing from their companies and doing as little work as possible whenever they can.

In this regard the unprecedented rise over the past few years in the compensation of corporate executives is extremely troubling. We may differ in our understanding of what a fair salary for executives should be, but certainly the increasing disparity between the wages and salaries of average workers and the inflated compensation packages of CEOs is unfair.

Consider these facts. "In 2004, the average CEO of a major company received $9.84 million in total compensation, according to a study by compensation consultant Pearl Meyer & Partners for the *New York Times*. This represents a 12 percent increase in CEO pay over 2003. In contrast, the average nonsupervisory worker's pay increased just 2.2 percent to $27,485 in 2004."[15]

From 1990 to 2000 the average hourly pay ratio between CEOs and workers rose from 100:1 to 500:1. Were CEOs in 2000 five times more effective than in 1990? There is no evidence to support such a claim, so it is hard to see how the increasing disparity between executives and workers can be justified.[16]

Character matters, in friendships as well as in our economic life. Integrity is important for both. We suspect that most people agree, although we all know stories of individuals who have "gotten ahead" by being ruthless and deceptive. Yet, if we are committed to economic justice, then we must act with integrity as well as compassion and encourage others to do likewise.

Consumers

One way consumers can act with integrity is to demand fair policies in the growing, making, and marketing of commodities. Consumers can exercise this responsibility by voting for legislators who will support economic policies that are fair and caring.

In addition, consumers can use their purchasing power to demand greater accountability by the corporations that produce and sell the products we all buy. A good example of exercising this moral option involves Fair Trade coffee. Coffee became a colonial cash crop in the nineteenth century. In tropical climates plantations were developed where laborers worked for low wages. Now, the expanding market for coffee generates income for about twenty-five million farm workers in nearly fifty countries.

In the United States coffee is the largest food import. Prices are set by what is known as the New York "C" Contract market, which fluctuates in response to factors affecting production, such as the weather and political instability in countries that are major exporters.

Large coffee producers usually process and export their own harvests, making substantial profits because they pay extremely low wages (two to three dollars a day) to their farm workers. Most small coffee farmers have had to sell their crops to exporters, who pay the farmers much less than the market price and then take the bulk of the profit when they sell the coffee to retailers.

The Fair Trade movement, however, has begun to change the coffee economy. To ensure small farmers a living wage for growing coffee, cooperatives have been organized that guarantee a minimum price of $1.26/pound regardless of the market price (which has fallen as low as 50 cents/pound), credit at reasonable interest rates, and long-term relationships with retailers.

This system has successfully created a market in the United States and Europe for Fair Trade certified coffee, because consumers in these countries have been willing to pay more for Fair Trade coffee so that those who grow it will receive a living wage for their labor.

In the United States more than one hundred companies now have licensing agreements to offer Fair Trade coffee, including Starbucks, Tully's, Peet's, Equal Exchange, Diedrich, and Green Mountain. Retailers, who receive requests from consumers to stock higher-priced Fair Trade coffee, are usually happy to do so, as they make their profit no matter what brand of coffee their customers buy.

This represents a significant victory in the struggle to ensure a living wage for coffee farmers. So far, however, companies such as Starbucks only sell packages of Fair Trade coffee, rather than selling brewed Fair Trade coffee by the cup. As a consequence, Fair Trade farmers are now able to obtain a living wage for only about 20 percent of their coffee, and have to accept a much lower market price for the rest of their crop.

Therefore, we urge coffee drinkers who visit Starbucks or similar coffee shops to request that Fair Trade coffee be served and not merely sold. If coffee chains like Starbucks begin to brew as well as sell packages of Fair Trade coffee, then small farmers will be more likely to achieve the living wage that economic justice requires.

Advocates for Fair Trade have extended the certifying process to other products. The Fairtrade Labeling Organizations International (FLO) was established in 1997 and now certifies a growing number of products including tea, cocoa, sugar, honey, bananas, and orange juice, as well as coffee. FLO is open to associations of small farmers who are poor and do not depend on hired labor. In addition, these farmer associations have to be managed using open and democratic procedures. Representatives from FLO annually inspect Fair Trade farms in producing countries.[17]

This new economic system for growing and marketing commodities is now only a small part of the global economy, but it demonstrates that consumers can help to ensure greater economic justice for those who labor to grow the commodities we consume.

RELATIONSHIPS: A SUSTAINING ECONOMY

Asserting that a just economy must involve caring for others resists the traditional distinction in moral philosophy between charity and justice. Most moral philosophers would argue that justice requires only equity, because justice means ensuring that people receive what they are due, whereas charity involves "giving above and beyond what is required."

We suggest, however, that economic justice requires more than giving others their due, at least as this "due" is generally construed. People in affluent countries may not have any legal obligation to help the poor in their own country or elsewhere. Yet, we believe that those (of us) who benefit more from the way the economic system works should support care for those who are victimized by this system.

Our moral presumption is that those who benefit the most from the global economy have a responsibility to care about those who benefit the least. We should support economic policies that will achieve greater justice by distributing income more fairly.

Most economists argue that the economy must reward the aggressive pursuit of self-interest in order to maximize benefits for all people, even if this means that some become much better off. This is, in fact, the argument made by Adam Smith in his famous book, *The Wealth of Nations*.[18] In the twenty-first century, however, there are reasons for challenging this nineteenth-century assumption. An economy driven only by self-interest, where power is unfairly distributed, will be unjust. Moreover, an economy driven only by self-interest, in an increasingly crowded world with limited resources, will be unsustainable.

Seeking not merely to maximize profits, but a sustainable as well as a just economy, is an ethical goal. We have seen that some consumers will pay more for a product when they have an ethical reason for doing so. To provide a living wage for farmers and their families, thousands of consumers pay a higher price for their coffee. Their relationship to the coffee growers moves consumers to make a decision that, according to neoclassical economic theory, is irrational, because they are paying more for coffee than the price set by the market.

Similarly, the Jubilee campaign to forgive the international debts of some developing countries also challenges conventional economic theory. Yet, after years of strenuous lobbying by charitable and religious organizations, the World Bank and the International Monetary Fund have forgiven fifty-five billion dollars in debts owed by eighteen of the world's poorest countries.

The World Bank and the IMF began managing this international debt after it ballooned to alarming levels in the 1980s. The debt crisis was created a decade earlier when banks with massive deposits from oil-producing countries promoted loans to developing countries with low but floating interest rates. In the early 1980s, however, the United States raised interest rates to fight inflation, which pushed up the cost of borrowing all over the world, and at the same time a surplus of raw materials in international markets depressed prices for commodities. With higher debt payments and decreased income, the developing countries were unable to pay the interest on their debts, much less repay the principal.

The IMF required that countries seeking to reschedule their debt repayments accept "structural adjustment programs" (SAPs) that severely reduce government spending. This has meant that governments with large foreign debts have had to slash funding for education, health, and social services, to limit food subsidies, and to cut jobs and wages in government. In many countries the result has been a recession or even a depression, and the poorest people in these countries have suffered the most.[19]

Moral philosophy is in agreement with economic theory that promises should be kept and debts repaid. It is unfair, however, to require people to repay bad debts incurred by their leaders, who often were not chosen by the people through free elections and who stole or squandered much of the money they borrowed. In addition, poor countries will never be able to repay these loans and at the same time invest in the economic development their people so desperately need.

We see in this example of forgiving international debt that the economy is greatly affected by the policies of national governments and also by the international institutions dominated by the most powerful economic interests. Yet, these policies may also be influenced by the lobbying efforts of committed groups of citizens. Government policies are not likely to ensure economic justice unless we all do our part by demanding that national and international policies be fair and caring.

Given the massive global poverty that mires billions of people in lives of deprivation, we are not persuaded that the *consequences* of our present global economy provide the greatest good for the greatest number of people. Therefore, we argue that those who do not believe economic justice includes caring for the most disadvantaged in our global economy should bear the burden of proof required to show that merely protecting "fair" competition in the marketplace will lead to results that are more just.

At stake are the human rights of more than a billion people. Therefore, we assert that *compelling* evidence is needed to set aside the presumption that economic justice should be fair and caring.

ECONOMIC RIGHTS: PROGRESSIVE REALIZATION

US workers are now protected by laws that provide a minimum wage, unemployment compensation for those out of work, social security for retirees, and health and safety standards in the workplace. Before these laws were passed in the middle of the twentieth century, many argued that workers did not have a right to such protection. Some advocates of "pure" capitalism even claimed the costs of providing employees with such benefits would undermine economic productivity, and thus reduce the income generated by the economy for its workers.

A disaster changed American thinking. The Great Depression in the 1930s proved that the economy is not simply a self-governing natural system, but instead is the result of human choices. Different choices in government economic polity were made under the New Deal. Laws were enacted that recognize the rights of working people, and every government since has protected (more or less) these economic rights.

Today there is strong support for the ethical presumption that a just economy must be committed to realizing economic rights.

Of course, the debate about the extent of these rights continues, and it is not clear that our economy can provide all the economic benefits some workers have come to expect as their due. Yet, economic justice must continue to mean the realization of social and economic rights, which are asserted by international human rights law and protected by the laws of most countries.

International Law

The standard under international law for securing economic rights is not immediate enforcement, but progressive realization. Economic and social rights require economic development and not simply the political will to enforce a right, as is the case with civil and political rights.

Thus, economic justice does not require the full realization of the economic rights asserted by international law, when economic conditions do not make this feasible. Instead, governments are to be held responsible for legislating policies and funding programs that reasonably may be expected to achieve the realization of these rights in a timely manner.

The United States has not ratified the International Covenant on Economic, Social and Cultural Rights, and so US courts do not recognize this treaty as having legal authority in the United States. Yet, many laws in the United States affirm similar standards of economic justice. Moreover, in most countries the ICESCR defines the law, and even in the United States its moral authority should not be ignored.

Therefore, we suggest that the standards of international law concerning economic rights should be affirmed everywhere as moral presumptions for economic justice.

Child Labor

The prohibition of child labor in international human rights law is one clear example of a moral presumption that most everyone defends, but many countries ignore. The International Labor Organization (ILO) estimates that 250 million children between the ages of five and fourteen are working in developing countries at least half time.

About two-thirds of these children are in Asia and a third in Africa. In rural areas children work in agriculture and as domestics. In cities children labor in trades, services, manufacturing, and construction. A working child often helps to support his or her family, but the benefits of child labor depend mainly on the age of the child, the conditions in which the child works, and whether working prevents the child from going to school.

Most of these children work long hours, often in dangerous and unhealthy conditions, and suffer both physical and psychological harm. Many of these children are deprived of an education and a normal childhood. Some are abducted, beaten, and treated as slaves.[20]

Recently, consumer groups in the US and Europe have begun to use their purchasing power to demand an end to child labor and abusive conditions for workers. To give only one example, university students lobbied the Follett bookstores on their campuses until Follett agreed to enforce a code of conduct on all its vendors, which states that:

- Manufacturers shall not require workers to work more than the lesser of 48 regular working hours per week, or the limit on regular working hours under applicable local law, and shall provide workers with at least one day off in every 7-day period.
- The use of child labor is not permissible and will not be tolerated. . . . Workers can be no less than fourteen years of age and not younger than the compulsory age to be in school in the country where the work is to be performed.
- Manufacturers shall treat workers with dignity and respect. No worker shall be subject to any physical, sexual, psychological or verbal harassment or abuse.[21]

As effective monitoring is essential for the implementation of such a code of conduct, Follett has authorized an independent third-party monitor to make unannounced visits to the facilities of Follett's vendors. Follett requires that its vendors provide the names and locations of production facilities where products are made for Follett stores, and that these vendors certify annually that they are in compliance with the code.

In the global economy violations of human rights are everywhere, and in too many countries there has been little progress. Nonetheless, few governments claim publicly that the moral presumptions now asserted by human rights law are unfair or unimportant. For instance, child labor is wrong, and we all know that it is wrong.

Moreover, as we have seen, consumer advocacy can make a difference in the global marketplace. We can use our buying power to promote economic policies that will help protect the economic and social rights of workers all over the world.

Surely, the burden of showing that economic human rights are an unwarranted or unreasonable aspiration rests on those who make such a claim. Moreover, given the violations of human rights throughout the global economy, *compelling* evidence should be required to set aside our moral commitment to securing economic and social human rights for every person.

It is not enough simply to claim that economic development through free trade will "trickle down" to improve the lives of most people in a poor society. We should aspire to realize a higher standard of economic justice.

JUSTICE AS FAIR AND CARING

Economic justice is often defined as ensuring that people receive what is due to them because of their labor, or their managerial skill, or their capital investment. From this perspective the whole debate is about what economic policies will deliver the greatest wealth for the greatest number of people. This approach reduces ethics to a cost-benefit analysis and ignores all the moral presumptions that we have argued should shape both political and economic policies.

We maintain, instead, that economic justice must be fair and caring. The ethical presumptions we have developed in this chapter include the following:

- We have a duty to ensure a fair and caring distribution of economic benefits.

- Free trade policies should be fair and fairly administered.
- Those disadvantaged by unfair economic policies should be compensated.
- A just economy will reward the character trait of integrity.
- Corporate executives should encourage more reasonable compensation.
- Consumers should lobby stores to sell Fair Trade products.
- Relationships must be strengthened for economic development to be sustainable.
- Those who benefit most from the economy have the greatest responsibility.
- Charity is necessary now to help offset the unfair distribution of resources.
- The unfair debts of developing countries should be forgiven.
- We should oppose the SAPs imposed by the IMF on developing countries.
- Economic justice requires the progressive realization of economic and social human rights.
- Consumers should demand that vendors protect workers' rights.
- Codes of conduct for manufactures should explicitly prohibit child labor.

Our economic system provides many benefits by harnessing the human energy that is expressed in the pursuit of self-interest, and economic competition is clearly important for allocating resources and stimulating innovation. As in sports, the desire to win and the thrill of competing may bring out the best in us. Nonetheless, the playing field needs to be level, and the rules of the game have to be enforced without bias, or these same motivations will bring out the worst in us.

To create economic justice in a global economy, there must be assistance for the least advantaged so they have a fair chance to compete. In response to the devastating consequences of a continuing transfer of wealth from many poor countries to affluent societies, economic justice requires acts of charity by those who derive greater benefits from this economic system. These acts of charity should not only seek to alleviate the suffering of the poor, but should also seek greater economic justice.

To be sustainable, economic justice must rest on human relationships, and these must protect individual freedoms as well as encourage affirmative action to assist the poor and those most disadvantaged by history and dominance by the West.

Finally, economic justice requires the progressive realization of economic and social human rights. When a global economy makes the rich even richer and the poor more numerous, we must call for affirmative action by governments, corporate leaders, shareholders, and consumers in order to realize economic and social rights, which are among the necessary conditions for human dignity.

DOING ETHICS TOGETHER

I. Moral presumptions about economic justice.

1. Who is responsible for making sure that the economy is just? Give one example of how economic justice might require caring and not simply "fair" rules.

2. How does the Fair Trade system help small farmers? What is guaranteed to the producer? Why is the consumer important in this alternative economic system?

3. What evidence is there for the claim that the recent increases in compensation for corporate executives are unfair? How do you think compensation for corporate leaders should be decided?

II. International institutions.

1. The IMF and the World Bank require countries to open their markets to foreign goods as a condition for economic development loans. Argue for or against this

requirement. What are the SAPs? Argue for or against these restrictions.

2. Make an argument in favor of the World Bank and IMF's decision to forgive fifty-five billion dollars in loans to eighteen poverty-stricken countries. Then offer an ethical argument opposed to this decision. Which argument do you find more convincing?

3. Explain why free trade agreements concerning a commodity, such as the NAFTA agreement that affects the sale of corn in Mexico, may be unfair.

III. Inequity in the globalized marketplace.

1. How would you persuade a Latin American consumer who values the lower prices of shopping at a megastore to buy goods from traditional markets? Would you make the same argument to someone in the United States about shopping at Wal-Mart? Explain your reasoning.

2. Who should have the power to decide whether or not the economic policies in a developing country are good for the majority of its people? (Consider the roles of international institutions as well as multinational corporations and national governments.)

3. Explain what US citizens can do to help people in other countries realize greater economic justice.

15

Our Natural World

LIVING ECOLOGICALLY

We depend on the natural world for our lives, and we are also part of the natural world. With our language and culture we can separate ourselves from nature, and yet we are natural. Even our language and culture is natural, for us. Therefore, doing ethics is also part of our human nature.

Living ecologically requires that we consider how to maintain the ecosystems of the earth that support life. This is an ethical issue as well as a matter of ecology, politics, and economics.

Those who are religious may embrace a duty to care for the natural world, as stewards (Jews and Christians) or vice-regents (Muslims) of God. Jains (in the Hindu tradition) affirm respect for all animal life, and Buddhists try not to cause suffering for sentient beings. Indigenous peoples respect the animals they observe, hunt, eat, and tell stories about.

Yet, anyone who has lived in Jewish, Christian, or Muslim cultures knows that nature today is primarily a resource for human life. Moreover, most Hindus, Buddhists, and indigenous peoples are all tempted now by the opportunities and technology of modern life to exploit their natural resources in ways that are environmentally damaging and unsustainable.

Perhaps, as some claim, ecology is fundamentally a spiritual issue. At first glance, however, living ecologically seems primarily to concern our material desires and habits as consumers.

DUTY: LIVING ECOLOGICALLY

To argue that all human beings have a duty to live ecologically, we need to understand what this would mean. We also need to consider what moral presumptions would be involved in acting on this duty.

Ecology is the study of living organisms in their environment. The word is derived from the Greek words *oikos* ("household") and *logos* ("study"), so we might say that ecology is the study of our natural household. In ecology, the word *ecosystem* refers to the natural organization and interaction of all the living and nonliving elements in a particular place. There are many ecosystems on earth, and the earth is also an ecosystem.

Living ecologically means living responsibly within our ecosystems. It does not mean preserving all other species or simply conserving nature, as ecosystems by their very nature are evolving. It does mean understanding our relationship to the other species in our environment as well as our dependence on ecosystems, and then supporting a flourishing way of life within the constraints of these ecosystems.

To live ecologically we need to create a culture that supports and celebrates this way of life.

Duty to Care

Our duty to respect other human beings does not by itself imply that we have a duty to the other species in our ecosystems or to the earth. Yet, if we were to say that we have a duty to care for the ecosystems of the earth, this affirmation would make sense to most of us. As we have a duty to care for our own home and a duty to do no harm to other homes, we may easily extend this notion to include a duty to care for our natural household.

Ecologist Holmes Rolston III writes: "Several billion years' worth of creative toil, several million species of teeming life, have been handed over to the care of this late-coming species in which mind has flowered and morals have emerged. Ought not this sole moral species do something less self-interested than count all the produce of an evolutionary ecosystem as nothing but human resources?" We concur with Rolston that: "Such an attitude hardly seems biologically informed, much less ethically adequate."[1]

Kant and Gandhi agreed that we have a duty to tell the truth, and certainly this is a duty we can act on, if we have a good will. The duty to live ecologically may be understood as the duty to live truthfully—to understand life as it is, both as ecosystems and as evolutionary change—and then to live as flourishing human communities on the basis of this understanding.

Living less wastefully, recycling more, and consuming less are all "more or less" propositions. Understanding the difference, however, between using renewable and nonrenewable resources will help us clarify our duty with respect to each.

Resources

Renewable resources, such as forests, offer us not only "stock" that may be harvested, but also essential life-supporting "fund-services" for our ecosystem. Trees are a source of wood, but also absorb carbon dioxide and add oxygen to the atmosphere, maintain animal habitats, and hold and replenish the soil.

"No one created renewable resources," Daly and Farley remind us, "therefore no single generation has the right to reduce the amount of the resource a future generation can sustainably consume. . . . "[2] This suggests that "resource stocks must be at least as large as that which provides the maximum sustainable yield."[3] We have a duty, therefore, to limit our human harvest of renewable, living resources to no more than the optimal scale in order to preserve the stock and also the fund-services provided by these species and their habitats.

What moral presumption should guide our use of nonrenewable resources, such as petroleum, minerals, and water in deep aquifers that can only be replenished over centuries, if at all?

"As long as the use of the resource generates waste no faster than the ecosystem can absorb it, the use of exhaustible resources by one generation will not reduce renewable natural capital. Keeping fossil fuel use within such limits would automatically limit our ability to extract other mineral resources."[4] (By "natural capital" we mean stocks or funds that provide either natural resources or natural services for the future. The "waste-absorption" capability of an ecosystem is a fund-service.)

It seems reasonable to assert that we also have a duty to recycle such resources as efficiently as possible, and to invest in research to develop substitutes for the nonrenewable resources we are using up. Specifically, through taxation policies we could "capture marginal user costs, the unearned income from nonrenewable resources,"[5] in order to invest in developing substitutes to replace the nonrenewable resources we are using up.

Our duty, therefore, to live more ecologically at least includes taking steps to:

Renewable resources

- Limit the harvest of biotic resources to the optimal scale for each stock.
- Preserve the stock for future generations.
- Maintain the fund-services provided to the ecosystem by biotic resources.

Nonrenewable resources

- Use at a rate no greater than the waste-absorption capability of the ecosystem.
- Capture and use the unearned income from natural capital to develop substitutes.

CHARACTER: LIVING MORE SIMPLY

We want to be persons of integrity, and this gives us another reason for facing the truth about the degradation of the environment and then acting on our awareness of this crisis. Also, we want to be caring, which means having the courage to do what is right even when it is not in our individual self-interest.

For reasons such as these, Aldo Leopold argues that those doing ethics need to have greater respect for the land. "All ethics so far evolved rest upon a single premise: that the individual is a member of a community of interdependent parts. . . . The land ethic simply enlarges the boundaries of the community to include soils, waters, plants, and animals, or collectively: the land."[6]

This means living ecologically. "In short, a land ethic changes the role of *Homo sapiens* from conqueror of the land-community to plain member and citizen of it."[7] This is more than a change in government policies, even more than a change in what we do as individuals. It is a change in who we are—a change in our character.

"No important change in ethics," Leopold argues, "was ever accomplished without an internal change in our intellectual emphasis, loyalties, affections, and convictions."[8] To live ecologically, we have to understand ourselves as part of the complex and diverse ecology of life that has evolved on earth.

Therefore, we must encourage greater respect for our ecosystems, for the regenerative power of nature, and also for the evolutionary process that has given us the capacity to care for the environment. Whether we see our life on earth as a divine gift or as a natural wonder, we need to cultivate a more caring attitude toward the ecological systems that sustain all life.

This means that we must change the *character* of our society. Rather than striving to consume more of the earth's resources, and to acquire more possessions for ourselves, we need to focus on being more creative in the ways that we care for the natural world.

In economic terms, this means working for a society that is no longer driven by policies that promote economic growth. Instead, our goal should be a steady-state economy functioning at an optimal scale. Economists Herman E. Daly and Joshua Farley explain what this would mean:

> The main idea of a steady-state economy is to maintain constant stocks of wealth and people at levels that are sufficient for a long and good life. The throughput by which these stocks are maintained should be low rather than high and always within the regenerative and absorptive capacities of the ecosystem. The system is therefore sustainable—it can

continue for a long time. The path of progress in the steady
state is no longer to get bigger, but to get better.[9]

The idea of a steady-state economy dates back to the nineteenth century. John Stuart Mill wrote that:

> . . . a stationary condition of capital and population implies
> no stationary state of human improvement. There would be
> as much scope as ever for all kinds of mental culture, and
> moral and social progress; as much room for improving the
> Art of Living and much more likelihood of its being im-
> proved, when minds cease to be engrossed by the art of get-
> ting on.[10]

In the twentieth century, neoclassical economists abandoned this idea,
believing it would mean an end to progress, and as a society we have come
to accept that continuous economic growth is necessary for a good life. An
economy using up nonrenewable resources, however, cannot grow forever
in the finite environment of the earth. Moreover, an economy generating
waste that exceeds the absorption capacity of nature will increasingly de-
grade the environment.

Therefore, we must resist the claim that we have to maintain or even increase our rate of consumption so the economy will continue to grow and
our wealth (if we are among the most fortunate) will increase.

A steady-state economy would continue to invest heavily in new technology, but the focus would be on technological advances that are more
ecologically sustainable. This is not simply a matter of improving efficiency, but of exploring new ways to use sources of energy that we have
ignored, because coal, oil, and gas have been so plentiful and readily
available.

As citizens, we now must persuade our political leaders that economic
policies be more sustainable. As consumers, we now must use our purchasing power to promote investment in more energy efficient technology. If
consumers are eager to buy more efficient cars, industry will produce

them. If, as citizens and consumers, we demand that governments should provide economic incentives to spur the development of more ecologically sustainable sources of power, legislatures will respond.

Therefore, our moral presumptions concerning character include living with greater respect for nature by:

- Reducing consumption and increasing thrift.
- Wasting less and recycling more.
- Supporting policies required for a steady-state economy.
- Investing in solar, wind, and geothermal power, and in renewable fuels.
- Providing incentives for more efficient and less polluting technology.

To act responsibly, in both our roles as citizens and as consumers, we need information that will enable us to understand what choices will encourage greater conservation of energy, less waste, more efficiency, decreased pollution, and new ways of recycling materials or rendering them biodegradable.

RELATIONSHIPS: LEARNING FROM ECOFEMINISM

The feminist critique of traditional ethics prompts us to reflect on how our humanity is shaped by our relationships with other species and with the ecosystems of the earth. Therefore, we consider the following moral presumptions as a way of living more ecologically. This ethical position is often described as "ecofeminism."

First, feminists argue, we should be suspicious of all "language of domination." Seeing how conceptions of justice and culture for so long allowed the domination of women by concealing this reality, and what this concealment was doing to the nature of both men and women, should make us suspicious of all similar language about our environment and its resources.

Our challenge, therefore, is not simply to use natural resources more efficiently, but to see that "resource" language reflects a tradition of domination.

Women have long been legal property valued for their utility. Trees, fish, birds, earthworms, and all the rest of nature continue to be "worth" something because of the uses we can make of these resources.

Yet, clearly women as well as other species are not simply resources for our use, but have worth in themselves and for themselves. Therefore, we should affirm the equality of women with men, but also be suspicious of language that refers to nature in a dominating manner. We need to accept that we are part of nature and are worthy to be stewards of the earth only if we respect other species and also the evolutionary process that has given human beings the ability to survive and thrive.

Similarly, we should be suspicious of what is often characterized as an objective or neutral point of view of the world. We need to ensure that valuing "objectivity" does not simply mean describing discrimination against women and the degradation of the environment as the way things are (and must remain), for our moral responsibility is to challenge and change unethical conduct and social injustice wherever we find it.

In this sense, ecofeminism: "is a social ecology. It recognizes the twin dominations of women and nature as social problems rooted both in very concrete, historical, socioeconomic circumstances and in oppressive patriarchal conceptual frameworks which maintain and sanction these circumstances."[11] In short, we cannot live ecologically without changing the way we live together as men and women. For example, environmentalists tend to endorse population control uncritically, as a way of preserving nature. Generally, men take the lead in arguing for government policies that will restrict the number of children in families in order to protect the environment. In contrast:

> The [feminist] critical perspective argues that ignoring co-requisites, such as economic and social justice and women's reproductive health and rights, also makes the overt target of population policies (a change in birth rates) difficult to achieve. . . . The women's health advocates argue for a different approach to population policy—one that makes women's health and other basic needs more central to policy and program focus, and by doing so increases human

welfare, transforms oppressive gender relations, and reduces population growth rates.[12]

Second, feminists suggest that we need to pursue a contextual approach
to ecological living, which means recognizing that we can only make ethical decisions by considering carefully our diverse historical and cultural circumstances. Living ecologically does not simply mean following a new set
of rules. Instead, it involves lifting up the various patterns of life, as they
emerge, that embody just and healthy relationships between men, women,
and our ecosystems. It means evolving our culture.

"With its emphasis on inclusivity and difference, ecofeminism provides
a framework for recognizing that what counts as ecology and what counts
as appropriate conduct toward both human and nonhuman environments
is largely a matter of context."[13] Our challenge is not to try reduce the
many voices raising concerns today to a single point of view, but to listen
in order to hear what those who have long been silenced have to say.

This is in part what we are trying to do in this chapter and throughout
the entire book. We are considering various suggestions as to who we
should be and what we should do by reflecting on our duty, our concern
for character and relationships, and our rights, in order to construct ethical
presumptions, which we then test against our predictions of the consequences of acting on them.

Third, by being suspicious of traditional arguments for justice and by
embracing the diversity of human experience, feminists are able to high-
light ethical acts that have been neglected, such as caring, love, friendship,
and forgiveness.

These neglected ethical lessons often take the form of narrative, which
is generally shunned by moral philosophers because it is imprecise. Yet, literature is our primary way of teaching ethics, and this is especially the case
for peoples that have been marginalized in our societies. Karen Warren
tells of a Sioux boy, who was taught by his grandparents:

> . . . to shoot your four-legged brother in his hind area, slow-
> ing it down but not killing it. Then, take the four legged's
> head in your hands, and look into his eyes. The eyes are

where all the suffering is. Look into your brother's eyes and feel his pain. Then, take your knife and cut the four-legged under his chin, here, on his neck, so that he dies quickly. And as you do, ask your brother, the four-legged, for forgiveness for what you do. Offer also a prayer of thanks to your four-legged kin for offering his body to you just now, when you need food to eat and clothing to wear. And promise the four-legged that you will put yourself back into the earth when you die, to become nourishment for the earth, and for the sister flowers, and for the brother deer.[14]

This powerful statement cannot be reduced to a moral rule or principle, but may stir us to have greater respect for the other species in our earth household.

We certainly need to be careful not to reduce the insights of ecofeminism to mere statements. Yet, we suggest that attending to our relationships with others and with the species of the earth's ecosystems, may help us construct (and act on) more creative ethical presumptions. Therefore, we should:

- Be suspicious of all language of domination.
- Address feminist and ecological issues together.
- Find diverse ways of living ecologically.
- Listen to the voices neglected by moral philosophy.
- Accept the challenge to be more caring and forgiving.

RIGHTS: PARTICIPATION AND PROTECTION

In chapter 7 we looked at provisions in the International Bill of Rights. The two main treaties under international law assert civil and political rights, as well as economic, social, and cultural rights. Neither of these treaties explicitly says anything about environmental rights, so we may wonder if a commitment to protect human rights will be helpful in considering ethical arguments about living more ecologically.

Reasoning by analogy from human rights, we might assert that some animals also have similar rights. If we were able to argue convincingly for these claims, we could try to resist the destruction of the environment by defending the rights of animals to a habitat that is necessary for them to survive and flourish.

Generally, however, those who assert environmental rights do so only for other human beings. Environmentalists are obviously concerned about the survival of other species, but most argue that the best strategy for preserving our natural habitats (and the species that live in them) involves relying on laws that create a duty to protect the environment and arguments about the consequences of environmental degradation.

Despite the lack of international treaties that specifically define and secure a human right to an environment that is healthy and sustainable, we will explore how human rights advocacy might support a more ecological way of life. To do this, we will look at several examples in order to construct moral presumptions concerning human survival, the conservation and the development of natural resources, and the enforcement of human rights.

Survival

In most countries a majority of people rely on the direct use of natural resources to survive. For instance, in Cambodia 80 percent of the population is rural, and per capita income for rural Cambodians is less than a dollar a day. To survive, these Cambodians depend on the lakes and streams for fishing and on the forests for wood and other resources.

Securing the right to use these environmental resources requires both just government policies and the just enforcement of these policies.

Under the National Environmental Action Plan of Cambodia, development is supposed to be sustainable and to improve the welfare of the poor. Companies that secure forest concessions are to treat local residents fairly, and commercial fishing lots are to be allocated in a way that does not encroach on the traditional livelihoods of communities living beside lakes and streams.

The reality, however, falls far short of the standards established by government policies. There is continued illegal fishing and logging by commercial interests, often with the complicity of the police or the military. More-over, courts lack the independence to uphold human rights standards, and so human rights advocates in Cambodia are often victims of intimidation and violence.[15]

Poor villagers in Cambodia continue to demand that the government enforce their right of access to natural resources, and their protest reminds us that environmental rights are not merely a concern of the affluent.

For people living in rural communities, access to environmental goods is necessary for survival. Improving food security in Cambodia will depend not only on substantive laws that are justly administered, but also on due process laws that recognize the right of poor people and their communities to participate in decision making about the use of natural resources where they live.

Environmental policies that protect individual and collective human rights are the primary way this can be accomplished. If civil and political rights are not protected, it will be impossible to protest effectively against the degradation of the environment and the unfair use of natural resources. Moreover, economic, social, and cultural rights cannot be realized without governments that are accountable and courts sufficiently independent to resist being corrupted.

Conservation

In Cambodia it seems clear that protecting the environment in order to sustain local livelihoods is good stewardship. Yet, in many countries there is conflict between those who are concerned with conservation and those who claim the right to use natural resources for their survival.

We see this in Kenya and Tanzania, where, in the past fifty years, large tracts of land have been set aside for parks to protect wildlife and generate tourist revenue for governments and businesses catering to foreign visitors. These conservation policies, however, have devastated the Maasai who roam the plain. More than one hundred thousand Maasai have been displaced, and the loss of access to the plain has led to overgrazing in the areas left to them, a decline in their life-sustaining herds, and hunger.

The plight of the Maasai is not unusual in Africa. The rural poor, who make up seventy percent of Africa's population, have been decimated by the policies of colonial and then independent governments, which have used the right of eminent domain to designate vast areas as public land and restrict access by the rural people who have long relied on this land for survival. These government decisions have failed to protect the procedural rights asserted by international law, which require participation in decision making by the people who are most affected by the decisions of their governments.

It is difficult to calculate the number of people displaced by these "conservation" strategies, but the total is estimated to be in the millions. In Africa, poorer countries have often set aside more land than nations with a higher standard of living, and generally there has been no compensation for those displaced. In Tanzania, after lengthy litigation, the High Court ruled in 1999 that the Maasai— who were displaced when the Mkomazi Game Reserve was established in 1952—are without customary land rights, and thus are not entitled to compensation for their loss of herds and income.[16]

Designating wildlife reserves is an effective strategy for preserving the natural environment. Moreover, many claim that "our" environmental right to ensure the survival of these natural areas should be given priority over the traditional claims of indigenous peoples to access these lands for food and other resources. It is not fair, however, that the poor pay a high cost for the conservation of natural resources, but receive few of the benefits. Moreover, it is wrong to ignore and violate their human rights.

Therefore, the rights of indigenous peoples must be asserted and protected. Peoples who seek access to the natural resources they depend on for their livelihood have claims that must be weighed against the demand of conservationists to exclude these peoples from their natural environments.

A settlement should be sought involving the participation of all concerned, with protection especially for those who have the fewest resources to advance their claims. Fortunately, there are examples in Africa of how this can be done.[17] As a last resort, when people are removed from their lands for legitimate public purposes, they must be fairly compensated and assisted in relocating and renewing a sustainable form of economic life.

The Communal Area Management Programme for Indigenous Resources (CAMPFIRE) in Zimbabwe is one of the best known examples of how local people will help protect wildlife in a nature park when they also benefit from the park. CAMPFIRE offers three incentives to local villagers. First, when the impala herds in the park are culled to reduce their numbers to a sustainable level, local people are offered the meat at less than market value but at a price that covers the cost of the cull. Second, the villages around the park also receive a portion of the revenue from the hunting allowed in the park, and each village decides how best to use these funds to meet the needs of its families. In addition, CAMPFIRE compensates villagers for the loss of livestock due to attacks by wild animals coming out of the park.[18]

Development

Achieving sustainable economic development that also protects the environment, and indigenous peoples living in harmony with it, is even more difficult, as the following case illustrates.

Before 1967 in Papua, the Kamoro people were living in relative peace below the Amungme people. Both communities existed, as they had for generations, on a subsistence economy that involved sustainable agriculture, using forest resources, and fishing and hunting. In 1967, however, the Freeport McMoRam Copper and Gold Company confiscated much of the land from these indigenous peoples in order to begin a massive mining operation.

Freeport's 1967 contract with the Indonesian government gave the corporation the right to take land, timber, water, and other natural resources, and to resettle the Kamoro and Amungme peoples. The company was not required to compensate local communities for the loss of their hunting and fishing grounds, forest products, food gardens, and drinking water.

The contract with the Indonesian government was enforced with the cooperation of the military, using coercion and intimidation. Large profits have been removed from the region for the benefit of foreign stockholders and a few cooperating Indonesians.

The impact on the environment has been devastating. Freeport decapitated one of the mountains held sacred by the Amungme and dumped into the local rivers millions of tons of mining waste. In addition, the area became the fastest growing "economic zone" in the Indonesian archipel-ago, and the town created to support the mining operation has grown to more than 120,000 people, many of whom live in crowded and unsanitary conditions.

Indonesian law, which has given the corporation free reign in the re-gion, does not meet international human rights standards. Community land rights are not recognized, and no protection is provided for traditional livelihoods and cultural rights.

In their struggle to preserve the natural environmental and their way of life, the Kamoro and Amungme have appealed to the Indonesian govern-ment, the UN, courts and governmental officials in the United States, and also directly to Freeport stockholders and management. These appeals in-clude interventions before the UN Commission on Human Rights and US congressional briefings, and two lawsuits filed in US courts on behalf of Amungme plaintiffs.[19]

This moral struggle reveals the importance of providing greater protec-tion for the habitats of indigenous peoples, and should motivate us to shame governments and corporations until they adopt the "best practice standards" set forth in international human rights law.

These standards are asserted by the International Labor Organization's Convention concerning Indigenous and Tribal Peoples in Independent Countries, the UN Draft Declaration on the Rights of Indigenous Peoples, and the Proposed American Declaration on the Rights of Indigenous Peo-ples being prepared by the Inter-American Commission on Human Rights.[20]

Enforcement

In addition to international human rights instruments, regional treaties and organizations that seek to enforce the law are important in Europe, Asia, Africa, and the Americas. The American Convention on Human Rights was adopted by American nations in 1969 and came into force in 1978. Its provisions are administered by the Inter-American Commission on Human Rights and the Inter-American Court of Human Rights, which are organs of the Organization of American States (OAS).

In 1988 the San Salvador Protocol to the American Convention asserted that everyone in the Americas has "the right to live in a healthy environment" (Article 11.1).[21] The Earth Summit held in Rio de Janeiro in 1992 raised awareness of environmental issues, and several Latin American nations incorporated the right from the protocol into their constitutions.

To date, however, this "environmental right" has not received the support within the OAS that many had hoped to see, and has been actively resisted by the United States government.

In 1998 the Inter-American Commission on Human Rights issued an injunction against illegal lumbering in indigenous territories of Nicaragua inhabited by the Awas Tingni people. When the Inter-American Court upheld the commission's ruling, it became clear that human rights advocacy and litigation might be an effective way of protecting at least some natural habitats.

Indigenous communities in the region are now preparing to use the tribunals of the Inter-American Human Rights system to seek protection for their ancestral lands.

Yet, specific environmental rights, such as the right to a healthy environment, remain vague and so courts are not likely to enforce them. Therefore, emphasizing the violation of established human rights, such as the right to life, the right to health, and the right to property, is probably a better strategy than asserting "environmental rights" per se.

We should try to protect the environment by resisting economic development wherever it: increases poverty, degrades the health of people, takes their property, denies them the procedural right to participate in such decisions, or deprives them of the substantive right to adequate compensation for any losses.

How might we state these moral presumptions about ecological living as assertions of human rights? Given the survival issues affecting the world's poor and the need both to conserve natural resources and promote economic development, we may agree, at least, that we should:

- Secure for all people the civil and political rights, as well as the economic, social, and cultural rights, guaranteed in the International Bill of Human Rights.

- Ensure that conservation measures protect access by people to natural resources necessary for their survival, or provide them just compensation for their losses.
- Require governments that permit economic development to involve communities in the decision making that will affect them.
- Hold corporations accountable for actions that deny the rights of people living in an environment to access and use its natural resources.

CONSEQUENCES: QUESTIONING OUR PRESUMPTIONS

We now ask if the possible consequences we foresee, of acting on the presumptions we have constructed in this chapter, seem either to support the presumptions or to call them into question.

We have a general *duty* to care for the earth's ecosystems, and specifically this includes limiting the harvest of renewable resources to the optimal scale for each stock and using nonrenewable resources in an ecologically responsible manner.

We cannot expect profit-making corporations to limit their harvesting of renewable resources to the optimal scale, except when they own the stock and thus have a direct interest in preserving it. Therefore, we must support laws that limit the harvesting of renewable resources, both to protect the stocks and also the fund-service contributions of the biotic resources to our ecosystems. It is hard to imagine a convincing consequential argument to the contrary.

Our presumptions about the use of nonrenewable resources are more controversial. For instance, limiting the mining and use of petroleum and minerals to a rate the ecosystem can absorb would mean curtailing the present extraction of both, as well as reducing our consumption of oil and coal. This would not only restrict the use of property that corporations have purchased or leased in order to extract these nonrenewable resources. It would also have significant and adverse consequences for our economy.

We presume, in addition, that we should capture the unearned income achieved by mining natural resources and use these funds to develop substitutes for the nonrenewable resources that we are depleting. Assessing a cost for the loss of our natural capital, which those who extract it have done nothing to create, would clearly lead to higher prices for these nonrenewable resources and everything made from them.

Would these adverse consequences outweigh using the funds to develop replacements? As our presumption does not assert a human right, the burden of proof only requires *convincing* evidence to set it aside. Those who disagree with our presumption are invited to present their arguments.

We have suggested that our moral presumptions concerning *character* include living with greater simplicity and respect for nature, and also supporting policies necessary for a steady-state economy.

The consequences of wasting less and recycling more seem clearly beneficial, as do policies that invest in solar, wind, and geothermal energy; renewable fuels like ethanol; and more efficient and less polluting technology. Yet, some will argue that reducing individual consumption and pursuing a steady-state economy would have very detrimental consequences for our way of life.

Those who take this position need only show *convincing* evidence, as no issue of human rights or retributive justice is at stake, that changing to a steady-state economy will have more adverse consequences than continuing to promote unsustainable growth in an ecosystem with finite resources.

Feminists urge us to be suspicious of all language of domination, to address feminist and ecological issues together, to look for diverse ways of living ecologically, and to listen to those who challenge us to be more caring and forgiving *in our relationships*.

There may well be adverse consequences in having increased sensitivity to others, but it seems reasonable to conclude that these negative outcomes are not likely to outweigh the positive benefits of knowing more and caring more about others and also the ecology of the earth. Only *convincing* evidence need be shown to overturn these presumptions.

We are left then to consider the likely consequences of acting on the moral presumptions we have constructed concerning *human rights*.

- That international human rights laws should be secured for all people.

The United States has tried to restrict international law to national standards, and this position is self-serving and thus morally untenable. There are, however, reasonable disputes about how a society might best strive to realize economic and social rights.

- Conservation measures should protect the rights of people to the natural resources they need for survival, even though this may result in less effective conservation.

Our moral presumption does not preclude restricting access to natural resources in some circumstances, as long as people and communities denied access are adequately compensated. Stated in this form, the presumption seems flexible enough to allow adjustments that will ensure that the positive outcomes of implementing a particular conservation measure will likely outweigh the possible negative consequences.

- Governments should implement participatory procedures enabling communities affected by economic development to have a voice in these decisions.

A participatory decision-making process is difficult to administer fairly and is time-consuming. Nevertheless, in Western countries such procedures are required by law for development projects, so how can anyone justify withholding this requirement of procedural justice from other peoples simply because their societies are less economically developed?

Of course, procedural justice does not guarantee substantive justice, but it does make it more likely that the decisions made by governments will be fair and more acceptable to those who are affected.

- Governments should hold corporations accountable for the environmental damage they cause.

Government regulation costs money, which must be raised by taxation. Environmental conditions imposed by governments on corporations are additional expenses that consumers will also have to pay, as companies raise prices on their products to cover these costs.

There is no world government to impose environmental costs equitably on corporations, but international treaties and intergovernmental organizations as well as national laws offer ways of trying to enforce corporate accountability for environmental damage. In addition, country reports under the terms of the International Covenant on Economic, Social and Cultural Rights allow public scrutiny of governmental plans for economic development and the procedures used in each country to ensure that corporations act responsibly.

Either consumers will pay taxes to cover the costs of cleaning up the environment, or the government must assess environmental costs to the corporations that created the damage. Generally, the latter approach will be better, as it gives corporations an incentive to minimize their damage to the environment in order to reduce the cost of making environmental improvements or compensating those who have suffered losses.

What burden of proof would those who oppose these moral presumptions have to meet in order to set them aside? As human rights are at stake, *compelling* evidence should be required.

The likely consequences we foresee of acting on these ethical presumptions seem to reinforce them. So, we conclude that these presumptions offer a more ecological way of living. We recognize that many people must be persuaded. We maintain, however, that those who oppose these moral presumptions bear the burden of showing that there are better alternatives.

DOING ETHICS TOGETHER

I. Duty.

1. State a moral presumption about using renewable resources and explain its importance.
2. Identify two nonrenewable resources. Argue in favor of the moral presumption that we should use these re-

sources at a rate no greater than the ecosystem can absorb the waste generated by their use. Then make an argument opposing this presumption.

3. Explain the ethical presumption that asserts that we should capture the unearned income realized by extracting a nonrenewable resource, and invest it to develop a substitute for the resource being depleted. As part of your explanation give an example.

II. Character and relationships.

1. Make an argument in favor of policies supporting a steady-state economy, and then criticize your reasoning. Does your argument in opposition to such policies concern consequences?
2. Illustrate the use of "language of domination" concerning the environment. Identify several different ways of thinking about living more ecologically.
3. What voices have been neglected by philosophy? Why is it important to hear these voices? Give an example from your experience of a situation in which someone's point of view was neglected.

III. Conservation and development.

1. Why might conservation strategies infringe on the rights of poor people to access the natural resources that they need to survive? Give an example and suggest a possible solution.
2. What measures should a government take to ensure that economic development preserves the environment? What responsibility does a government have for the local people who will be affected by economic development?

3. How might governments hold corporations accountable for the damage they cause to natural environments? What policies and enforcement systems might be necessary?

IV. Human rights strategies.

1. Why is it likely that advocating explicitly for environmental rights will not be effective? Give an example.
2. What specific human rights under international law might be asserted to protect poor and indigenous peoples from economic development that causes damage to their environment?
3. How might you define "the right to live in a healthy environment" that is asserted by the Protocol of San Salvador to the American Convention on Human Rights?

Notes

CHAPTER 1   OUR CHALLENGE: DOING ETHICS IN A PLURALISTIC SOCIETY

1. Anthony Weston writes: "We know that we really ought to listen to other people. We know that we ought not to act out of impatience or anger or indifference or prejudice. We know that we ought to take special care when making decisions that deeply affect not only our own lives but the lives of many others too. This is what ethics itself requires." Anthony Weston, *A 21st Century Ethical Toolbox* (New York: Oxford University Press, 2001), 2.

2. William Butler Yeats, *The Collected Poetry of William Butler Yeats* (New York: Macmillan, 1961), 184–185.

3. Robert Kane, *Through the Moral Maze: Searching for Absolute Values in a Pluralistic World* (Armonk, NY: North Castle Books, 1996), 1.

4. Sandra Blakeslee, "This is Your Brain Under Hypnosis," *The New York Times* (22 Nov. 2005).

5. What is known in physics as "Bell's theorem" proves mathematically that quantum mechanics is correct in asserting that at the quantum level our knowledge is limited to probabilities. Bell's theorem may be stated as holding that: "No physical theory of local hidden variables can ever reproduce all of the predictions of quantum mechanics." If hidden variables might explain our inability to predict at the quantum level the exact location of a particle, then we could conclude that we live in a deterministic world and simply have yet to identify all the variables that cause things to be where they are. Bell's theorem has been proven experimentally in the laboratory to be true.

"Bell's Theorem," *Wikipedia*, http://en.wikipedia.org/wiki/Bell's_theorem. See also "Bell's Theorem," Stanford Encyclopedia of Philosophy, online at htpp://plato.stanford.edu/entries/bell-theorem.

6. Benton Lewis, quoted in Wayne C. Booth, *The Company We Keep: An Ethics of Fiction* (Berkeley, CA: University of California Press, 1988), 324.

7. "There are an unlimited number of valid ways to interpret or evaluate any fiction, any historical event or historical account of events, any philosophy, any critical work. And there are even more ways to get it wrong." Anonymous, quoted in Wayne C. Booth, *The Company We Keep*, 324.

8. Simon Blackburn, professor of philosophy at Cambridge University, writes: "Human beings are ethical animals. I do not mean that we naturally behave particularly well, nor that we are endlessly telling each other what to do. But we grade and evaluate, and compare and admire, and claim and justify. . . . Events endlessly adjust our sense of responsibility, our guilt and shame and our sense of our own worth and that of others." Simon Blackburn, *Being Good: A Short Introduction to Ethics* (Oxford: Oxford University Press, 2001), 4.

9. *The Sayings of Confucius*, translated by James R. Ware (New York: New American Library, 1955), 27.

CHAPTER 2   REASONING TOGETHER: MAKING SENSE OF OUR EXPERIENCE

1. Anthony Weston writes: "Feeling right does not guarantee rightness. Feeling is part of the story, yes. Care, concern, passion—these are what make ethics so engaging and so compelling. . . . Still, we must also examine and temper our feelings too, even the strongest feelings. Take prejudice. To be prejudiced is to have a strong negative feeling about someone who is of a different ethnicity or gender or age or social class. . . . Ethics asks us to challenge those feelings instead." Anthony Weston, *A 21st Century Ethical Toolbox*, 9–10.

2. Michael Schulman and Eva Mekler, *Bringing Up a Moral Child: A New Approach for Teaching Your Child to Be Kind, Just, and Responsible* (Reading, MA: Addison-Wesley Publishing Company, 1985), 8.

3. Patrick J. Hurley, *A Concise Introduction to Logic*, seventh edition (Stamford, CT: Wadsworth, 2000), 33–39.

4. Ibid.

5. Sissela Bok, *Lying: Moral Choice in Public and Private Life* (New York: Vintage Books, 1999).

6. Deuteronomy 6:4–5 in the *Tanakh, A New Translation of The Holy Scriptures According to the Traditional Hebrew Text* (Philadelphia, PA: The Jewish Publication Society, 1985).

7. Swami Prabhavananda and Christopher Isherwood, *The Song of God: Bhagavad Gita* (New York: Mentor Books, 1951).

8. Surah 1 in *The Glorious Qur'an*, translated by Mohammed Marmaduke Pickthall (Elmhurst, NY: Tahrike Tarsile Qur'an, Inc., 2000).

9. *The Lotus Sutra*, chapter 3, at http://www.lioncity.net/buddhism/index .php?showtopic=3854.

10. Luke 6:30 in the New Revised Standard Version of the Bible.

11. Robert Kane, *Through the Moral Maze*, 34.

12. C. E. Harris writes: "*Good* refers to a wider range of phenomena than *right* does. *Good* refers to actions and the motives of actions, but it can also describe people or things. *Right*, on the other hand, refers primarily to actions. We can speak of good people and good things, as well as good actions and good intentions, but we cannot substitute 'He is a right man' for 'He is a good man.' Nor can we say that knowledge or courage is *right*, although we can say either is *good*." C. E. Harris Jr., *Applying Moral Theories*, fourth edition (Belmont, CA: Wadsworth, 2002), 12.

13. Anthony Weston says: "There are no surefire ways to avoid rationalizing. It takes a kind of self-confidence, honesty, and maturity that develop slowly, and even then we seldom escape the temptation entirely." He suggests four strategies for guarding against rationalizations: recalling that rationalizations are self-defeating, not trying too hard to win a moral argument, watching for irritation when challenged, and avoiding the automatic comeback. Anthony Weston, *A 21st Century Ethical Toolbox*, 14–15.

CHAPTER 3   RULE OF LAW: THE ETHICS OF JUSTICE

1. International human rights instruments are online at http://www .unhchr.ch/html/intlinst.htm.

CHAPTER 4   DUTY: DOING WHAT IS RIGHT

1. An introduction to the writings of Kant, online at http://www .philosophypages.com/ph/kant.htm.

2. James Ellington, translator, "Introduction" to Immanuel Kant, *Grounding for the Metaphysics of Morals*, third edition (Cambridge, MA: Hackett Publishing Company, 1993), vi. Ellington adds that the categorical imperative "is a working criterion supposedly employed by any rational agent as a guide for making his own choices and judgments but without necessarily being able to formulate it and make it explicit."

3. Swami Prabhavananda and Christopher Isherwood, *The Song of God: Bhagavad Gita*, 37.

4. Gandhi, Young India (8 Jan. 1925), in Robert Traer, *Faith in Human Rights: Support in Religious Traditions for a Global Struggle* (Washington, DC: Georgetown University Press, 1991), 132.

5. Gandhi, Young India (5 Mar. 1925), in Robert Traer, *Faith in Human Rights*, 132.

6. Gandhi, Young India (8 Aug. 1929), in Robert Traer, *Faith, Belief, and Religion* (Aurora, CO: The Davies Group, 2001), 83.

7. Gandhi, Young India (5 Mar. 1925), in Robert Traer, *Faith, Belief, and Religion*, 82.

CHAPTER 5   CHARACTER: BEING A GOOD PERSON

1. Sophocles, *Antigone*, online at http://classics.mit.edu/Sophocles/antigone.html.

2. Martin Luther King, Jr. *Letter from a Birmingham Jail*, online at http://almaz.com/nobel/peace/MLK-jail.html.

3. An introduction to Aristotle is online at http://www.ucmp.berkeley.edu/history/aristotle.html.

4. An introduction to Aquinas is online at http://www.philosophypages.com/ph/aqui.htm.

5. Lao Tsu, *Tao Te Ching*, a new translation by Gia-Fu Feng and Jane English (New York: Vintage Books, 1972), number 21.

6. *The Way of Life*, a new translation of the *Tao Te Ching* by R. B. Blakney (New York: Mentor, 1955), 91, number 38.

7. Ibid.

8. *Tao Te Ching*, Feng and English, number 67.

9. *The Sayings of Confucius*, James R. Ware, 36, number 4:14.

10. Ibid., 47, number 6:22.

11. Ibid., 53, number 7:25.

12. Ibid., 41, number 5:16.

13. Ibid., 47, number 6:18.

14. Herbert Fingarette, *Confucius: The Secular as Sacred* (New York: Harper & Row, 1972), 55.

15. Ibid., 14.

16. Ibid., 16.

17. Ibid., 28, quoting the *Analects*, number 2:3.

18. *The Sayings of Confucius*, Ware, 56, number 8:2.

CHAPTER 6   RELATIONSHIPS: CARING AND
LETTING GO

1. Carol Gilligan, *In a Different Voice: Psychological Theory and Women's Development* (Boston, MA: Harvard University Press, 1983), 26. The Heinz Dilemma, as described by Kohlberg, is in Lawrence Kohlberg, *Philosophy of*

Moral Development: Essays in Moral Development, vol. 1 (San Francisco, CA: Harper, 1981), 12.

2. Ibid., 28.

3. Virginia Held, *Feminist Morality: Transforming Culture, Society, and Politics* (Chicago, IL: University of Chicago Press, 1993).

4. Eshin Nishimura, *Unsui: A Diary of Zen Monastic Life*, drawings by Giei Sato, edited and an with introduction by Bardwell L. Smith (Honolulu: The University Press of Hawaii, an East-West Center Book, 1973).

CHAPTER 7   HUMAN RIGHTS: AUTONOMY AND HUMAN DIGNITY

1. Robert Traer, "U.S. Ratification of the International Covenant on Economic, Social, and Cultural Rights," *Promises to Keep: Prospects for Human Rights*, ed. Charles S. McCoy (Pinole, CA: Literary Directions, 2002), 1–47. If the United States were to ratify the ICESCR, "the United States would be obligated to take legislative, executive, and other measures . . . 'with a view to achieving progressively the full realization' of those rights. Since there is no definition or standard in the Covenant, the United States would largely determine for itself the meaning of 'full realization' and the speed of realization, and whether it is using 'the maximum of its available resources' for this purpose." *Restatement (Third) of the Foreign Relations Law of the United States*, Section 701, Reporters' Note 8 (1987).

2. General Comment No. 4 (191), UN ESCOR, Supp. (No. 3), Annex III, at 115, para 7., in Matthew Craven, *The International covenant on Economic, Social and Cultural Rights: A Perspective on its Development* (Oxford: The Clarendon Press, 1998), 335.

3. Ronald Munson, *Intervention and Reflection: Basic Issues in Medical Ethics* (Belmont, CA: Wadsworth, 2004), 511–512.

4. Robert Traer, "The Cornerstone," *Faith in Human Rights*, 173–186.

5. *Pacem in Terris: The 1963 Encyclical of John XXIII on World Peace*, in Joseph Gremillion, ed., *The Gospel of Peace and Justice: Catholic Social Teaching since Pope John* (Maryknoll, NY: Orbis, 1976), number 9 and number 145.

6. *Gaudium et Spes*, number 26, in Gremillion, *The Gospel of Peace and Justice*, 339.

7. Robert Traer, *Jerusalem Journal: Finding Hope* (Aurora, CO: The Davies Group, 2006), 171.

8. Ibid., 168.

9. Ilan Pappé, ed. *The Israel/Palestine Question* (London: Routledge, 1999).

10. Robert Traer, *Jerusalem Journal*, 165.

11. Abul A'la Mawdudi writes: "When we speak of human rights in Islam we mean those rights granted by God. Rights granted by kings or legislative

assemblies can be withdrawn as easily as they are conferred; but no individual and no institution has the authority to withdraw the rights conferred by God." Abul A'la Mawdudi, *Human Rights in Islam*, second edition (Leicester, UK: Islamic Foundation, 1980), 15.

12. Riffat Hassan, "On Human Rights and the Qur'anic Perspective," in *Human Rights in Religious Traditions*, ed. Arlene Swidler (New York: The Pilgrim Press, 1982), 63 and 65.

13. Surah 4:34. The translation by Mohammed Marmaduke Pickthall is: "Men are in charge of women, because Allah hath made the one of them to excel the other, and because they spend of their property (for the support of women). So good women are the obedient, guarding in secret what Allah hath guarded. As for those from whom ye fear rebellion, admonish them and banish them to beds apart, and scourge them." *The Glorious Qur'an* (Elmhurst, NY: Tahrike Tarsile Qur'an, 2000). The translation of this text by A. J. Arberry ends with the words: "banish them to their couches, and beat them." *The Koran Interpreted* (New York: Simon & Schuster, 1955).

14. Gandhi, quoted in German Arciniegas, "Culture—A Human Right," in *Freedom and Culture*, ed. Julian Huxley (London: Wingate, 1951), 32.

15. Gandhi, *Young India* (8 Jan. 1925), in Robert Traer, *Faith in Human Rights*, 132.

16. Sangharakshita, *Ambedkar and Buddhism* (Glasgow, Scotland: Windhorse Publications, 1986), 157.

17. Masao Abe, "Religious Tolerance and Human Rights: A Buddhist Perspective," in *Religious Liberty and Human Rights in Nations and in Religions*, ed. Leonard Swidler (Philadelphia, PA: Ecumenical Press, Temple University, 1986), 202.

18. Tilokasundari Kariyawasam, "Feminism in Theravada Buddhism," paper presented at the conference, *Buddhism and Christianity: Toward the Human Future*, Berkeley, CA, 8–15 Aug. 1987, 6.

19. Wei Jingsheng, "The Fifth Modernization," in *The Fifth Modernization: China's Human Rights Movement, 1978–1979*, ed. James D. Seymour (Stanfordville, NY: Human Rights Publishing Group, 1980), 68.

20. Wm. Theodore de Bary, "Human Rites—An Essay on Confucianism and Human Rights," *China Notes* 23, number 4 (Fall 1984): 308. A shorter version of this essay is published as "Neo-Confucians and Human Rights," in *Human Rights and the World's Religions*, ed. Leroy S. Rounder (Notre Dame, IN: University of Notre Dame Press, 1988, 183–198.

21. Martin Luther King Jr., "Nobel Prize Acceptance Speech," in *A Testament of Hope: The Essential Writings of Martin Luther King, Jr.*, ed. James Melvin Washington (San Francisco, CA: Harper & Row, 1986), 226.

22. In Africa women have lobbied for a "Protocol to the African Charter on Human and Peoples' Rights on the Rights of Women in Africa," and as of the

end of 2006 ten of the required fifteen countries have ratified the Protocol. Governments ratifying this Protocol, once it is in force, are obliged to: protect women against sexual harassment in the workplace and in schools, enact and enforce laws prohibiting violence against women, protect women's reproductive rights by permitting abortion in case of rape and incest, and ensure increased participation of women in peace processes and post-conflict reconstruction and rehabilitation. The text of the Protocol and its status are available online at http://www.africa-union.org/root/au/Documents/Treaties/treaties.htm.

23. In 1961 the World Council of Churches approved a statement distinguishing proselytism from witness: "Witness is corrupted when cajolery, bribery, undue pressure or intimidation is used—subtly or openly—to bring about seeming conversion." Four years later the Roman Catholic hierarchy came to a similar conclusion in the Declaration on Religious Freedom adopted by the Second Vatican Council. A footnote to *The Documents of Vatican II* makes clear the new Catholic position: "Proselytism is a corruption of the Christian witness by appeal to hidden forms of coercion or by a style of propaganda unworthy of the Gospel. It is not the use but the abuse of the right to religious freedom." This understanding is now reflected in Barrett's *World Christian Encyclopedia: A Comparative Study of Churches and Religions in the Modern World*, which defines proselytism as "a manner of behaving contrary to the spirit of the gospel" and making "use of dishonest methods to attract" others "by exploiting their ignorance or poverty." Robert Traer, "Religious Freedom in Central and Eastern Europe," online at http://www.religionhumanrights.com/Culture/Europe/mission.nationalists.htm.

CHAPTER 8   POSSIBLE CONSEQUENCES: UTILITARIAN AND COST/BENEFIT ARGUMENTS

1. Jeremy Bentham, Introduction to *The Principles of Morals and Legislation* (New York: Oxford University Press, 1789), quoted in Barbara MacKinnon, *Ethics: Theory and Contemporary Issues*, second edition (Belmont, CA: Wadsworth Publishing Company, 1998), 35.

2. John Stuart Mill, *Utilitarianism* (London, 1861), quoted in James Rachels, *The Elements of Moral Philosophy*, fourth edition (New York: McGraw-Hill, 2003), 168. An introduction to John S. Mill is online at http://www.philosophypages.com/ph/mill.htm.

3. F. H. Knight, *Risk, Uncertainty, and Profit* (Boston, MA: Houghton Mifflin, 1921), quoted in Herman E. Daly and Joshua Farley, *Ecological Economics: Principles and Applications* (Washington, DC: Island Press, 2004), 95.

4. Herman E. Daly and Joshua Farley, *Ecological Economics*, 95.

5. Jeremy Bentham, Introduction to *The Principles of Morals and Legislation*, Chap. 17, Sect. 1, note, quoted in James Rachels, *The Elements of Moral Philosophy*, fourth edition, 122–23.

6. Peter Singer, *Writings on an Ethical Life* (New York: HarperCollins, 2000), 70.

7. Ibid., 71.

8. Robin Attfield, *Environmental Ethics: An Overview for the Twenty-First Century* (Cambridge, UK: Polity Press, 2003), 44.

9. Ronald Munson, *Intervention and Reflection*, 694.

CHAPTER 9   MAKING DECISIONS: HIV/AIDS

1. Tracy McVeigh, "Nurse Exodus Leaves Kenya in Crisis," *Observer* (21 May 2006).

2. Sharon LaFraniere, "Mandatory Testing Bolsters Botswana in Combating AIDS," *The New York Times* (14 June 2004).

3. Sissela Bok, *Lying*, 244.

4. Donald G. McNeil Jr., "Plan to Battle AIDS Worldwide is Falling Short," *The New York Times* (28 Mar. 2004). McNeil reports: ". . . few people in poor countries have been able to get lower-priced generic antiretroviral drugs. While the generic drugs have been approved by the World Health Organization, endorsed by the World Bank and used in several African countries, the Bush administration has so far paid only for medicines that are still under patent and cost much more." On a more hopeful note, McNeil notes that: "Two pharmaceutical giants, Glaxo and Boehringer-Ingelheim, agreed to grant licenses to produce AIDS drugs to four generic companies from India and South Africa. The companies will be allowed to sell the drugs anywhere in sub-Saharan Africa. In return, Glaxo, and Boehringer will get royalties of 5 percent of sales. Under the threat of heavy fines, the companies had backed down from their original plan: a license for one small generic maker supplying only South Africa's public hospitals and royalties of 15 percent to 30 percent." See also Allison Langley, "African AIDS Drug Plan Faces Collapse," *The Observer* (14 Mar. 2004).

CHAPTER 10   PUBLIC MORALITY: SEEKING THE
COMMON GOOD

1. Robert Kane, *Through the Moral Maze*, 101.

2. *Roe v. Wade* (1973), online at http://www.tourolaw.edu/patch/Roe/. The *Gonzales v. Carhart* ruling (April 18, 2007) by the US Supreme Court bans the "intact dialation and extraction" procedure.

3. *Planned Parenthood v. Casey* (1992), online at http://www.oyez.org/oyez/resource/case/306/.

4. "China Bans Abortion Based on Baby's Gender," online at http://www
.infowars.com/print/life/china_bans_abortion.htm.

5. "India's Abortion Gender Gap," online at http://www.cbsnews.com/
stories/2006/01/09/world/main1190138.shtm.

6. Ronald Munson, *Intervention and Reflection*, 767–768.

7. Ibid., 572.

8. "Spain: Group appeals gay marriage law," online at http://www.gay
.com/news/article.html?2005/09/19/2.

9. David Brooks, "The Power of Marriage," *The New York Times* (22 Nov.
2003).

10. Doug Struck, "Canadian Prime Minister Loses Bid to Revisit Gay Marriage
Law," *The Washington Post* (8 Dec. 2006), online at http://www.washington
post.com/wp-dyn/content/article/2006/12/07/AR2006120701684.html,
and Laura Mansnerus, "Legislators Vote for Gay Unions in N. J.," *The New
York Times* (14 Dec. 2006), online at http://www.nytimes.com/2006/12/
15/nyregion/15union.html?hp&ex=1166245200&en=4201828902b533be&ei
=5094&partner=homepage.

11. Jason Szep, "Battle Over Gay Marriage Deepens," *Yahoo! News* (9 Nov.
2006), online at http://news.yahoo.com/s/nm/20061109/ts_nm/rights_
gays_dc_1.

12. Helen Prejean, CSJ, *Dead Man Walking: An Eyewitness Account of the
Death Penalty in the United States* (New York: Vintage Books, 1993), 197.

13. *The Truth and Reconciliation Commission*, online at http://www.doj
.gov.za/trc/.

14. Helen Prejean, *Dead Man Walking*, 197. However, she notes: "The July
26, 1991, CNN/Gallup public opinion poll indicated that of the 76 percent
who said they were in favor of the death penalty, 13 percent cited deterrence as
a reason, 19 percent cited protection, and 50 percent, revenge."

15. Ted Goertzel, "Capital Punishment and Homicide," online at
http://www.csicop.org/si/2004-7/capital-punishment.html.

CHAPTER 11   HEALTH CARE: LIFE AND DEATH

1. *Code of Ethics for Nurses* (Washington, DC: American Nurses' Association,
2001).

2. The *Nuremberg Principles* are online at http://deoxy.org/wc/wc-nurem
.htm.

3. The Donald Cowart case is from Ronald Munson, *Intervention and Reflection*, 101–104.

4. This recommended selection process for allocating organs for transplantation is from Ronald Munson, *Intervention and Reflection*, 496. The waiting list

for organ transplants is long and growing. "As of Oct. 23, the waiting list for donor organs in the U. S. was made up on 87,210 individuals, and more than 40,000 additional individuals will join the waiting list this year, or about one every 13 minutes. The waiting list grows about five times as fast as the rate of organ donation. It is estimated that more than half of the people on the waiting list will die while awaiting transplant, and about 6,000 such individuals in the U. S. died last year, or about one every 90 minutes." *Medscape* (25 Oct. 2004).

5. Information on the Canadian health care system is from Ronald Munson, *Intervention and Reflection*, 523–528. Eduardo Porter explains how the United States could convert to a health care system similar to Canada's: "The new universal insurance could be provided by government. One simple way would be to extend Medicaid coverage up to the desired income level and to require people above that point to buy into the system according to a price scale that rose proportionately to income. Because Medicaid has lower administrative costs than private insurance, this would be efficient. But the new regime could be run privately as well, to take advantage of the private sector's superior track record on innovation. The government could give tightly focused tax credits so that lower-income people could buy health insurance on the market. And it could organize pools by, say, requiring insurers to charge the same for similar policies sold to people of the same age group who live in the same area." Eduardo Porter, "Health for All, Just a (Big) Step Away," *The New York Times*, (18 Dec. 2005), online at http://nytimes.com/2005/12/18/business/yourmoney/18view.html ?incamp=article_popular.

6. The 1985 "Baby Doe" regulations and the quotes concerning euthanasia are from Ronald Munson, *Intervention and Reflection*, 645, 706, and 707.

7. The definition of what Catholic ethicists mean by "ordinary care" is from Ronald Munson, *Intervention and Reflection*, 769.

8. *Cruzan v. Director, MDH* (1990), online at http://www.tourolaw.edu/patch/Cruzan.

9. Lonnie R. Bristow, "Physician-Assisted Suicide," in Munson, *Intervention and Reflection*, 730–732. Statement by Lonnie R. Bristow, President of the American Medical Association, before the United States House of Representatives Committee on the Judiciary, Subcommittee on the Constitution, *Congressional Record*, 29 April 1996.

10. The Dutch practice of physician-assisted suicide is described in Ronald Munson, *Intervention and Reflection*, 706–708. In January 2005 Canon Professor Robin Gill, a chief advisor to the Archbishop of Canterbury, suggested to a UK parliamentary committee investigating euthanasia that a person assisting in the death of a relative, who is terminally ill and in pain, should not be prosecuted. "There is a very strong compassionate case for voluntary euthanasia,"

Gill said. Jamie Doward, "Church Ends Taboo on Mercy Killings," *The Observer* (16 Jan. 2005).

11. *Gonzalez v. Oregon* (2006), online at http://caselaw.lp.findlaw.com/scripts/getcase.pl?court=US&vol=000&invol=04–623.

12. Lonnie R. Bristow, "Physician-Assisted Suicide," in Ronald Munson, *Intervention and Reflection*, 731.

13. Report by the New York State Task Force on Life and Law, in Lonnie R. Bristow, "Physician-Assisted Suicide," in Ronald Munson, *Intervention and Reflection*, 732.

14. Lonnie R. Bristow, "Physician-Assisted Suicide," in Ronald Munson, *Intervention and Reflection*, 731.

CHAPTER 12   SEX: CONSENT PLUS WHAT?

1. "Congregation for the Doctrine of the Faith," (22 Feb. 1987) in Ronald Munson, *Intervention and Reflection*, 398.

2. Hanna Rosin, "Reform Rabbis Sanction Gay Unions," *The Washington Post* (30 Mar. 2000), online at http://www.washingtonpost.com/wp-srv/WPcap/2000–03/30/103r–033000-idx.html, and Laurie Goodstein, "Conservative Jews Allow Gay Rabbis and Unions," *The New York Times* (7 Dec. 2006), online at http://www.nytimes.com/2006/12/07/us/07jews.html?hp&ex=11655540000&en=391277b1ab56f3cd&ei=5094&partner=homepage.

3. Benjamin Cohen, "Liberal Judaism launches gay marriage ceremonies in UK" (28 Nov. 2005), online at http://www.gmax.co.za/look05/11/28-UKgay-jews.html.

4. "Sodomy Laws: India," online at http://www.gmax.co.za/look05/11/28-UKgayjews.html.

5. Robert Kane, *Through the Moral Maze*, 105 and 106. Kane credits Joel Feinberg, author of *Social Ethics* and *The Moral Limits of the Criminal Law*, with formulating the moral criterion of "reasonable avoidability."

6. Peter Landesman, "The Girls Next Door," *The New York Times* (25 Jan. 2004). Landesman quotes Kevin Bales of Free the Slaves: "The physical path of a person being trafficked includes stages of degradation of a person's mental state. A victim gets deprived of food, gets hungry, a little dizzy and sleep-deprived. She begins to break down; she can't think for herself. Then take away her travel documents, and you've made her stateless. Then layer on physical violence, and she begins to follow orders. Then add a foreign culture and language, and she's trapped." Landesman notes that there is one more oppressive layer: "a sex-trafficking victim's belief that her family is being tracked as collateral for her body. All sex-trafficking operations, whether Mexican, Ukrainian or Thai, are vast criminal underworlds with roots and branches that reach back to the countries, towns and neighborhoods of their victims."

7. Nicholas D. Kristof, "Girls for Sale," *The New York Times* (17 Jan. 2004).

8. Alexander McKay, "Common Questions about Sexual Health Education," *SIECCAN Newsletter*, vol. 35, number 1 (Summer 2000, revised to Mar. 2001).

CHAPTER 13   WAR AGAINST TERRORISM: JUSTICE AND FREEDOM

1. Ron Fournier, "Bush Vows to 'Rid the World of Evil'," (14 Sep. 2001), online at http://www.fredericksburg.com/News/terrorism/0914bushvisit/printer_friendly.

2. Deuteronomy 7:1–2, *Tanakh: A New Translation of the Holy Scriptures According to the Traditional Hebrew Text* (Philadelphia, PA: The Jewish Publication Society, 1985).

3. "The Just War Theory," *The Internet Encyclopedia of Philosophy*, online at http://www.utm.edu/research/iep/j/justwar.htm.

4. Information on the Geneva Conventions from "A Brief History of the Laws of War," *Society of Professional Journalists*, online at http://www.genevaconventions.org/.

5. "Iraq Faces Massive U. S. Missile Barrage," *CBS Evening News* (24 Jan. 2003), online at http://www.cbsnews.com/stories/2003/01/24/eveningnews/main537928.shtml.

6. Alexander G. Higgins, "Red Cross: Iraq Abuse Widespread, Routine," *Yahoo! News*, (10 May 2004), online at http://story.news.yahoo.com/news?tmpl=story&u=/ap/20040510/ap_on_re_mi_ea/red_cross_prisoner_abuse&cid=540&ncid=1480. The *New York Times* also reported: "Hundreds of Iraqi prisoners were held in Abu Ghraib prison for prolonged periods despite a lack of evidence that they posed a security threat to American forces, according to an Army report completed last fall." *The New York Times* (30 May 2004).

7. The Convention against Torture and Other Cruel, Inhuman or Degrading Treatment or Punishment, online at http://www.unhchr.ch/html/menu3/b/h_cat39.htm.

8. The McCain amendment prohibiting torture uses the language of the Universal Declaration of Human Rights. In supporting this amendment, Senator McCain refers to the prohibition of torture in the International Covenant on Civil and Political Rights and in the Convention Against Torture. "McCain Statement on Detainee Amendments" (5 Oct. 2005), online at http://www.taylormarsh.com/archives_view.php?id=1010.

9. As general counsel of the US Navy, Alberto J. Mora strenuously argued against violating US and international prohibitions by sanctioning torture. "Well before the exposure of prisoner abuse in Iraq's Abu Ghraib prison, in April,

2004, Mora warned his superiors at the Pentagon about the consequences of President Bush's decision, in February, 2002, to circumvent the Geneva Conventions, which prohibit both torture and 'outrages upon personal dignity, in particular humiliating and degrading treatment.' He argued that a refusal to outlaw cruelty toward US-held terrorist suspects was an implicit invitation to abuse. Mora also challenged the legal framework that the Bush Administration has constructed to justify an expansion of executive power, in matters ranging from interrogations to wiretapping. He described as 'unlawful,' 'dangerous,' and 'erroneous' novel legal theories granting the President the right to authorize abuse. Mora warned that these precepts could leave U.S. personnel open to criminal prosecution." Jane Mayer, "The Memo," *The New Yorker* (27 Feb. 2006), online at http://www.newyorker.com/printables/fact/060227fa_fact.

10. "Bush Signs Statements to Bypass Torture Ban, Oversight Rules in Patriot Act," *Democracy Now* (27 Mar. 2006), online at http://www.indybay.org/news/2006/03/1811176.php.

11. Burton J. Lee III, "The Stain of Torture," *The Washington Post* (30 June 2005), online at http://www.washingtonpost.com/wp-dyn/content/article/2005/06/30/AR2005063001680.html.

12. Ibid.

13. Ibid.

14. "About that Rebellion . . . ," The *New York Times* (11 Mar. 2006), online at http://www.nytimes.com/2006/03/11/opinion/11sat1.html?_r=1&hp&oref=slogin.

15. "Rushing Off a Cliff," *The New York Times* (28 Sep. 2006), online at http://www.nytimes.com/2006/09/28/opinion/28thu1.html?_r=1&hp&oref=slogin. In contrast, on February 24, 2007, Canada's highest court "unanimously struck down a law that allows the Canadian government to detain foreign-born terrorism suspects indefinitely using secret evidence and without charges while their deportations are being reviewed. . . . The decision reflected striking differences from the current legal climate in the United States. In the Military Commissions Act of 2006, Congress stripped the federal courts of authority to hear challenges, through petitions for writs of habeas corpus, to the open-ended confinement of foreign terrorism suspects at Guantánamo Bay, Cuba." The constitutionality of this US law has been upheld by a federal appeals court, but this decision is being appealed to the US Supreme Court. Jan Austen, "Canadian Court Limits Detention in Terror Cases," *The New York Times* (24 Feb. 2007), online at http://www.nytimes.com/2007/02/24/world/americas/24ottawa.html?em&ex=1172552400&en=37cb5e99fe5fa541&ei=5087%0A.

16. "End of Secret Detention Urged," *The Washington Post* (29 Jul. 2006), online at http://www.washingtonpost.com/wp-dyn/content/article/2006/07/28/AR2006072800512.html.

17. Paul Rieckhoff, "Do Unto Your Enemy . . . ," *The New York Times* (25 Sep. 2006), online at http://www.nytimes.com/2006/09/25/opinion/25rieckhoff.html?hp.

18. The authors do not question that some wars may meet the minimal requirements of the just war tradition and international law and agree with the president that Al Qaeda is an enemy of the United States. Nonetheless, the authors also agree with a recent editorial in the New York Times: "At a crucial moment, the Bush administration diverted America's military strength, political attention and foreign aid dollars from a necessary, winnable war in Afghanistan to an unnecessary, and by now unwinnable, war in Iraq." An unnecessary war is certainly an unjust war. "Al Qaeda Resurgent," The New York Times (25 Feb. 2007), online at http://www.nytimes.com/2007/02/25/opinion/25sun1.html ?_r=1&hp&oref=slogin.

19. George W. Bush, *Second Inaugural Address*, 2004, online at http://www .whitehouse.gov/inaugural/.

20. Abraham Lincoln, *Second Inaugural Address*, 1865, online at http://www .bartleby.com/124/pres32.html.

CHAPTER 14   ECONOMIC JUSTICE: FAIR AND CARING?

1. Charitable acts by governments not only aid those who are in need, but also involve economic benefits for those who administer assistance programs. Aaron Glantz reports that agribusiness sees government charity in the form of food aid as a source of income. In 2006, when the Bush administration proposed earmarking 25 percent of US food aid for local suppliers in recipient countries, the agribusiness lobby persuaded Congress to continue the mandate that; "all food and grain [for aid] be bought from U.S. farmers, packaged in U.S. exporters, and shipped on U.S.-flagged vessels." The United States is not alone in limiting its food aid to homegrown commodities for this is true of 70 percent of the food distributed by the UN. Nonetheless, "The European Union, Canada, and Australia have, in recent years, increased their flexibility to buy their food aid from developing countries. . . . Canada now permits 50 percent of its food aid to be bought locally while up to 67 percent of Australian food aid is bought near the site of the emergency." Aaron Glantz, "Food Aid 'Overhaul' Would Save Money and Lives—Report," *OneWorld US* (26 July 2006), online at http://news.yahoo.com/s/oneworld/20060726/wl_oneworld/45361370371153951499.

2. Jim Lobe, "NGOs Rally Behind UN Plan to Slash World Poverty," *OneWorld.net* (15 Jan. 2005), online at http://story.news.yahoo.com/news ?tmpl=story&u=/oneworld/20050119/wl_oneworld/45361017541106154327.

3. *Economic Justice for All*, the tenth anniversary edition of the *Pastoral Letter on Catholic Social Teaching and the U.S. Economy* (Washington, DC: United States Catholic Conference, Inc., 1997), 1.

4. Monica Campbell and Tyche Hendricks, "Mexico's Corn Farmers See Their Livelihoods Wither Away," *The San Francisco Chronicle* (31 Jul. 2006), online at http://www.sfgate.com/cgi-bin/article.cgi?f=/c/a/2006/07/31/MNGIVK8BHPI.DTL&hw=Mexico+corn&sn=001&sc=1000.

5. Tina Rosenberg, "Why Mexico's Small Corn Farmers Go Hungry," *The New York Times* (3 Mar. 2003).

6. "About That Free Trade . . . ," *The New York Times* (15 May 2006).

7. Herman E. Daly and Joshua Farley, *Ecological Economics*, 320.

8. Ibid., 334.

9. Ibid., 335.

10. Celia W. Dugger, "Supermarket Giants Crush Central American Farmers," *The New York Times* (28 Dec. 2004), online at http://www.truthout.org/docs_04/122904J.shtml.

11. Ibid.

12. Peter S. Goodman, "The Persistently Poor," *The Washington Post* (7 Dec. 2006), online at http://www.washingtonpost.com/wp-dyn/content/article/2006/12/07/AR2006120700427.html.

13. Ibid.

14. An introduction to John Rawls is online at http://www.erraticimpact.com/~20thcentury/html/john_rawls.htm.

15. "2004 Trends in CEO Pay," online at http://www.aflcio.org/corporatewatch/paywatch/pay/index.cfm. At the end of 2006 the Securities and Exchange Commission (SEC) promulgated new regulations requiring companies to explain clearly the compensation packages provided their executives. This action by the SEC came: "in response to a rising backlash against annual double-digit percentage increases in executive pay." Terence O'Hara, "Executive Compensation Comes Into the Clear," *The Washington Post* (15 Dec. 2006), online at http://www.washingtonpost.com/wp-dyn/content/article/2006/12/14/AR2006121401816.html.

16. Robert J. Samuelson writes: "no one should be happy with today's growing inequality. It threatens American's social compact." He says that living standards in the US for the past decade have risen for almost everyone. Yet, it is clear, he argues, that "productivity gains (improvements in efficiency) are going disproportionately to those at the top." Robert J. Samuelson, "Trickle-Up Economics?" *Newsweek*, (2 Oct. 2006), 40.

17. Fair Trade information, online at http://www.globalexchange.org/campaigns/fairtrade/coffee/.

18. Adam Smith, *The Wealth of Nations*, online at http://www.bibliomania
.com/2/1/65/112/frameset.html. Economist Duncan K. Foley says he wrote
A Guide to Economic Theory "to give people more confidence in their own
moral judgments" about economics. He disputes claims that economic laws
are universal and asserts that all economic theories are conditioned by class
conflicts and historical circumstances. Moreover, he does not agree that simply
pursuing self-interest will generate the best world for the greatest number of
people or that capitalism will, by itself, "solve the problems of poverty and inequality." Peter Steinfels, "Economics: The Invisible Hand of the Market," *The
New York Times*, (25 Nov. 2006), A11.

19. "The International Debt Crisis," online at http://www.osjspm.org/
debt.htm.

20. Child Labor," *Human Rights Watch*, online at http://www.hrw.org/
children/labor.htm.

21. "Follett's Commitment to Fairness: Key Messages for the Child Labor
and Sweatshop Issue," and "Vendor Labor Practice Code of Conduct," Follett
Higher Education Group, obtained from the Follett Bookstore at Dominican
University of California, 2005.

CHAPTER 15   OUR NATURAL WORLD: LIVING
ECOLOGICALLY

1. Holmes Rolston III, "Values in and Duties to the Natural World," *Environmental Ethics: What Really Matters, What Really Works*, eds. David Schmidtz
and Elizabeth Willott (NY: Oxford University Press, 2002), 35, originally published in *Ecology, Economics, Ethics: The Broken Circle*, ed. F. Bormann and S.
Kellert (New Haven: Yale University Press, 1991), 73–96.

2. Herman E. Daly and Joshua Farley, *Ecological Economics*, 270.

3. Ibid.

4. Ibid.

5. Ibid.

6. Aldo Leopold, "Ecocentrism: The Land Ethic," *Environmental Ethics:
Readings in Theory and Application*, ed. Louis P. Pojman, fourth edition, (Belmont, CA: Wadsworth, 2005), 141.

7. Ibid.

8. Ibid., 143.

9. Herman E. Daly and Joshua Farley, *Ecological Economics*, 55.

10. John S. Mill, *Principles of Political Economy*, Book IV, Chapter VI (1848),
quoted in Daly and Farley, *Ecological Economics*, 54, online at http://www
.econlib.org/library/Mill/mlPbl.html.

11. Karen J. Warren, "The Power and the Promise of Ecological Feminism," in *Environmental Ethics: What Really Matters, What Really Works*, 244, originally published in *Environmental Ethics* 12 (1990): 125–146.

12. Gita Sen, "Women, Poverty, and Population: Issues for the Concerned Environmentalist," in *Environmental Ethics: What Really Matters, What Really Works*, 251, originally published in *Feminist Perspectives on Sustainable Development*, ed. W. Harcourt (London: Zed, 1994), 216–225.

13. Karen J. Warren, "The Power and the Promise of Ecological Feminism," in *Environmental Ethics: What Really Matters, What Really Works*, 244.

14. Ibid., 246.

15. Blake D. Ratner, "Environmental Rights as a Matter of Survival," *Human Rights Dialogue: Environmental Rights* (Spring 2004), online at http://www.globalpolicy.org/socecon/envronmt/2004/0617envtlrights.htm.

16. Peter G. Veit and Catherine Benson, "When Parks and People Collide," *Human Rights Dialogue: Environmental Rights* (Spring 2004), online at http://pdf.wri.org/vb_parks_people.pdf.

17. Raymond Bonner, "At the Hand of Man: Peril and Hope for Africa's Wildlife," *Environmental Ethics: What Really Matters, What Really Works*, 306–319, originally published as *At the Hand of Man: Peril and Hope for Africa's Wildlife* (New York: Alfred A. Knopf, 1993), 253–278.

18. Abigail Abrash Walton, "Mining a Sacred Land," *Human Rights Dialogue: Environmental Rights* (Spring 2004), online at http://www.minesandcommunities.org/Company/freeport12.htm.

19. Jorge Daniel Taillant, "A Nascent Agenda for the Americas," *Human Rights Dialogue: Environmental Rights* (Spring 2004), online at http://www.cceia.org/resources/publications/dialogue/2_11/section_4/4461.html.

20. The American Convention on Human Rights, online at http://www.oas.org/juridico/english/Treaties/b-32.htm.

21. Additional Protocol to the American Convention on Human Rights in the Area of Economic, Social and Cultural Rights, "Protocol of San Salvador," *OAS Treaty Series* 69 (17 San Salvador 1988), online at http://www.oas.org/juridico/english/Treaties/a-52.html.

Bibliography

"2004 Trends in CEO Pay," http://www.aflcio.org/corporatewatch/paywatch/pay/index.cfm.

Abe, Masao. "Religious Tolerance and Human Rights: A Buddhist Perspective," in *Religious Liberty and Human Rights in Nations and in Religions*, ed. Leonard Swidler (Philadelphia, PA: Ecumenical Press, Temple University, 1986).

"About that Free Trade . . . ," *The New York Times* (15 May 2006).

"About that Rebellion . . . ," *The New York Times* (11 Mar. 2006), online at http://www.nytimes.com/2006/03/11/opinion/11sat1.html?_r=1&hp&oref=slogin.

"A Brief History of the Laws of War," *Society of Professional Journalists*, online at http://www.genevaconventions.org/.

"Al Qaeda Resurgent," *The New York Times* (25 Feb. 2007), online at http://www.nytimes.com/2007/02/25/opinion/25sun1.html?ex=1330059600&en=9c7056f191f8a73d&ei=5088&partner=rss.

Arciniegas, German. "Culture—A Human Right," in *Freedom and Culture*, ed. Julian Huxley (London: Wingate, 1951).

Attfield, Robin. *Environmental Ethics: An Overview for the Twenty-First Century* (Cambridge, UK: Polity Press, 2003).

Austen, Ian. "Canadian Court Limits Detention in Terror Cases," *The New York Times*, (24 Feb. 2007), online at http://select.nytimes.com/gst/abstract.html?res=F60E14FR73B5A0C778EDDAB0894DF404482.

"Bell's Theorem," *Stanford Encyclopedia of Philosophy*, online at http://plato.stanford.edu/entries/bell-theorem/.

"Bell's Theorem," Wikipedia, http://en.wikipedia.org/wiki/Bell's_theorem.

Bentham, Jeremy. "Introduction" to *The Principles of Morals and Legislation* (New York: Oxford University Press, 1789).

Blackburn, Simon. *Being Good: A Short Introduction to Ethics* (Oxford: Oxford University Press, 2001).

Blakeslee, Sandra. "This Is Your Brain Under Hypnosis," *The New York Times* (22 Nov. 2005).

Bok, Sissela. *Lying: Moral Choice in Public and Private Life* (New York: Vintage Books, 1999).

Bonner, Raymond. "At the Hand of Man: Peril and Hope for Africa's Wildlife," *Environmental Ethics: What Really Matters, What Really Works*, (New York: Oxford University Press, 2002), 306–319.

Booth, Wayne C. *The Company We Keep: An Ethics of Fiction* (Berkeley, CA: University of California Press, 1988).

Bristow, Lonnie R. "Physician-Assisted Suicide," in Ronald Munson, *Intervention and Reflection*, 730–732. Statement by Lonnie R. Bristow, President of the American Medical Association, before the United States House of Representatives Committee on the Judiciary, Subcommittee on the Constitution, *Congressional Record*, 29 April 1996.

Brooks, David. "The Power of Marriage," *The New York Times* (22 Nov. 2003).

Bush, George W. *Second Inaugural Address*, 2004, online at http://www.white house.gov/inaugural/.

"Bush Signs Statements to Bypass Torture Ban, Oversight Rules in Patriot Act," *Democracy Now* (27 Mar. 2006), online at http://www.indybay.org /news/2006/03/1811176.php.

Campbell, Monica and Tyche Hendricks. "Mexico's Corn Farmers See Their Livelihoods Wither Away," *The San Francisco Chronicle* (31 Jul. 2006), online at http://www.sfgate.com/cgi-bin/article.cgi?f=/c/a/2006/07/31 /MNGIVK8BHPI.DTL&hw=Mexico+corn&sn=001&sc=1000.

"Child Labor," Human Rights Watch, online at http://www.hrw.org/children /labor.htm. *Code of Ethics for Nurses* (Washington, DC: American Nurses' Association, 2001).

"China Bans Abortion Based on Baby's Gender," online at http://www.infowars.com/print/life/china_bans_abortion.htm.

Cohen, Benjamin. "Liberal Judaism launches gay marriage ceremonies in UK" (28 Nov. 2005), online at http://www.gmax.co.za/look05/11/28-UKgayjews.html.

The Convention against Torture and Other Cruel, Inhuman or Degrading Treatment or Punishment, online at http://www.unhchr.ch/html /menu3/b/h_cat39.htm.

Craven, Matthew. *The International Covenant on Economic, Social and Cultural Rights: A Perspective on Its Development* (Oxford: The Clarendon Press, 1998).

Cruzan v. Director, MDH (1990), online at http://www.tourolaw.edu/patch/Cruzan.

Daly, Herman E. and Joshua Farley. *Ecological Economics: Principles and Applications* (Washington, DC: Island Press, 2004).

de Bary, Wm. Theodore. "Human Rites—An Essay on Confucianism and Human Rights," *China Notes* 23, no. 4 (Fall 1984): 308.

Doward, Jamie. "Church Ends Taboo on Mercy Killings," *The Observer* (16 Jan. 2005).

Dugger, Celia W. "Supermarket Giants Crush Central American Farmers," *The New York Times* (28 Dec. 2004), online at http://www.truthout.org/docs_04/122904J.shtml.

Economic Justice for All, the tenth anniversary edition of the *Pastoral Letter on Catholic Social Teaching and the U.S. Economy* (Washington, DC: United States Catholic Conference, Inc., 1997).

Ellington, James W. "Introduction" to Immanuel Kant, *Grounding for the Metaphysics of Morals*, third edition (Cambridge, MA: Hackett Publishing Company, 1993).

"End of Secret Detention Urged," *The Washington Post* (29 Jul. 2006), online at http://www.washingtonpost.com/wp-dyn/content/article/2006/07/28/AR2006072800512.html.

Fingarette, Herbert. *Confucius: The Secular as Sacred* (New York: Harper & Row, 1972).

Fournier, Ron. "Bush Vows to 'Rid the World of Evil'" (14 Sep. 2001), online at http://www.fredericksburg.com/News/terrorism/0914bushvisit/printer_friendly.

Gandhi, *Young India* (8 Jan. 1925).

———, *Young India* (5 Mar. 1925).

———, *Young India* (8 Aug. 1929).

Gaudium et Spes, no. 26, in Joseph Gremillion, ed., *The Gospel of Peace and Justice: Catholic Social Teaching since Pope John* (Maryknoll, NY: Orbis, 1976).

Gilligan, Carol. *In a Different Voice: Psychological Theory and Women's Development* (Boston, MA: Harvard University Press, 1983).

Glantz, Aaron. "Food Aid 'Overhaul' Would Save Money and Lives–Report," *OneWorld US* (26 July 2006), online at http://news.yahoo.com/s/oneworld/20060726/wl_oneworld/45361370371153951499.

The Glorious Qur'an, translated by Mohammed Marmaduke Pickthall (Elmhurst, NY: Takrike Tarsile Qur'an, Inc., 2000).

Goertzel, Ted. "Capital Punishment and Homicide," online at http://www.csicop.org/si/2004-7/capital-punishment.html.

Gonzalez v. Oregon (2006), online at (http://caselaw.lp.findlaw.com/scripts/getcase.pl?court=US&vol=000&invol=04–623.

Goodman, Peter S. "The Persistently Poor," *The Washington Post* (7 Dec. 2006), online at http://www.washingtonpost.com/wp-dyn/content/article/2006/12/07/AR2006120700427.html.

Goodstein, Laurie. "Conservative Jews Allow Gay Rabbis and Unions," *The New York Times* (7 Dec. 2006), online at http://www.nytimes.com/2006/12/07/us/07jews.html?hp&ex=11655540000&en=391277b1ab56f3cd&ei=5094&partner=homepage.

Gremillion, Joseph, ed. *The Gospel of Peace and Justice: Catholic Social Teaching since Pope John* (Maryknoll, NY: Orbis, 1976).

Harris, C. E., Jr. *Applying Moral Theories*, fourth edition (Belmont, CA: Wadsworth, 2002).

Hassan, Riffat. "On Human Rights and the Qur'anic Perspective," in *Human Rights in Religious Traditions*, ed. Arlene Swidler (New York: The Pilgrim Press, 1982).

Held, Virginia. *Feminist Morality: Transforming Culture, Society, and Politics* (Chicago, IL: University of Chicago Press, 1993).

Higgins, Alexander G. "Red Cross: Iraq Abuse Widespread, Routine," Yahoo! News, (10 May 2004), online at http://story.news.yahoo.com/news?tmpl=story&u=/ap/20040510/ap_on_re_mi_ea/red_cross_prisoner_abuse&cid=540&ncid=1480.

Hurley, Patrick J. *A Concise Introduction to Logic*, seventh edition (Stamford, CT: Wadsworth, 2000).

"India's Abortion Gender Gap," online at http://www.cbsnews.com/stories/2006/01/09/world/main1190138.shtml.

"The International Debt Crisis," online at http://www.osjspm.org/debt.htm.

"Iraq Faces Massive U. S. Missile Barrage," *CBS Evening News* (24 Jan. 2003), online at http://www.cbsnews.com/stories/2003/01/24/eveningnews/main537928.shtml.

Jingsheng, Wei. "The Fifth Modernization," in *The Fifth Modernization: China's Human Rights Movement, 1978–1979*, ed. James D. Seymour (Stanfordville, NY: Human Rights Publishing Group, 1980).

"The Just War Theory," *The Internet Encyclopedia of Philosophy*, online at http://www.utm.edu/research/iep/j/justwar.htm.

Kane, Robert. *Through the Moral Maze: Searching for Absolute Values in a Pluralistic World* (Armonk, NY: North Castle Books, 1996).

Kant, Immanuel. *Grounding for the Metaphysics of Morals*, translated by James W. Ellington, third edition (Indianapolis, IN: Hackett Publishing Company, 1993).

Kariyawasam, Tilokasundari. "Feminism in Theravada Buddhism," paper presented at the conference *Buddhism and Christianity: Toward the Human Future*, Berkeley, CA, 8–15 Aug. 1987.

King, Martin Luther, Jr. *Letter from a Birmingham Jail*, online at http://almaz.com/nobel/peace/MLK-jail.html.

———. "Nobel Prize Acceptance Speech," in *A Testament of Hope: The Essential Writings of Martin Luther King, Jr.*, ed. James Melvin Washington (San Francisco, CA: Harper & Row, 1986).

Knight, F. H. *Risk, Uncertainty, and Profit* (Boston, MA: Houghton Mifflin, 1921).

Kohlberg, Lawrence. *Philosophy of Moral Development: Essays in Moral Development*, vol. 1 (San Francisco, CA: Harper, 1981).

Kristof, Nicholas D. "Girls for Sale," *The New York Times* (17 Jan. 2004).

LaFraniere, Sharon. "Mandatory Testing Bolsters Botswana in Combating AIDS," *The New York Times* (14 June 2004).

Landesman, Peter. "The Girls Next Door," *The New York Times* (25 Jan. 2004).

Langley, Allison. "African AIDS Drug Plan Faces Collapse," *The Observer* (14 Mar. 2004).

Lao Tsu, *Tao Te Ching*, a new translation by Gia-Fu Feng and Jane English (New York: Vintage Books, 1972).

Lee, Burton J. III. "The Stain of Torture," *The Washington Post* (30 June 2005), online at http://www.washingtonpost.com/wp-dyn/content/article/2005/06/30/AR2005063001680.html.

Leopold, Aldo. "Ecocentrism: The Land Ethic," *Environmental Ethics: Readings in Theory and Application*, ed. Louis P. Pojman, fourth edition (Belmont, CA: Wadsworth, 2005).

Lobe, Jim. "NGOs Rally Behind UN Plan to Slash World Poverty," *OneWorld.net* (15 Jan. 2005), online at http://story.news.yahoo.com/news?tmpl=story&u=/oneworld/20050119/wl_oneworld/45361017541106154327.

The Lotus Sutra, chapter 3, online at http://www.lioncity.net/buddhism/index.php?showtopic=3854.

MacKinnon, Barbara. *Ethics: Theory and Contemporary Issues*, second edition (Belmont, CA: Wadsworth Publishing Company, 1998).

Mansnerus, Laura. "Legislators Vote for Gay Unions in N.J.," *The New York Times* (14 Dec. 2006), online at http://www.nytimes.com/2006/12/15/nyregion/15union.html?hp&ex=1166245200&en=4201828902b533be&ei=5094&partner=homepage.

Mawdudi, Abul A'la. *Human Rights in Islam*, second edition (Leicester, UK: Islamic Foundation, 1980).

Mayer, Jane. "The Memo," *The New Yorker* (27 Feb. 2006), online at http://www.newyorker.com/printables/fact/060227fa_fact.

McKay, Alexander. "Common Questions about Sexual Health Education," *SIECCAN Newsletter*, vol. 35, no. 1 (Summer 2000, revised to Mar. 2001).

McNeil, Donald G. Jr. "Plan to Battle AIDS Worldwide is Falling Short," *The New York Times* (28 Mar. 2004).

McVeigh, Tracy. "Nurse Exodus Leaves Kenya in Crisis," *Observer* (21 May 2006).

Mill, John Stuart. *Principles of Political Economy*, Book IV, Chapter VI (1848).

_____. *Utilitarianism* (London, 1861), quoted in James Rachels, *The Elements of Moral Philosophy*, fourth edition (New York: McGraw-Hill, 2003).

Munson, Ronald. *Intervention and Reflection*, seventh edition (Belmont, CA: Wadsworth, 2004).

Nishimura, Eshin. *Unsui: A Diary of Zen Monastic Life*, drawings by Giei Sato, edited and with introduction by Bardwell L. Smith (Honolulu: The University Press of Hawaii, an East-West Center Book, 1973).

O'Hara, Terence. "Executive Compensation Comes Into the Clear," *The Washington Post* (15 Dec. 2006), online at http://www.washingtonpost.com/wp-dyn/content/article/2006/12/14/AR2006121401816.html.

Pacem in Terris: The 1963 Encyclical of John XXIII on World Peace, in Joseph Gremillion, ed., *The Gospel of Peace and Justice: Catholic Social Teaching since Pope John* (Maryknoll, NY: Orbis, 1976).

Pappé, Ilan, ed. *The Israel/Palestine Question* (London: Routledge, 1999).

Planned Parenthood v. Casey (1992), online at http://www.oyez.org/oyez/resource/case/306/.

Porter, Eduardo. "Health for All, Just a (Big) Step Away," *The New York Times*, (18 Dec. 2005), online at http://nytimes.com/2005/12/18/business/yourmoney/18view.html?incamp=article_popular.

Prabhavananda, Swami and Christopher Isherwood. *The Song of God: Bhagavad Gita* (New York: Mentor Books, 1951).

Prejean, Helen, CSJ, *Dead Man Walking: An Eyewitness Account of the Death Penalty in the United States* (New York: Vintage Books, 1993).

"Protocol to the African Charter on Human and Peoples' Rights on the Rights of Women in Africa," online at http://www.africa-union.org/root/au/Documents/Treaties/treaties.htm.

Rachels, James. *The Elements of Moral Philosophy*, fourth edition (New York: McGraw-Hill, 2003).

Ratner, Blake D. "Environmental Rights as a Matter of Survival," *Human Rights Dialogue: Environmental Rights* (Spring 2004), online at http://www.globalpolicy.org/socecon/envronmt/2004/0617envtlrights.htm.

Restatement (Third) of the Foreign Relations Law of the United States, Section 701, Reporters' Note 8 (1987).

Rieckhoff, Paul. "Do Unto Your Enemy . . . ," *The New York Times* (25 Sep. 2006), online at http://www.nytimes.com/2006/09/25/opinion/25rieckhoff.html.

Roe v. Wade (1973), online at http://www.tourolaw.edu/patch/Roe/.

Rolston, Holmes, III. "Values in and Duties to the Natural World," *Environmental Ethics: What Really Matters, What Really Works*, eds. David Schmidtz and Elizabeth Willott (New York: Oxford University Press, 2002).

Rosenberg, Tina. "Why Mexico's Small Corn Farmers Go Hungry," *The New York Times* (3 Mar. 2003).

Rosin, Hanna. "Reform Rabbis Sanction Gay Unions," *The Washington Post* (30 Mar. 2000).

"Rushing Off a Cliff," *The New York Times* (28 Sep. 2006), online at http://www.nytimes.com/2006/09/28/opinion/28thu1.html?_r=1&hp&oref=slogin.

Samuelson, Robert J. "Trickle-Up Economics?" *Newsweek*, (2 Oct. 2006), 40.

Sangharakshita. *Ambedhar and Buddhism* (Glasgow, Scotland: Windhorse Publications, 1986).

The Sayings of Confucius, translated by James R. Ware (New York: New American Library, 1955).

Schulman, Michael and Eva Mekler. *Bringing Up a Moral Child: A New Approach for Teaching Your Child to Be Kind, Just, and Responsible* (Reading, MA: Addison-Wesley Publishing Company, 1985).

Sen, Gita. "Women, Poverty, and Population: Issues for the Concerned Environmentalist," in *Environmental Ethics: What Really Matters, What Really Works*.

Singer, Peter. *Writings on an Ethical Life* (New York: HarperCollins, 2000).

"Sodomy Laws: India," online at http://www.gmax.co.za/look05/11/28-UKgayjews.html.

Sophocles, *Antigone*, online at http://classics.mit.edu/Sophocles/antigone.html.

"Spain: Group appeals gay marriage law," online at http://www.gay.com/news/article.html?2005/09/19/2.

Steinfels, Peter. "Economics: The Invisible Hand of the Market," *The New York Times*, (25 Nov. 2006), A11.

Struck, Doug. "Canadian Prime Minister Loses Bid to Revisit Gay Marriage Law," *The Washington Post* (8 Dec. 2006), online at http://www.washingtonpost.com/wp-dyn/content/article/2006/12/07/AR2006120701684.html.

Szep, Jason. "Battle Over Gay Marriage Deepens," Yahoo! News (9 Nov. 2006), online at http://news.yahoo.com/s/nm/20061109/ts_nm/rights_gays_dc_1.

Taillant, Jorge Daniel. "A Nascent Agenda for the Americas," *Human Rights Dialogue: Environmental Rights* (Spring 2004), online at http://www.cceia .org/resources/publications/dialogue/2_11/section_4/4461.html.

Tanakh, *A New Translation of The Holy Scriptures According to the Traditional Hebrew Text* (Philadelphia, PA: The Jewish Publication Society, 1985).

Traer, Robert. *Faith, Belief, and Religion* (Aurora, CO: The Davies Group, 2001).

———. *Faith in Human Rights: Support in Religious Traditions for a Global Struggle* (Washington, DC: Georgetown University Press, 1991).

———. *Jerusalem Journal: Finding Hope*, (Aurora, CO: The Davies Group, 2006).

———. "Religious Freedom in Central and Eastern Europe," online at http://www.religionhumanrights.com/Culture/Europe/mission .nationalists.htm.

———. "U. S. Ratification of the International Covenant on Economic, Social, and Cultural Rights," *Promises to Keep: Prospects for Human Rights*, ed. Charles S. McCoy (Pinole, CA: Literary Directions, 2002), 1–47.

Veit, Peter G. and Catherine Benson. "When Parks and People Collide," *Human Rights Dialogue: Environmental Rights* (Spring 2004), online at http://pdf.wri.org/vb_parks_people.pdf.

Walton, Abigail Abrash. "Mining a Sacred Land," *Human Rights Dialogue: Environmental Rights* (Spring 2004), online at http://www.minesand communities.org/Company/freeport12.htm.

Warren, Karen J. "The Power and the Promise of Ecological Feminism," in *Environmental Ethics: What Really Matters, What Really Works*, 234–247

The Way of Life, a new translation of the *Tao Te Ching* by R. B. Blakney (New York: Mentor, 1955), 91, number 38.

Weston, Anthony. *A 21st Century Ethical Toolbox* (New York: Oxford University Press, 2001).

Yeats, William Butler. *The Collected Poetry of William Butler Yeats* (New York: Macmillan, 1961).

Index